Studies in Evangelicalism

Edited by Donald W. Dayton, Northern Baptist Theological Seminary, and Kenneth E. Rowe, Drew University Theological School

"Logical" Luther Lee and the Methodist War against Slavery

Paul Leslie Kaufman

Studies in Evangelicalism Series, No. 17

The Scarecrow Press, Inc.
Lanham, Maryland, and London
2000

SCARECROW PRESS, INC.

Published in the United States of America
by Scarecrow Press, Inc.
4720 Boston Way, Lanham, Maryland 20706
http://www.scarecrowpress.com

4 Pleydell Gardens, Folkestone
Kent CT20 2DN, England

British Library Cataloguing in Publication Information Available

Library of Congress Cataloging-in-Publication Data
Kaufman, Paul Leslie, 1944–
    "Logical" Luther Lee and the Methodist war against slavery / Paul
Leslie Kaufman.
        p.   cm. — (Studies in evangelicalism ; no. 17)
    Includes bibliographical references and index.
    ISBN 0-8108-3710-2 (cloth : alk. paper)
    1. Lee, Luther, 1800–1889. 2. Methodist Episcopal Church—Clergy
Biography. 3. Abolitionists—United States Biography. I. Title. II. Series.
BX8495.L45K38   2000
287'.6'092—dc21   99-41934
    [B]   CIP

Contents

Foreword

For generations of scholars and students of American religious history, the holiness movements have lurked in misunderstanding and lived in the shadows of the Puritan, Anglican, and Congregational/Baptist traditions. Only in the last two decades have pietistic, holiness, and pentecostal influences been recognized in the works of historians like Ernest Stoeffler, Timothy Smith, and Walter Hollenwager, respectively.

Thus, the publication of this book is a scholarly landmark. Luther Lee (1800-1889) is a figure of no small stature to Methodists, Wesleyans, those interested in social reform, particularly antislavery, and religious biographers. Enlarging our view of social change in the nineteenth-century United States, Lee's career parallels other contemporary reformers, notably William Lloyd Garrison, William H. Brisbane, Theodore Weld, and Elijah P. Lovejoy. By following Luther Lee through the several phases of reform, both in his church affiliations and in the context of the national social trends, Kaufman has done us a great service. The author's theological insights and careful attention to prevailing political issues finally sets the record straight on this forgotten man of the Wesleyans. Moreover, Lee's return to the religious mainstream should be a lesson to contemplate, especially in the continuing debate over institutional reform and "come-outerism."

Dr. Kaufman's study provides a readable historical account and extensive bibliography that challenges the reader throughout. Based solidly upon Lee's 1882 *Autobiography*, his sermons, and 1886 published *Theology*, plus numerous letters and cross-references, he gives us a treasury of new material. I commend this volume to serious students of American religious development.

William H. Brackney, Ph.D.
McMaster University
Hamilton, Ontario

Acknowledgments

One cannot research and write a monograph such as this without accumulating an immense debt of gratitude to those who helped to bring such an enterprise to fruition. To those who assisted in uncovering literary sources and rendered valuable advice in organizing and writing this work, I am immeasurably indebted. To those who provided the encouragement and prodding needed to keep me moving, I offer sincere thanks. I appreciate the help of the librarians and archivists at Boston Public Library, Arthur and Elizabeth Schlesinger Library on the History of Women in America at Radcliffe College, Houghton Library at Harvard University, Olin Library at Cornell University, Grand Lodge of Free and Accepted Masons of the State of New York Library and Museum, Delaware County Historical Society, Utica Public Library, Northville Historical Society, Oswego Historical Society, Andover Historical Society, Pollard Public Library at Lowell, Lowell Historical Society, Lynn Historical Society and Museum, North Andover Historical Society, Madison County Historical Society, Jefferson County Historical Society, St. Lawrence County Historical Association, Oneida County Historical Society Library, Herkimer County Historical Society, Clermont County Historical Society, New England Historic Genealogical Society, Worcester Public Library and Central Massachusetts Regional Library System, American Antiquarian Society Library at Worcester, New York Historical Society Library, Onondaga Historical Association, E. S. Bird Library at Syracuse University, Syracuse Public Library, Schoharie County Historical Society, Fulton Public Library, Oswego Public Library, Adrian Public Library, Chagrin Falls Historical Society, and Stark County Public Library.

Special thanks are in order to Donna Watson of the Archives and Historical Library and International Center of the Wesleyan Church in Indianapolis, Charyl Frounfelter of the Flint Public Library, Bob Buckeye of the Starr Library at Middlebury College, Doris Reinke of the Elkhorn Historical Society, Daniel Wheeler of the New York City

Law School, Professor Eugene Mahan of Mater Dei College, Edwin N. Cotter Jr. of the John Brown Farm at North Elba, Professor James Geary of the Kent State University Library, Ronald Brunger, retired archivist of the Methodist Collection at the Shipman Library at Adrian College, and Professor Kenneth Rowe of the General Commission on Archives and History of the United Methodist Church at Drew University.

John Blackwell, of Boston, has graciously granted me permission to quote from the letter between Antoinette Brown Blackwell (his great aunt) and Luther Lee.

I am deeply indebted to Professor Robert P. Swierenga, who influenced this book from its inception to completion. His vast knowledge of the period of American history that spanned the life of Luther Lee added depth and meaning to this book. His perceptive observations and insights kept me from erroneous interpretations and outrunning the available evidence on Lee. Any historical and literary skills that I may possess reflect his guidance. I am also deeply indebted to Professor Frank Byrne, whose course in Sectional Conflict and Civil War awakened my interests in slavery and abolitionism and who steered me through my first graduate seminar at Kent State University. Professor D. Ray Heisey, past chair of the Department of Speech Communications at Kent State, provided invaluable assistance in the analysis of Luther Lee's debating skills. Additionally I wish to thank Professors Leone M. Hudson and David Odell-Scott for their contributions to this project. I am grateful to Professor Henry Leonard, chair of the Department of History, and to the Graduate College of Kent State University for providing me with the History Teaching Fellowship and the research award that made this volume possible. My colleagues at Ashland Theological Seminary and Allegheny Wesleyan College have contributed invaluable suggestions and criticisms of the work. Professor William Brackney of the McMaster Divinity College and Professor William Kostlevy of Asbury Theological Seminary have sharpened my interpretations of Lee. My thanks are due to Professors Kenneth Rowe and Donald Dayton of Drew Theological Seminary, editors of the Studies in Evangelicalism series, who invited me to publish this volume to provide students and scholars with a better understanding of Lee's involvement in the antislavery struggles of the Methodist Episcopal Church and the subsequent rise of Wesleyan Methodism.

Special thanks are due to Miss Angela Reynolds, my secretary at

Allegheny Wesleyan College for her arduous hours of labor in getting this volume into camera-ready format. Also worthy of mention is Miss Connie Gessner who assisted in preparing the manuscript and the index.

To my family and friends I offer special thanks. I am grateful to my daughter Lorilee, the nurse who helped keep me healthy while I researched and wrote, and to my other daughter Louisa Mae, professor at Malone College and a history teaching fellow and doctoral candidate at Kent State University, who encouraged me to keep writing when I needed the boost. To my wife, Pearl Marlene, goes my deepest gratitude for her unfailing support. She was my traveling companion and research assistant throughout this entire project. I hope now to become a full-time husband.

Chronology

1800	Born, Schoharie, N.Y.
1804	Family moved to Delaware County, N.Y.
1809	Family moved to Ulster County, N.Y.
1813	Mother died; family broken up, Lee on his own; Middletown, N.Y., hired as summer laborer; learned milling business
1817	Served as an apprentice tanner to Daniel H. Burr (a Deist) until 1821 (had no religious influence during those years)
1819	Converted, joined the ME church Middletown, N.Y.
1821	Preached first sermon in home of Jacob Dubois of Andes, N.Y.; local preacher for next six years
1823	Assigned as local preacher at Plymouth, N.Y. (Lebanon Circuit, Genesee Conference)
1825	Met Mary Miller—married July 31, 1825; moved that fall to Conquest, N.Y.; moved family to Victory; organized the first Sunday School in that vicinity; recommended by Victory quarterly conference after six years service as local preacher
1826	Received on trial (Wilkes-Barre, Pa. Conference); assigned to Malone Circuit—Franklin County, N.Y.
1829	Attended his first conference at Cazenovia, Madison

County, N.Y.; Lee examined there and ordained a deacon; appointed to Waddington Circuit

1830   Second Conference held at Utica; Bishop Hedding presided

1831   Third Conference Lowville, Lewis County; Bishop Soule presided; Lee ordained an elder at age thirty-one; appointed to Heuvelton Circuit; had first public debate with Universalists

1832   Fourth Conference Manlius, Onondaga County, Bishop Hedding presided; Lee returned to Heuvelton Circuit

1835   Lee began his book on Universalism; Mary Lee contracted typhus; Lee appointed Watertown Circuit

1836   Eighth Conference Watertown—Bishop Waugh presided; first session Black River Conference; Lee appointed to Fulton Circuit

1837   Ninth Conference at Potsdam, St. Lawrence County; Bishop Hedding presided; Lee reappointed to Fulton Circuit; Elijah Lovejoy murdered—Lee preached a sermon against mobocracy

1838   Utica antislavery convention, Orange Scott keynote speaker; Lee defended C. K. True on abolition charges by Methodist Episcopal church; Black River Conference held at Fulton, Lee hosted; Peck preferred charges against Lee; Lee appointed Oswego Circuit; refused to serve, requested relocation; accepted antislavery agency in New York Anti-Slavery Society; relocated family to Utica

1839   Lee met Gerrit Smith; resigned New York agency; delivered most severe speech to date at Broadway Tabernacle at American Anti-Slavery Society, May 7, 1839; Lee and Scott split on female delegate issue; accepted general agency of Massachusetts Anti-Slavery Society; moved family to Charlestown, Mass.; Garrisonian split in Anti-Slavery

Society; debated Theodore Parker on inspiration of scripture

1840   Lee campaigned for Birney and Van Buren; resigned Massachusetts agency; Methodist Episcopal church moved to purge ranks of abolitionism; Orange Scott at Lowell, Mass., began the *New England Christian Advocate*, Lee accepted editorship of the paper; Lee supplied Lowell First ME Church; Lee at Augusta, Maine, addressed legislature committee; he also published *The Sword of Truth*

1842   Moved to Andover, Mass., to supply vacant ME church; October 1842, Scott secedes from ME church

1843   Andover (Mass.) Convention, February 1843; Utica (N.Y.) Convention, May 31, 1843, organizing convention; Lee appointed president *pro tem*, also president of New York Conference, and appointed to Syracuse Wesleyan Methodist Church; wrote articles for the *True Wesleyan*

1844   Oct 3—Elected president of Wesleyan Methodist Connection, Cleveland; elected editor of *True Wesleyan* and *Juvenile Wesleyan*; moved to New York to pastor; published *Immortality of the Soul*

1847   Preached funeral of Orange Scott

1848   Second General Conference held in New York City; reappointed as editor of *True Wesleyan*; move to censure Lee for his Liberty Party activity failed; Dec 20-29 involved in the Belt slave case in New York

1852   Resigned editorship of *True Wesleyan*; left New York City for pastorate at Syracuse church; Third General Conference held at Syracuse in October; preached ordination sermon of Antoinette Brown

1854   Feb 28-Mar 23, debated Rev. Samuel J. May in Syracuse City Hall

1855   Moved to Fulton Wesleyan Methodist Church; finished
        Elements of Theology

1856   Moved to Leoni College; assumed professorship and presi-
        dent of faculty; Fourth General Conference, Cleveland,
        Ohio; Lee elected president for second time

1857   Felicity, Clermont County, Ohio, pastor; conferred with
        an honory D.D. from Middlebury College, Vt.; president of
        Miami Conference of the Wesleyan Methodist Connection

1858   Professor at Michigan Union College

1859   Chagrin Falls, Ohio, pastor Wesleyan Methodist church

1860   Delivered oration at cornerstone laying, Adrian College,
        Mich.; July 4 gave oration overlooking John Brown's grave,
        North Elba, N.Y.; Fifth General Conference, Fulton, N.Y.;
        Lee elected a general missionary (church extension supervi-
        sor), relocated family to Syracuse

1861   Lee resigned general missionaryship in April, accepted
        pastorate of Sprague's Corners Wesleyan Methodist Church
        in Jefferson County, N.Y.

1864   Adrian College, Professor of Theology; Sixth General Con-
        ference, Lee elected president for third time

1867   Lee resigned from Adrian College, returns to ME church;
        Detroit conference at Saginaw, Mich.; supplied Port Huron
        ME charge, later appointed to Court Street ME Church for
        two years

1869   Appointed to the Ypsilanti ME Church (Ann Arbor District)

1870   Appointed to Northville ME Church (Detroit District)

1871   Superannuated

1872   Preached semi-centennial sermon at East Saginaw at annual ME conference; appointed supply to Milford ME charge

1874   Appointed pastor to Petersburgh ME Church

1875   Superannuated; visited dying son in Syracuse; fiftieth wedding anniversary

1882   Lee's *Autobiography* published

1885   Death of Mary Lee

1889   December 13, Lee died at the age of eighty-nine in Flint, Michigan

Introduction

This study offers a biography of Luther Lee within the context of nineteenth-century revivalism and reform movements. Lee is known to most Methodist historians as a Methodist Episcopal minister who deserted the church that had brought him to spiritual birth and ordination. Whitney Cross refers to Lee as a typical itinerant preacher serving within the "burned-over district."[1] Wesleyan Methodist church historians know him as the first president of their denomination, an editor of their periodical, and, unfortunately, a traitor who betrayed and then subsequently walked away from the church he had helped to establish. His significance in American history has not heretofore been observed: he does not appear in the *Dictionary of Christianity in America*, the most recent publication that concerns itself with leaders in reform and religion.[2] It was not until I began visiting manuscript and rare book collections of academic and historical society libraries that the true impact of this nineteenth-century reformer began to unfold.

Born of pure English stock in the Schoharie Valley of New York, Lee was a true son of the early national period. His parents were typical Yankee immigrants from Connecticut, hardworking souls who knew nothing but grinding poverty, and their son had no reason to expect anything better than the same lot in life. Owing to the family's extreme poverty, Luther's formal education was practically nonexistent. By the age of nineteen his only boast was that he had mastered spelling, grammar, and little else. His mother's piety, however, had deeply influenced him. He recounted in later life that as she read him the narrative of Freeborn Garrettson, the itinerant Methodist preacher credited with introducing Methodism into New England, Lee had the distinct impression that someday he was to be a minister. After a conversion experience at the age of nineteen, Lee was baptized into the Methodist Episcopal church and shortly thereafter began traveling as a local

1

preacher.

Lee's life was typical of a small town cleric until news of the murder of Elijah Lovejoy in 1837 swept across the burned-over district. Lured into the antislavery movement, he began to preach sermons denouncing slave holding and condemning mobs and violence such as the murder of Elijah Lovejoy in Alton, Illinois. In 1838 he emerged as a prominent abolitionist lecturer in northern New York and a contributor to *Zion's Watchman*, a Methodist periodical whose editor had agreed to run antislavery articles. The next year, after several incidents in which Lee was either the accused or the defender of antislavery advocates being tried within the Methodist Episcopal church, he accepted the position of general agent for the Massachusetts Abolition Society. He moved his family to Lowell, Massachusetts, and there he developed a strong attachment to Orange Scott and La Roy Sunderland, two other Methodist preachers who were already in trouble with the church for their "modern abolitionist" agitation.

These men, along with Orson Murray and George Storrs, were New England members of Theodore Weld's "seventy" who had stood trial in annual conferences for refusing to acquiesce to the gag rule that the bishops had imposed on the church. James G. Birney had covered the 1836 General Conference of the Methodist Episcopal church in Cincinnati as a newspaper editor of *The Philanthropist*. It was through the relationship with Scott that Lee later linked up with Birney. In 1840 these three men were the moving spirits behind the *New England Christian Advocate*, which Lee edited.

As pressure continued to mount against the abolitionist clergy in the Methodist Episcopal church, the idea of secession and the formation of an antislavery church became more widespread throughout New England and beyond. The split within the American Anti-Slavery Society had placed William Lloyd Garrison and his women's rights, peace, and antichurch following on a divergent course from the remaining clerical agents of the society. The time seemed propitious for secession from the mother church. In 1842, Lee, Scott, Sunderland, and Horton published their reasons for withdrawing from the Methodist Episcopal church. Those who flocked to their banner assembled in the Andover Methodist Episcopal church in 1843 and began the Wesleyan Methodist Connection. The new denomination adopted a congregational/presbyterian type of government that had no bishops, Masons, or slave holders, and it prohibited use of malt, wine, or spirituous liquors. At its first general conference, Luther Lee was elected president.

In addition to that office, Lee simultaneously served as pastor of churches in Syracuse and Fulton, New York, where he became active in issues other than saving souls and presiding over a new denomination. While Lee's autobiography reveals little of his activity in the formation and support of the Liberty Party, his later writings shed more light on his political activities with James G. Birney, Gerrit Smith, William Goodell, and other moving spirits in the political phase of abolitionism. During Lee's years in New York City and in Syracuse, he rendered support to the women's rights movement. In 1853 Lee preached the ordination sermon of Antoinette Brown who became the first female Congregationalist minister. On July 4, 1860, Lee delivered a most radical antislavery speech at the grave of John Brown in North Elba, New York.

In the 1850s Lee served Ohio pastorates with the Wesleyan Methodists in Felicity and Chagrin Falls. Always a prodigious laborer, Lee not only ministered to congregations, but busied himself as a writer. His main literary productions, *Lee's Theology, Universalism Examined, Immortality of the Soul,* and *Slavery Examined in the Light of the Scriptures,* resulted in his call to teach in Leoni College, a fledgling school in Michigan. When that institution closed for lack of finances, he later was summoned to Adrian College, Michigan, as professor of moral and intellectual philosophy, where he served from 1864 to 1867. Struggles to save the college from financial ruin, in addition to problems over governance, caused him to leave Adrian College and return to the Methodist Episcopal church after an absence of nearly twenty-five years. After pastorates at Flint, Ypsilanti, Northville, and Petersburg, Michigan, he retired in 1870 from the active ministry and died in 1889.

Lee was one of several prominent leaders who left the Wesleyan Methodists after the passage of the Fifteenth Amendment. It is apparent that many members within the ranks of the clergy of the Methodist Episcopal church had entered the early stages of a discernible shift toward a more liturgical worship service and less emotional evangelistic fervor. The secession of the Free Methodists in 1860 from the Methodist Episcopal church, led by B. T. Roberts of the Genesee Conference, had ostensibly taken place as a result of complaints that the Methodist doctrine of entire sanctification had been progressively less emphasized. Lee, along with many revivalist preachers, turned to something less emotional, and several abolitionists found something completely non-Christian. For example, Antoinette Brown separated from Congregationalism and embraced Unitarianism. Elizabeth Cady Stanton came to be identified as an infidel in the *New York Observer*. James Birney in his last letter to Gerrit Smith revealed that he had long since "lost all confidence in mere beliefs as necessary to happiness hereafter." When Theodore Weld temporarily lost his speaking voice in 1842, he understood the loss as a sign of displeasure by God and from that point, he began a shift in theology that ultimately led him into Unitarianism, the very system he decried in his preaching years. Angelina Grimké dabbled in Millerism and La Roy Sunderland became a practitioner of mesmerism and in later years he renounced Christianity in toto.[3] Elizur Wright traded his evangelical fervor to become a self-proclaimed infidel and atheist. Lee's experience in later life differed from those. The shift in Lee's ministry never reached a point of such radical departure from his earlier style and focus. His final decades witness one who had settled into a discourse of a quiet homily rather than the earlier passion-filled oratory of one bent on saving Christianity from drowning in perdition for tolerating the sin of slave holding.

Historians offer a myriad of interpretations of antebellum reformers. James Ford Rhodes presented Wendell Phillips and William Lloyd Garrison as the New England storm center of abolitionism. Gilbert Barnes countered with his revisionistic interpretation of the religious revivals of the West with Theodore Weld, protégé of Charles G. Finney, as the driving force of abolitionism. Dwight Lowell Dumond essentially agreed with Barnes. David Donald, influenced by Richard Hofstadter's *Age of Reform,* put forth the "status anxiety" thesis that Robert Skotheim demolished. Frank Thistlethwaite and Richard Carwardine argued for the British influence in abolitionism, whereas Russell Nye viewed these reformers as far-sighted realists. Martin Duberman and Donald Mathews essentially agreed with his thesis.[4]

In this book we shall observe that Lee was no myopic idealist, a career in search of an issue, but, indeed, a far-sighted reformer that historical events such as the passage of the Thirteenth, Fourteenth, and Fifteenth Amendments and other civil rights legislation have vindicated. While he conforms well to the abolitionist profile essentially drawn by Nye, Duberman, and Mathews, Lee presents a challenge to historians when he is tested against the contrasting interpretations of Rhodes and Barnes. Whereas Rhodes argued for a Garrisonian, Eastern-centered abolition movement, and Barnes stressed a Weld, Western-centered movement, Lee is a curious blend of both of these two movements. He had his initial foray into abolitionism as a result of local antislavery activities in the area of Fulton and Oswego, New York, within Cross's burned-over district. After several confrontations with church bishops, Lee spent a year traveling the length and breadth of the district as an agent of the New York Anti-Slavery Society. His area of activity and the men with whom he labored in that agency reflect well the thesis of Gilbert Barnes. Curiously, however, Lee crossed into New England the next year and linked up with Garrison, a man with whom he shared many public events in the cause of abolitionism. Thus, in Lee we have an anomaly who transcends the profile of Rhodes and Barnes in the East versus West historiography.

Students of Lee find him on the surface to be one among a kaleidoscopic cadre of antebellum reformers. Without a doubt, Lee shared the stigma with many church leaders who could boast no formal education. What sets him apart from the others, however, was the level to which he mastered the use of logic and rhetoric—and did so with such precision that his peers and superiors labeled him "Logical Lee." Coupling the argumentative rules of Richard Whately to the rhetoric of reformism, Lee argued for and aided the establishment of the Wesleyan Methodist Connection, a seceder church that reflected the Jacksonian egalitarianism of his day. Lee mirrors perfectly the argument of Nathan Hatch that populistic religious leaders made up the cutting edge of reform. Furthermore, the Second Great Awakening produced a marked shift from aristocratic control of the churches toward one that brought the laity into the leadership. Lee's methods and his message fit well within the society of the 1830s and 1840s. Religion was the engine that not only initiated reform but kept it moving forward. Lee, deprived of formal education, serves as a classic example of Richard Hofstadter's arguments concerning anti-intellectualism that pervaded the Jacksonian era. Lee educated himself at the precise time in our nation's history when the leadership in evangelical ranks had passed from intellectuals to commoners. He mastered the tools of the mental elitists and used them to become a convincing speaker and leader in the cause of reform.[5]

Few are free of some inherent self-contradiction, and Lee was no exception. While he happily participated in a seceder church movement, he refused to resign from the Masons, even though most of his peers were leaving the ranks of the lodges in droves!

Luther Lee was an abolitionist first and foremost. Within that context he can be seen as a church builder, organizer, administrator, editor, and Christian apologist. Beyond that, he reflected an early interest in women's rights and an avid interest in the Liberty Party. Despite the opinion of some historians that the subject of abolitionism has "run dry," the story of Lee deserves to be told.[6]

NOTES

1. Whitney R. Cross, *The Burned-over District: The Social and Intellectual History of Enthusiastic Religion in Western New York, 1800-1850* (Ithaca N.Y.: Cornell University Press, 1950), 42, 45, and 50. The term "burned-over district" is a term of common usage from the literature of the Second Great Awakening, that describes the upstate section of New York between Buffalo and Albany on the east and west and Lake Ontario on the north and to the counties south of the Erie Canal. This area experienced numerous waves of religious revivals and is the area from which numerous cults and denominations have sprung.

2. *Dictionary of Christianity in America,* Daniel Reid, Robert D. Linder, Bruce L. Shelley, Harry S. Stout, eds. (Downers Grove, Ill.: InterVarsity Press, 1990).

3. See Whitney Cross, 283; cf., "Mysterious Rappings at La Roy Sunderland's," *True Wesleyan,* January 25, 1851, for an account of the writer's visit to Sunderland's home at which he observed Sunderland conduct a spiritualist meeting, claiming, "several spirits were hovering [in the room]"; *True Wesleyan,* May 13, 1857, in which Sunderland responded to Prindle for the article, "Fall of Le Roy [*sic*] Sunderland," in which Sunderland asserts that he left the

Wesleyans when they passed the rule on Masons. He assures Prindle that he still holds Scott, Horton, Prindle, and Lee in high esteem. His "peculiar work, at present, as it has been for the past seventeen years, is 'doing good to the souls and bodies of men.'"; Lawrence B. Goodheart, *Abolitionist, Actuary, Atheist: Elizur Wright and the Reform Impulse* (Kent, Ohio: Kent State University Press, 1990), 192.

4. James Ford Rhodes, *History of the United States from the Compromise of 1850*, 9 vols. (New York: Macmillan & Co., 1906) I: 53-63; Gilbert Hobbs Barnes, *The Antislavery Impulse 1830-1844* (New York, 1933; repr., New York: Harcourt, Brace & World, 1964); Dwight Lowell Dumond, *Antislavery: The Crusade for Freedom in America* (Ann Arbor: University of Michigan Press, 1961); David Donald, *Lincoln Reconsidered* (New York: Alfred A. Knopf, 1956); Robert A. Skotheim, "A Note on Historical Method: David Donald's 'Toward a Reconsideration of Abolitionists,'" *Journal of Southern History* 25 (August 1959): 356-65; Frank Thistlethwaite, *The Anglo-American Connection in the Early Nineteenth Century* (Philadelphia: University of Pennsylvania Press, 1959); Richard Carwardine, *Trans-atlantic Revivalism: Popular Evangelicalism in Britain and America, 1790-1965* (Westport, Conn.: Greenwood Press, 1978); Russell B. Nye, "The Slave Power Conspiracy, 1830-1860," *Science and Society* 10 (Summer 1946): 262-74; Martin B. Duberman, "The Abolitionists and Psychology," *The Journal of Negro History* 47 (July 1962): 183-92; Donald G. Mathews, *Slavery and Methodism: A Chapter in American Morality 1780-1845* (Princeton, N.J.: Princeton University Press, 1965).

5. Richard Whately, *Elements of Rhetoric: Comprising an Analysis of the Laws of Moral Evidence and of Persuasion, with Rules for Argumentative Composition and Elocution* (n.p., 1828), repr. Douglas Ehninger, ed., foreword by David Potter (Carbondale, Ill.: Southern University Press, 1962); George Campbell, *The Philosophy of Rhetoric* (London and Edinburgh, 1776), repr., Lloyd F. Bitzer, ed., *The Philosophy of Rhetoric by George Campbell* (Carbondale, Ill.: Southern Illinois University Press, 1963); Richard Hofstadter, *Anti-intellectualism in American Life* (New York: Alfred A. Knopf, 1966); Nathan O. Hatch, *The Democratization of American Christianity* (New Haven, Conn.: Yale University Press, 1989); John William Ward, *Andrew Jackson: Symbol for an Age* (New York: Oxford University Press, 1955).

6. Lawrence J. Friedman, "'Historical Topics Sometimes Run Dry': The State of Abolitionist Studies," *Historian* 43 (February 1981): 177-94.

Chapter 1

1800-1826: Formative Years

"The hand that rocks the cradle rules the world" is a statement whose truth is self-evident. From Monica, the sainted mother of Augustine who refused to abandon her son to a dissipated life, to Susanna Wesley, the Puritan mother of John and Charles whose piety influenced them beyond her earthly days, society understands the indelible impress of a mother upon her offspring. Hannah Williams Lee, the mother of Luther Lee, used the thirteen years from his birth until her death to fashion his character and to inculcate Christian ideals in her son.[1] Students of Lee observe that her efforts were not unavailing; Lee never strayed far from her ideals as a teenager or later in life as a mature minister.

The Lee family name of the first generation arriving from England may well have been Leigh. The grandfather of Luther Lee arrived in Boston in relative obscurity. The immediate cause of his immigration cannot be established, and the exact date of his arrival is just as tentative—perhaps in the period 1748 to 1750. His marriage to Deborah Bundy produced two sons, Samuel and Moses. Samuel, born in 1754, was Luther's father. In 1775 Samuel answered the call to serve in the patriot army and remained until American independence was secured. At the close of the war he moved to Woodbury, Connecticut, where he met his bride, Hannah Williams.[2]

Luther Lee's maternal grandfather Williams, whose first name was unknown, was also an Englishman. He came to America in the French and Indian War as one of his majesty's soldiers, and his was the hapless misfortune of participating in the tragedy at Fort Duquesne when General Edward Braddock was ambushed and routed. Miraculously, Williams lived until the time of his discharge when he, too, made his way to Woodbury, Connecticut, where he met and married Thankful Spencer. Hannah, a daughter born to them in Woodbury, became the mother of Luther. Owing to the death of her father and her mother's inability to provide for her, she found herself in the home of the famous Reverend Dr. Joseph Bellamy, who had agreed to raise the lass. Such a towering figure in the Congregational Church and a strong leader in the New Divinity Movement must have had significant effect upon Hannah Williams. Bellamy had been a student of Jonathan Edwards when the latter's shaping influence in the First Great Awakening was at its zenith. Without question, young Hannah reflected many of the pious qualities of Bellamy. Samuel Lee and Hannah Williams were married while she still resided in the parsonage of the Congregational Church in Bethlehem, Connecticut.[3]

No evidence remains to inform us about the couple until they reappear in upstate New York. By that time seven sons and two daughters had blessed their home, all surviving to adulthood. Luther Lee, next to the youngest, was born in Schoharie, New York, in 1800. That year proved to be significant in the annals of antislavery. Before the year came to a close, Gabriel Prosser led a slave revolt, Denmark Vesey purchased his freedom, and Nat Turner, John Brown, Orange Scott, and Luther Lee first saw the light of day.

Yankee immigrants into the frontier country of Schoharie County proved to be a rugged lot. People such as Samuel and Hannah Lee shared the town of Schoharie with descendants of original German families who had first settled the area in 1711. Dutch settlers later arrived from Albany, following the Schoharie River, the largest tributary of the Mohawk River. Schoharie County, officially organized by the New York legislature in 1795, was primarily under the influence of the Lutherans and Dutch Reformed.

Methodism also entered America in New York. In 1768 the first local society to develop enough numerical strength to build a church was the John Street Methodist Church of New York City. The thrust of expansion from that beginning tended toward the South and the West. Methodism numbered into the thousands by the time of the Cane Ridge camp meeting of 1801 in Bourbon County, Kentucky. While the ubiquitous circuit riders were following the frontier toward the Cumberland and Ohio River valley, their penetration into the North and New England enjoyed significantly slower progress. The established Congregationalists and their comrades in spiritual arms, the Presbyterians, presented the followers of Asbury a more unified body of opposition, especially after the Plan of Union in 1801. By the last decade of the eighteenth century, Methodism began to push up the Hudson Valley.[4]

In 1791 Francis Asbury preached to three hundred people in a barn in Coeymans Patent on the eastern shore of the Hudson in Albany County. Reflecting the earlier successes utilizing the camp meeting in the West, Methodists conducted similar events north of New York. In 1805 and 1806 as many as six thousand gathered at Stillwater, west of the Hudson near Troy, and at Philips Manor in New Rochelle. People as far away as Brooklyn and Manhattan came to hear the preachers. By 1792 circuit riding preachers penetrated into Schoharie County. Traversing the area west of Albany, they entered the valley of the Mohawk River and preached their way up its tributaries. Other Methodist preachers from Pennsylvania reached the headwaters of the Delaware and Susquehanna Rivers into the area surrounding Schoharie. These two groups converged in Schoharie at approximately the same time. From that point the ubiquitous itinerant preachers exerted a continuous Methodist influence on the area.[5]

Nothing in print sheds light as to where and how Samuel Lee and his growing family worshipped and nourished their souls while living in Schoharie—much less how they managed to feed their physical bodies. Unable to find an enduring means of providing for his wife and children, Samuel Lee proved typical of so many who relocated frequently from town to town, barely eking out a subsistence.[6]

At the dawn of young Luther's recollection, the Lee family moved into Delaware County, settling for a period of time in the township of Kortwright.[7] The distinguished Bangs family resided in that neighborhood. John Bangs, a noted member of the Bangs clan and a blacksmith who worked his trade during the week and preached on Sundays, conducted meetings in the Lee home.[8] Using current Methodist methods, Bangs exhorted in groves, barns, schoolhouses, and private dwellings. Writing of these cottage meetings in later life,

Lee recalled how his youthful heart of seven or eight was profoundly affected by the loud, earnest exhortations of this Methodist Episcopal gentleman. During the family's residence in Kortwright, Hannah Lee's religious influence on young Luther was profound. It cannot be stated with certainty at which point she had come under the influence of the Methodists. Lee recalls his emotional response as his mother read him accounts from the life of Freeborn Garrettson, one of the prominent names in American Methodism in the late eighteenth century. Lee wrote that the persecutions of Garrettson had moved him to tears. During those stirring moments in his tender years, he underwent profound "religious feeling," while at the same time he sensed that some day he would be a minister. "That impression never left me, nor was I ever after without religious feeling," he stated later.

When Lee reached the age of nine (1809), the family migrated again, this time to Ulster County. Nothing is known about the events of this last move, except for the fact that Hannah Lee died there when Lee was thirteen years old. As if that blow to the family were not sufficiently tragic, Samuel Lee passed away in the following year just as the War of 1812 was reaching a climax.

Most Americans had hoped to avoid war; only the "war hawks" manifested much enthusiasm for another war with the English. Unfortunately, the issue of neutral rights had not been solved with Great Britain by 1812. Other issues also troubled the nation. The matter of seizing American sailors and impressing them into the British royal navy, the rising tensions with the native tribes in the West, new sectional alignments in Congress, and the desire to seize Canada had all culminated in the "second war for independence" with the English. The Lake Erie battles and the bloody affair at Fort Niagara proved to be as close as young Lee ever got to the war. The summer witnessed the disastrous campaign against Washington and the stand-off of the British at Fort McHenry. Then in September of 1814, Commodore Thomas Macdonough, commander of the American Naval squadron on Lake Champlain, managed to end the threat of British invasion from the north by a brilliant victory at Plattsburgh, New York. As far as Lee and most of the country could see, the war had wound down. Lee, however, had his own battles to fight, the struggle to make a living in an unfriendly world.

Thus at the age of fourteen, Lee was cast upon the harsh realities of orphanhood. For reasons not now clear, he decided to return to Delaware County, and crossing over Hemlock Mountain, he settled in Middletown, located along the eastern branch of the Delaware River. Backbreaking labor was the lot of young men as poor as Lee. He contracted to work temporarily for the summer and in the autumn took a job at Smith's gristmill that lasted until he reached the age of seventeen. Moving four miles away, Lee subsequently entered into a tanner apprenticeship with Daniel H. Burr, a man he had met while grinding Burr's grain.

This employment proved to be an interesting challenge to young Lee. Not only did Burr busy himself as a farmer and a tanner; he was a Deist.[9] Lee remained true to his mother's strict Methodist instruction, however, and did not permit himself to be influenced by Burr's unorthodox religious views. In the four years that Lee remained at the tannery, he constantly had to withstand the temptation to drink along with most of his peers. Despite the absence of any pastor or church in the immediate area of Middletown, Lee managed to observe the rules of Methodism such as keeping the Sabbath. He later stated that he was by no means perfect and did indulge in "some of the immoral habits of the neighborhood," but he reached adulthood without ever being drunk.[10]

During the time of Lee's employment at the tannery, the nation experienced its first major confrontation with slavery. Although the institution of slavery had nearly ceased north of the Mason-Dixon Line and the Ohio River, no one knew for sure where the dividing line would run beyond the Mississippi River. The application of Missouri for statehood forced the issue and unwittingly initiated the first sectional alignment in Congress until that time.

From 1819 to 1821, the nation witnessed the polarization of its leaders in Congress over the issue of slavery. Free-state men wanted to stop the expansion of slavery into the western territories. Already ten thousand slaves had been carried into the area of Missouri. Finally, Henry Clay began to earn his sobriquet as the "Great Compromiser," and the congressional deadlock broke.

After two years of controversy, the nation sighed in relief. In actuality, only a truce with slavery had been declared. The aging

Thomas Jefferson wrote to a friend that the issue "like a firebell in the night awakened and filled me with terror. I considered it at once as the knell of the Union." Lee evidences no concern or even knowledge of the Missouri Compromise at the time. Little could he have understood the implications of the institution of slavery for his own life. In 1821 he focused on spiritual matters as though completely oblivious to national issues.

Lee finally mustered the courage to make a public acknowledgment of his desire to fellowship with the Methodist Episcopal church. At the age of nineteen he sought the nearest church of that denomination on the Delaware Circuit and joined the Middletown Society. Still harboring the earlier compulsion to someday preach, he began to take some part in public meetings wherever he could. Methodist meetings presented opportunity for testimony, exhortation, and public prayers. As he continued to overcome his early hesitancy and bashfulness, his gift of speaking and his ready, quick mind impressed those who gathered to worship in Delaware County. Lee's first real sermon took place on November 25, 1821, just six days prior to attaining his majority and fulfilling the terms of his contract with Burr. The service had been scheduled in the town of Andes in the home of an elderly Dutch Methodist class leader by the name of Jacob Dubois.[11] The scheduled speaker on that occasion for some reason failed to appear. Lee's first public introduction to his hearers came in a unique manner. The class leader turned to Lee and announced: "Broder Luter [*sic*] you must talk to the people."[12] While nothing of that extemporaneous sermon remains, it met with the approval of its auditors. As Lee wrote, "It was not much of a sermon, but it was a beginning."[13]

The days of the common school for all of the counties of New York lay in the future, and Lee operated at a decided disadvantage because of his unsettled home life. One of his older brothers had managed to attend school and, adapting Lancastrian methods to his needs, taught young Luther the letters of the alphabet with a penknife on a pine shingle. Later, the same brother secured a copy of the *American Spelling-book* from which Lee learned enough spelling to enable himself to read the Bible and hymnbook, to write on a rudimentary level, and to perform basic mathematical computations including long division. In his later teens, Lee agreed to work for three days clearing land in exchange for a coveted copy of *Murray's Grammar*. Such was the sum of his education before embarking on a life in the Methodist ministry.[14]

Education for Methodist preachers had never been much of a priority. Nathan Bangs, a contemporary of Lee, lamented later in his ecclesiastical history that by the turn of the century, "it had become proverbial that the 'Methodists were enemies to learning.'"[15] Bishop Francis Asbury, the Father of American Methodism, reflected his attitude toward the education of the ministry in his words, "I have not spoken against learning. I have only said that it cannot be said to be an essential qualification to preach the gospel."[16]

At that time Lee took one further step on the pathway to maturity and manhood; he joined the Masonic lodge. He writes nothing of the context nor of where he found the finances for membership fees and subsequent dues. Some lodges waived membership fees in order to gain the support of local clerics and perhaps that enabled Lee to affiliate. The act of joining the lodge became for Lee a source of unending disputes with later churchmen and students.[17]

With this humble beginning and no formal classroom education, Lee entered the ranks of the Methodist exhorters and preachers. He had conquered his reticence in public speaking to the point that he felt comfortable before a frontier congregation. As a local preacher, Lee must have struggled to provide his hearers with a sermon. Most of those who assembled to listen, however, would have been relatively poor judges of homiletics.

Shortly after the sermon in the home of Dubois, the Methodist presiding elder of the Hudson River District, Reverend Eben Smith, signed Lee's local preacher's license. He immediately began traveling the Delaware Circuit of the New York Conference, an enterprise that encompassed parts of three counties and required travels that averaged ten miles a day, seventy-five miles per week, or a total of more than three hundred miles, to visit the established preaching points. Men such as Lee had little other than their own experiences on which to draw for preaching material. But in a country that was expanding faster than regular preachers could be found, the ubiquitous Methodist preacher met the needs of its hardy inhabitants.[18]

Until 1823 he trudged the rugged terrain of the circuit. In that year he left behind the Delaware country and took up clerical labors in Chenango County, making his home in the town of Plymouth. Here he labored under the presiding elder of the Lebanon Circuit of the Genesee Conference. While busying himself as a local preacher, he met the woman who was to become his bride, Mary Miller, the daughter of John Miller. She had received a substantial education and had been hired by the town as a teacher. The young preacher became her star pupil, doing his best to make up for the severe deficiencies in his education. On July 31, 1825, he married his teacher.[19]

In the autumn of that year as the Erie Canal was opening for business, Lee moved with his bride to Cayuga County. Finding the neighborhood less than congenial morally, the Lees responded to the invitation of some Methodists and relocated in the town of Victory, roughly midway between Syracuse and Rochester. In that place Lee, for the first time in his life, found himself in a strong Methodist community. He busied himself assisting the two preachers who had been assigned to the Victory Circuit of the Genesee Conference. Lee's aggressiveness can be observed at that place. He took it upon himself to organize the first Sunday School, a phenomenon that he had never seen before. Thus, in 1826 he can be credited with making the first attempt to teach religion to children in that area. He served as both superintendent and sole teacher to twenty or thirty youth. Actually his innovative step met with everyone's satisfaction except that of the presiding elder. Reverend George Gary viewed the enterprise as a diversion and a distraction to Lee, who might better spend his time finding places without regular clergy to preach on the circuit. Lee argued that as a local preacher he had no regular assignment and was free to use his religious talents in whatever manner he saw fit. The presiding elder ultimately acquiesced and Lee continued his work among the children of Victory.[20]

His future as a preacher, however, was already an accomplished fact in the minds of his fellow church members. After two years the quarterly conference of the Victory Circuit manifested its confidence in Lee's abilities. The membership recommended him as a "traveling preacher" to the Genesee Annual Conference, meeting that year in Wilkes Barre, Pennsylvania. This step was taken, however, without Lee's knowledge. Furthermore, the congregation at Victory desired that he be assigned as one of their preachers. But their request availed nothing; he was sent more than two hundred miles to the northeast part of New York. Thus in 1827, Lee entered the ranks of the traveling ministry.

Two Methodist rules need to be understood. The "two-year rule" mandated that each parish pastor move after two years at any given appointment. Another rule held that only ordained elders and bishops could attend the annual conferences. Lee, not being present for the session, had no way of knowing of his appointment to the Malone Circuit, one that encompassed all of Franklin County and portions of St. Lawrence and Clinton Counties, as well as the lower sections of Lower Canada. Several suspense-filled weeks passed. Finally a copy of the Methodist publication, the *Christian Advocate and Journal*, arrived and only then did Lee discover that his assignment would take him far to the north.[21]

The road that Lee had traveled to this point in life had not taken him very far in the world—in fact his world was quite small. Nothing in his heritage and life had prepared him for future leadership in the church, yet he would become the president of a denomination. With little formal education, he would rise to a college professorship, lead a college faculty as its president, and defeat a Harvard-trained theologian in debate. From an inauspicious beginning, he set high standards for himself. With his appointment to the distant northern reaches of New York, he stepped across the threshold of his formative years into the challenging world of the Methodist ministry.

NOTES

1. Philip Greven Jr., *The Protestant Temperament: Patterns of Child-Rearing, Religious Experience, and the Self in Early America* (New York: Knopf, 1977), 15-25, convincingly argues the value of understanding the temperament in not only interpreting persons and events, but also the latent influence of one's upbringing.

2. William Lee, *John Leigh of Agawam (Ipswich) Massachusetts 1634-1671 and His Descendants of the Name of Lee with Genealogical Notes and Biographical Sketches of ALL His Descendants, so Far as Can Be Obtained: Including Notes on Collateral Branches* (Albany, N.Y.: Joel Munsell's Sons,

1888), 26; Luther Lee, *Autobiography of the Rev. Luther Lee, D.D.* (New York: Phillips & Hunt, 1882; Cincinnati, Ohio: Walden & Stowe, 1882), 15; hereinafter *Autobiography*; *Historical Collections, Collections and Researches Made by the Michigan Pioneer and Historical Society, Michigan Historical Commission*, vol. XVII (Lansing, Mich.: Robert Smith & Co., 1892), 87-88.

3. The name of Woodbury had subsequently been changed to Bethlehem; S. T. Logan, "Bellamy, Joseph," *Dictionary of Christianity in America* (Downers Grove, Ill.: InterVarsity Press, 1990), 126; *Autobiography*, 16; see Henry K. Rowe, *History of Andover Theological Seminary* (Newton, Mass.: Andover Theological Seminary, 1933), 9, for a discussion of the many students that Bellamy indoctrinated and influenced toward the Arminianized New Divinity of Hopkinsianism and Taylorism.

4. William Ralph Ward Jr., *Faith in Action: A History of Methodism in the Empire State, 1784-1984* (Rutland, Vt.: Academy Books, 1984), 14-15.

5. Ward, *Faith in Action*, 14-15.

6. Jeptha R. Simms, *History of Schoharie County and Border Wars of New York*, facsimile reprint (Bowie, Md.: Heritage Books, n.d.), 601-33; William E. Roscoe, *History of Schoharie County, New York* (Syracuse, N.Y.: D. Mason & Co, 1882), 74-85, 354-83; J. H. French, *Gazetteer of the State of New York: Embracing a Comprehensive View of the Geography, Geology, and General History of the State, and a Complete History and Description of Every County, City, Town, Village, and Locality* (Syracuse, N.Y.: R. Pearsall Smith, 1860), 600-07; Emory Stevens Bucke, gen. ed., *The History of American Methodism in Three Volumes* (New York: Abingdon, 1964), I: 407-408.

7. Lee spelled the name of the town "Courtwright," as it is today; however, records from that era used the spelling as it appears in the text.

8. Bangs is credited with founding several Methodist Episcopal churches in that area. Most of these churches were begun first as "classes" or "societies," after which a regular church usually was organized. Reverend John Bangs was born in 1779 and died in 1848. *History of Delaware County, N. Y. with Illustrations, Biographical Sketches and Portraits of Some Pioneers and Prominent Residents* (New York: W. W. Munsell & Co., 1880), 240; *Autobiography*, 17; cf., Bertram Wyatt-Brown, *Lewis Tappan and the Evangelical War against Slavery* (New York: Atheneum, 1971), 1-17, for the lasting spiritual legacy that Sarah Tappan left her children, especially Lewis.

9. Burr appears to have been a prominent citizen in that area. In 1810 he was elected and served for ten years as the town supervisor. Interestingly, when a Methodist Episcopal church building was erected in January 1823, Burr's name appears as one of the three trustees—evidence the Methodist preachers were successful in converting Deists to orthodox Christianity. *History of Delaware County, N. Y. with Illustrations, Biographical Sketches and Portraits of Some Pioneers and Prominent Residents* (New York: W. W. Munsell & Co., 1880), 292.

10. *Autobiography*, 19-20.

11. Lee spelled the name Duboys in his *Autobiography* but other sources in the town of Andes give Dubois as the spelling. This Dutchman appears to have been of considerable means. He owned and operated a sawmill on the east branch of the Delaware River that existed for more than forty years as the Dubois Mill. *History of Delaware County, N.Y. with Illustrations, Biographical Sketches and Portraits of Some Pioneers and Prominent Residents* (New York: W. W. Munsell & Co., 1880), 106.

12. *Autobiography*, 23.

13. It was not uncommon for a young man to be pushed into the itinerant ministry in that era, e.g., Jessie Lee, a prominent Methodist circuit rider wrote that Asbury came to him at the conference of 1872 and asked Lee if he was willing to take a circuit. Lee responded rather hesitantly, "fearful of hurting the cause, [and] being very sensible of my own weakness." When the assignments were given, Asbury announced in public, "I am going to enlist brother Lee," cited by Menton Thrift, *Memoir of the Rev. Jessie Lee with Extracts from His Journals,* in Nathan O. Hatch, *The Democratization of American Christianity* (New Haven, Conn.: Yale University Press, 1989), 267; *Autobiography*, 23.

14. *Historical Collections, Collections and Researches Made by the Michigan Pioneer and Historical Society, Michigan Historical Commission, vol. XVII*, 87-88; *Autobiography*, 22-24.

15. Nathan Bangs, *A History of the Methodist Episcopal Church*, 4 vols. (New York: Mason and Lane, 1840), 1: 249.

16. Francis Asbury, *The Journal and Letters of Francis Asbury*, ed. Elmer C. Clark, J. Manning Potts, and Jacob S. Payton, 3 vols. (Nashville, Tenn.: Abingdon, 1958), vol. 3, *Letters*, August 5, 1813.

17. Dorothy Ann Lipson, *Freemasonry in Federalist Connecticut* (Princeton, N.J.: Princeton University Press, 1977), 312-40; *Autobiography*, 248-49.

18. *Autobiography*, 27-28.

19. *Autobiography*, 27-28.

20. *Autobiography*, 29.

21. F. W. Conable, *History of the Genesee Annual Conference of the Methodist Episcopal Church,* (New York: Nelson & Phillips, 1876), 257; *Autobiography*, 28-30.

Chapter Two

1827-1835: Learning to Debate

Luther Lee had been stationed in a territory that boasted no deep roots in Methodism. Presbyterians, whose tradition stemmed from staunch New England Congregationalists who had drifted west, and Baptists composed the strength of the orthodox denominations in the territory south of the St. Lawrence River. Universalism had also taken root in the area. Methodism had made inroads, but its development had only recently begun. Although Lee's route into the area led him near Adams, the place where Charles G. Finney had his conversion and first revivals in the early 1820s, there is little evidence of such revivals in the counties to the north and east. Religion had spread, to be sure, but not with the same intensity as in the burned-over district nearer the Erie Canal country.

Using the old military road built during the War of 1812, Lee made his way through the adjoining counties of upstate New York. He passed through numerous villages and hamlets where Methodist societies had begun over three decades before. As early as 1792, Reverend William Losee had ridden through the territory and even preached across the St. Lawrence River to Methodists on the Canadian side, competing for the souls of newly arriving Yankees. By 1793 the Methodists were conducting services in the Ogdensburg garrison. Reverend Chandley Lambert, the first Methodist preacher to travel the area regularly, had been assigned by Bishop Asbury in 1808. He reported forty-three professed Methodists on the three-county circuit. Being an austere fellow and a sharp judge of those who professed more religion than they possessed, he subsequently expelled eight or ten who

21

were "lacking in grace."[1]

The Methodist Episcopal denomination was the first to organize a church in that place. The St. Lawrence Circuit with eighty-four members was formed in 1811. From 1804 to 1824 circuit riders were sent to hold meetings wherever they could assemble a group of hearers. Congregationalists, Presbyterians, Universalists, and some Roman Catholics composed the ecclesiastical landscape in St. Lawrence County. As recently as 1816 only one small meeting house existed in the entire northern part of New York, and none in the next county to the east where Lee had been assigned.[2]

In 1827 Lee discovered in Franklin County an even more remote, undeveloped area where the twenty dollar bounty on wolves and panthers had only recently been dropped by the town authorities. On the Malone Circuit he found that religion in general, and Methodism in particular, had not progressed beyond the formative stages. After an arduous search Lee succeeded in locating Reverend J. M. Brooks, the preacher in charge. Between the two of them they designed a plan for the year's campaign to push the Methodist banner in that sparsely settled area. Their circuit would normally require one man to cover the territory in four weeks, delivering thirty sermons in that period of time. The itinerary they devised called for each man to speak at all the preaching points in the course of one month, but they would travel with one preacher two weeks behind the other. In that manner each congregation could hear a preacher at least twice per month.[3]

Church facilities were nonexistent throughout the circuit. In the village of Malone none of the denominations had a meeting house. The problem was solved by each group sharing the county courthouse on alternating Sundays: the Presbyterians (mostly these were Congregationalists from Vermont and New Hampshire who became Presbyterians after crossing into New York in keeping within the Plan of Union of 1801) occupied the building two Sundays per month, while the Baptists (also immigrants from New England) and the Methodists each had access the other two worship days. On weeks when they could not use the courthouse, Lee's congregation met in "the old academy," an unused building with no platform or speaker's desk.

At the same time that Lee and Brooks were drawing their strategy for attacking and defeating the devil, Charles G. Finney and his friends from the West were locked in a methodological debate with Lyman Beecher, Asahel Nettleton, and others from the East at the New Lebanon Conference in July of 1827. Even as Finney won a solid victory for his "New Measures" at that meeting, Lee and Brooks hoped to strike the right key to produce results along the St. Lawrence.[4]

Methodism, in time, outgained every competing religion on the frontier. In upper New York it entered the religious fray behind the Presbyterians and Baptists who brought their religion with them. The Methodists were forced to produce their congregations by converting sinners out of the rough. The Methodist organization, however, proved quite utilitarian and the denomination quickly surpassed all religious competitors. Traveling preachers within the ranks of Methodism clearly viewed themselves as "professional organizers." These hardy men set up spiritual shop any place where someone would listen to their preaching. Frequently, they did not know even one person in their congregation. The venerable Jessie Lee, a rugged preacher in the early national period, confided to his journal in 1789, while preaching in Milford, Connecticut: "This is the third time I have preached at this place, and have not yet become acquainted with any person."[5]

Patterned on the Wesleyan form in England, the preacher would arrive at the appointed place, either a home, barn, grove, schoolhouse, or even a borrowed building from another denomination. Some hymns would be sung with the leader using the hymnal of Charles Wesley. Next the preacher would select a scriptural text and expound from it as best as his education would permit. At the conclusion of the message he would invite those who wished to be saved from their sins and flee from the wrath to come, to step forward. These converts formed the nucleus of a society in that place. The preacher recorded the members of these societies and reported them to his superior and eventually to the next session of the annual conference. Societies came to be called classes and from these churches eventually formed with their own leaders. After the itinerant preacher moved to the next point, a local preacher, steward, or exhorter had oversight of things until the "traveling preacher" arrived on his next trip through the area. The local preacher or exhorter had the task of instructing the classes from the scriptures and the *Discipline,* which contained the general rules Wesley had established as early as 1740. Worship services took place on

Sunday morning and evening, sometimes in the afternoon. At Methodist "love feasts" all the worshippers rejoiced in praise, prayer, and testimony. If an ordained elder presided, the sacrament of holy communion concluded the service. Since Lee was only a traveling preacher and not an ordained deacon or elder, he could not serve communion during his tenure at Malone Circuit.[6]

In February 1828 Lee suffered an accident that depressed him, but it also illustrates the magnanimous spirit of cooperation that often manifested itself on the frontier. Lee had traveled to the town of Fort Covington with a deliriously high fever, arriving on Saturday. Clearly unable to preach on the next day, friends arranged to have his horse hitched to a cutter and have someone drive him home. On the icy road home, the harness somehow came loose and caused the sleigh to strike the horse, breaking its leg. Just when despair set in, Lee received a visit from Esquire Parkhurst of Fort Covington, a wealthy lawyer and a distinguished member of the Presbyterian Church. After assuring Lee, who possessed no means to replace the horse, that Providence would supply the need, Parkhurst returned home and mounted a subscription drive to replace the horse. Events of that nature transpired on occasion, and they reveal a spirit of unity among the various denominations that otherwise were poles apart on theology and practice.[7]

Lee's first year in the ministry drew to a close without further event, other than the arrival of his first child, a daughter Loretta.[8] Methodist men on trial for the ministry did not attend annual conference until the year of their ordination. Thus Lee remained at home to await developments. In time he received notice that his colleague, having served two years on the circuit, must be transferred elsewhere. Lee, with the consent of the quarterly conference, chose a local preacher to assist him for the 1828-29 circuit year. Because poverty pinched many of his parishioners, his annual salary amounted to $100, far below that of Reverend Timothy Dwight, the Yale-educated grandson of Jonathan Edwards. In 1784 Dwight, pastor of the Fairfield Hill, Connecticut, Congregational church, earned $500, plus the use of the manse. The Lees had no parsonage while serving the Malone Circuit. Whatever accommodations were available to the young preacher and his small family must have been severely limited because he was forced to keep his horse in a neighbor's barn.[9]

The spiritual results of Lee's labors included "some revival during the year, and some additions to the Church." While Finney enjoyed vast popularity for his incomparable Western revival, Lee labored in obscurity. He did, however, encounter some of the same bizarre phenomena in the Malone area as other frontier revivalists had witnessed.[10]

At a camp meeting just south of Malone, Lee observed a "brawling infidel" declaring his doubts about the existence of God. He continued to monopolize the meeting with his challenges that should such a supreme Being actually exist, he wanted proof by having God "knock me down without hands," professing that afforded such evidence, he would become a believer in God. Lee wrote that as the God-challenger passed in front of the preachers' stand, he fell "as suddenly as though he had been knocked down with a blacksmith's hammer." After being in that position for two or three hours, he revived and subsequently testified to receiving forgiveness for his many sins. Nothing is known of the man's life after that day. Most revivalists reported events just as inexplicable during the course of emotionally charged meetings.[11]

At the close of his second year on the Malone Circuit, Lee became eligible to attend the annual conference to be received into full connection with the Methodist Episcopal church; there he presented himself for examination. Mary Lee and two children remained near the conference at her parents' home. While en route, Lee was asked to visit a camp meeting in Gouverneur, where a shortage of preachers existed. Although he had enough time to render assistance, he declined. After all, Mary Lee had not visited her parents during the intervening four years and Lee felt constrained to press on to their home. On the way, however, as they neared the eastern end of St. Lawrence County, about sixty miles from Malone, their spooked horse upset the buggy. While Lee and the children narrowly escaped serious injury, Mrs. Lee sustained a severely injured knee. Fortunately, relatives of the presiding elder lived nearby and provided rooms in which she might recover. The same elder seized the opportunity to press Lee into service as an evangelist, even offering to pay him to preach. Lee finally acquiesced and preached three sermons at the camp meeting at Gouverneur. Traveling again toward the conference, he happened upon another camp meeting at Lowville in Lewis County. There, once again, Lee permitted himself to be pressed into service as a public speaker. Feeling that the crowds, including the Methodist preachers from those areas that did not know him, had been favorably impressed with his message and delivery, Lee finally arrived at the conference where the ordaining committee awaited him. To his chagrin, Lee made a dismal showing due mainly to a lack of the needed study books. The members of the committee would not recommend him to the conference for ordination.[12]

What saved the day for him, however, was his preaching at the camp meetings. His hearers were favorably impressed with the youthful Lee's preaching and protested the action of the committee. With their backing, Lee was elected deacon and the venerable old Bishop Robert Roberts ordained him to that office. Methodist rules mandated that he serve at least two more years before being examined and ordained an elder. Lee determined to let nothing hinder his making a strong showing at that examination. He promptly purchased books on natural philosophy and rhetoric, as well as a theological dictionary. To his way of thinking, if he could not boast a classical education at a college, at least he would develop himself into the very best "practical scholar" possible.[13]

As the 1829 session ended, Lee discovered that his next appointment was to Waddington Circuit of the Potsdam District, located in eastern St. Lawrence County. After a particularly arduous trip on an old corduroy road that had rotted since its construction during the War of 1812, Lee and his family arrived in Lisbon, a sprawling hamlet comprised mostly of small log cabins. Lee reported spending the night with large families of a dozen that all shared one room. On one occasion he spent the night with a family that had replaced the older log cabin shanty with a more modern two-room cabin. With two feet of snow on the ground and the temperature hovering between thirty-five and forty degrees below zero, he spent the night without a lantern or fireplace on a mattress with linen sheets. Contrastingly, on hot summer nights, he sometimes chose to sleep on the floor rather than be consumed by bedbugs.[14]

After traversing the Waddington Circuit several times, Lee decided to locate nearer the center of his circuit. That placed him in the town of Waddington, and shortly thereafter, he moved to Grass River, a village where one of his regular preaching points was located. During his tenure on this circuit, Lee gave additional credence to the growing popularity of camp meetings, a chief weapon in Methodism's spiritual armory. Bishop Francis Asbury looked with great approbation upon the protracted services held throughout the country. Wherever people could be assembled en masse, away from the routine grind of life, a camp meeting could be staged with the assurance of success. A forest clearing, an empty lot near a village, or an unused meadow could easily accommodate a roisterous crowd of rural folks who might otherwise be bored with the monotony of life far from the cities. Asbury described many such spiritual camps which usually lasted for an extended weekend of four days, where several thousand people gathered to listen to three or four preachers exhort souls from very crude platforms or brush arbors. As early as 1811, Asbury estimated that upwards of three or four million Americans gathered annually for such religious gatherings. [15]

Lee's first task was to oversee a local camp meeting. As he directed in clearing the area, setting up the tents and constructing the platform, his extremely youthful looks made him appear to the strangers as anyone but the preacher in charge. He presided over the first services and did the preaching until other ministers began to arrive later in the week to share the duties. The converts provided many, if not most, of the new members in Lee's congregations. Almost singlehandedly, the Methodists seized the forefront in utilizing that frontier institution in northern New York. Baptists and Presbyterians appeared anxious to help, but one gets the impression from the literature of the day that the Methodists built the camp meeting into the great soul-gathering mechanism of the early republic. [16]

Some members of Lee's congregations proved to be rather picky. On one occasion Mrs. Lee needed a replacement bonnet for the one lost in the buggy accident. The couple rode to Ogdensburg where a Methodist woman operated a millinery shop. Lee parted rather gingerly with five dollars for the bonnet, but that proved not to be the worst part of the incident. Somehow, word of the price came to the knowledge of one of Lee's strongest supporting families, and the result heaped further injury on the Lees: the pious couple refused to pay any support toward Lee for an entire year. The lady of that family deplored any finery, and went to great lengths to demonstrate her own frugality and humility. She purchased a common calico dress and sewed it so that the material was inside out, as Lee wrote, "lest she should be proud of its bright colors." Such people composed Lee's membership within the circuit.[17]

Lee attended the annual conference that met in Utica in July of 1830. Bishop Elijah Hedding presided over the proceedings. In that session the topic of temperance was brought up. As early as 1753 the Methodists in England had established a general rule by which members could be subjected to disciplinary measures for "drunkenness, buying or sell spirituous liquors, or using them, unless in cases of extreme necessity." American Methodists in the 1780 general conference dealt with the matter by asking: "Shall we disapprove of the practice of distilling grain into liquor? Shall we disown our friends who will not renounce the practice?" The delegates voted an affirmative answer. In 1783 the conference urged its members not to manufacture, sell, or use spirituous liquors. The general conference in 1816 passed a resolution that any local preacher found guilty of distilling or selling spirituous liquor would forfeit his license. The Congregationalists, however, seized the national spotlight on temperance. Responding to the constant pressure of Lyman Beecher, members of the American Tract Society were encouraged to call for a state convention in Boston. That meeting wrote a constitution for the American Society for the Promotion of Temperance.[18]

In 1828 the general conference evidenced a willingness to further tighten the rules. It advised all members to cease manufacturing and selling ardent spirits as well as to cease dispensing liquor to their employees. The Oneida Conference at Utica debated a change in the General Rule, which had prohibited ". . . drinking them unless in cases of necessity." A large majority favored the passage of a resolution that added the word "extreme" before the word "necessity." Thus, the Methodists were doing their part to stamp out the evil of drink. Bishop Hedding, clearly pleased that the resolution had carried, announced the vote and then trumpeted its epitaph: "Now let whisky die an eternal death." If John Barleycorn has died, we have yet to read his obituary or visit his grave.[19]

Lee, along with two others, was reassigned to Waddington for the

1830-31 conference year. By then, Lee was maturing as a preacher, and felt more comfortable with his understanding of Wesleyan theology. With that confidence he evidenced a man willing to stand firmly against heresy. During that year he had opportunities to demonstrate such a bent. Whenever Baptists had taunted Methodists for not baptizing their converts by immersion rather than by sprinkling, Lee resorted to preaching apologetical and polemical sermons against them. Early in that year, however, pressure from another source developed.

Universalism had made significant headway in northern New York. On occasion, whenever it appeared that some theological showdown might develop, Presbyterians and Baptists tended to fall in behind the Methodist clergy and the three groups presented a unified front against the unorthodox teachings of the Universalists. Lee managed to get himself into one of those situations in the little hamlet of De Peyster located on a neighboring circuit. A meeting house, built by the community at large, was to be dedicated. By common consent, since the Methodists and the Universalists were the strongest numerically in that place, the Presbyterians, the only other group of any size there, contacted Lee to preach a dedicatory sermon representing their side. A Universalist preacher would preach a similar sermon for their side.[20]

After drawing straws to determine who should preach first, Lee mounted the pulpit, determined not to be confrontational. His sermon seemed innocuous enough and he sat down satisfied that he had not started a quarrel. He had mentioned neither Universalism nor its key doctrine that denied eternal punishment. Unfortunately, the other preacher did not return the favor. He harangued upon his pet themes until confrontation could not be avoided. Since no meeting had been scheduled for that evening, Lee proceeded to announce that he intended to review part of the Universalist's sermon in an evening service. Word spread through the village and into the country. By evening a large host had assembled to hear what the young Methodist preacher would say.[21]

By that time, Universalism had been in America for over half a century, having arrived through the influence of several different mystical and pietistical groups from Germany. An American strain can be traced to John Murray and two later writers, Elhanan Winchester and Hosea Ballou. These three, in various ways, had attempted to conjoin the predestination of Calvinism with the benevolence of God. Behind this struggle, of course, lay their problems with eternal punishment for nonbelievers. Since the gospel taught that Christ died for the sins of everyone, Universalists insisted that all men must go to heaven upon death. Winchester, holding to a restorationist view, argued for the soul passing through a purgatory-like place (although he did not use that term), in which the human soul suffers for a period of time, after which it passed into a happy abode. Ballou, who represented the ultra-Universalists, maintained that upon death the soul immediately proceeded to heaven. Obviously, any teaching that instructed humankind that despite living like the devil, or slightly better, one would be assured of heaven, was bound to be received with great joy on the frontier, or anywhere for that matter. Lee knew that he would need to be at his best if he were to save people in De Peyster from such rank heresy. It was also his first opportunity for a prearranged public debate. The Universalist preacher, hearing Lee's lecture on that Sunday night, challenged him to a set debate on the proposition "Will all men be finally holy and happy?" The showdown between the two preachers would take place in four weeks. Lee willingly obliged him.[22]

As noted above, after such a poor performance at his examination for admission to the deaconate, Lee set about to develop himself into a self-made scholar. Since that conference in 1829 at Cazenovia, his studies and practice in the pulpit had enabled him to develop a style of argument shaped by the philosophy of discourse attributed to George Campbell and Bishop Richard Whately. Nineteenth century rhetorical theory in America was chiefly molded by the influence of those two British scholars. Their textbooks on logic and rhetoric were standard college reading and are observed on the required reading lists of men studying for ordination in most of the major denominations of antebellum America. The level of mastery of the contents of such books by aspiring preachers of the day cannot be ascertained with any certainty. Evidence reveals in the case of Lee, however, that he honed his public discourse and debating skills to such a degree of perfection that he rightfully earned for himself the sobriquet "Logical Lee" from his colleagues, and the recognition of contemporary scholars as a solid example of evangelical reform rhetoric.[23]

Campbell's *Philosophy of Rhetoric* developed a theory of discourse based upon human nature. In it he emphasized the ends of discourse as they related to the nature of the audience, giving special attention to the aim of rhetoric as persuasion. He was concerned with audience analysis, sources of evidence, and the qualities of perspicuity and vitality in eloquence.[24]

Whately tended to focus on argumentation as central to the rhetorical process. Solidly Aristotelian in his theory, Whately placed great emphasis on the logical mode of proof. He provided modern theory with the concepts of presumption and the burden of proof, as well as advocating the natural manner of delivery rather than the elocutionary method then prevalent. Ernest Bormann, a modern analyst of Whately, has identified the major characteristic of religious rhetoric to be romantic pragmatism in communication style. That literary form, so evident in Lee's sermons and books, celebrated nature, the importance of the imagination, and effectiveness. Concern with these elements typified nineteenth century speakers in general and preachers in particular. Bormann cites three branches of this style: the colloquial or "ungenteel" style that emphasized personal experience, the Puritan style that focused on orthodoxy, and the evangelical reform style that stressed effectiveness.[25]

Lee adopted the evangelical reform style, which was characterized by establishing common ground with the audience, using factual evidence and rhetorical proof, and celebrating the American experience. At De Peyster, Lee had no problem in engaging his audience's sympathy, a group that already harbored suspicions about Universalist teaching. Of course the thought that they no longer needed to fear hell, as the Universalists taught, must have sounded wonderful to their sinful ears! Following a carefully planned strategy, Lee proved himself a master craftsman, skillfully applying the rules of logic and rhetoric, and adapting them to his hearers as well as his debating opponents.

When the appointed day for the debate arrived, Lee and his young colleague in the ministry traveled to De Peyster. The combatants set about to settle the issue as to whether or not "all men will be finally holy and happy." Each side was allotted alternate speaking times of fifteen minutes. Lee discovered that two preachers would do the debating for the Universalists, while he must defend orthodoxy alone. According to rules of debate, his opponents, having the affirmative, should have presented their views first. They refused, however, so Lee began. In discussing his methodology, Lee utilized standard nomenclature of logic such as "chain of arguments" and "direct argument." Citing every scripture that bore on the topic, Lee built a solid, unassailable defense of the endless punishment of sinners. Since he set the tone by going first, he managed to keep the Universalist preachers on the defensive. That "being their first hand to hand grapple with Methodist theology," they appeared somewhat bewildered, denying all punishment after death, affirming that one's virtue or vice has no effect on what happens in the afterlife, stressing that all are immediately both holy and happy at the moment of death. Stating the standard teachings of Murray, Winchester, and Ballou, they argued against the doctrine of Christ's atonement, denied the doctrine of pardon, and finished by asserting that persons receive in this life all the punishment that their sin deserves.[26]

After two days and evenings of debate, the affair came to a close by mutual consent. A full house witnessed the concluding remarks. Unfortunately for the Universalists, several people were present who had celebrated Lee's strong showing by imbibing ardent spirits. To the embarrassment of Lee's opponents, they then declared with thick tongues and weakened brains that they supported the Universalists, who would certainly have preferred not to have that support just then. Lee's supporters raised an offering for his expenses. Not to be outdone, one of the drunks removed his filthy coat and handed it to Lee's opponents, claiming that he had no money but that the subdued debater was welcome to it. As Lee wrote, "It was the climax of ridiculousness." The community of De Peyster claimed that Lee had won for them a great victory, and even the Universalists admitted that Lee was the best debater. The commendation of the place must have been sincere; they invited Lee to be their pastor in the coming year.[27]

Later in the year, Lee engaged in another debate with the Universalists on the same topic. He spared nothing in preparation for the public event that lasted three days and three evenings. Lee described the "chain of logic-linked arguments" which appears to have been constructed as a lawyer's brief, but he depended upon his memory or his extemporizing power for filling out the case. He came to be known through such public debates and later through his writings that grew out of the debates. Doubtless, it was at this time that he began to think about writing a book in refutation of Universalism, which he published in 1836.[28]

The balance of the year passed quickly and for his labors Lee had received just under $200. Soon it was time for the Lees to pack their furniture and household items. His second son had been born that year; Lee's family responsibilities were growing. The two-year rule still applied and Lee knew the conference would send him elsewhere. He had worked hard to prepare himself for the committee of examination, determined that he would not be humiliated as he had been two years earlier. His pluck and determination paid off handsomely. He passed his examination for ordination as an elder.[29]

The Oneida Conference met that year in Lowville, Lewis County. Bishop Joshua Soule presided over the session, and had charge of the service in which Lee and thirteen others received ordination into elder's orders. At the close of the conference, Lee found to his satisfaction that he had been assigned to the Heuvelton Circuit in St. Lawrence County. Located six miles above Ogdensburg on the Oswegatchie River, Heuvelton village gave the Methodist circuit its name.[30]

Vanden Heuvel, the wealthy founder of the town, built a church for the use of the Episcopalians. In 1818, a regular preaching circuit had been formed in Heuvelton and the first Methodist class, organized in 1826 and known as the "Irish Settlement Class," began meeting in the stone schoolhouse in the town. A Methodist church had to wait until 1843, ten years after Lee left the area. While Lee cannot be credited with building a meeting house, he busied himself building a solid congregation, as well as an imposing reputation for his ministerial abilities.[31]

When Lee arrived in 1831 at Heuvelton Circuit, he located his family in the town of De Peyster, the battlefield where he had put to flight the spiritual enemy, the Universalists. The people there did not need an introduction to the new Methodist preacher; he enjoyed a solid reputation among them already. Except for a single public encounter, the Universalists whom Lee had vanquished in earlier debates made no problems for him. They had fallen on hard times locally. But the funeral of a drunk who had hanged himself brought Lee and his former adversary together for another round.[32]

The community agreed that the poor wretch needed a Christian funeral, but who should preach the sermon? A meeting of the dead man's friends produced no unanimity; a compromise solution called for Lee and the Universalist preacher both to preach at the funeral. At the appointed hour the Universalist minister spoke from Psalm 97:1 as his text: "The Lord reigneth; let the earth rejoice; let the multitude of the isles be glad thereof." The gist of his sermon held that since God controls every event that transpires, then He must have ordered the events surrounding the hanging of the deceased. This predestination of God was the last in a series of predetermined acts of divinity that always leads to eternal bliss. The conclusion reached was aimed at comforting the surviving friends; the suicide proved God's providence as much as would death by fever, consumption, or even old age. Such teaching, of course, reflected accurately the position of Elhanan Winchester, the Baptist preacher who devised the theological position of Universal Restoration. Throughout the Universalist's harangue, his sharpest barbs were pointed toward his opponent. Then it was Lee's turn to preach.[33]

Applying rules of logic, Lee carefully laid his groundwork of orthodoxy with which to silence his nemesis. Taking Hebrews 10:31 for his text: "It is a fearful thing to fall into the hands of the living God," Lee agreed that all humanity, good or bad, is in the hands of God. He then pointed out that "falling into the hands" of God must be something different from merely resting in the hands of a providential creator. Then he pointed out that good men do not "fall" into God's hands because He is their friend and defender. Therefore, the text must refer only to wicked men who are called into account before God. Continuing with a series of statements that established humanity's period of probation on earth, and the folly of sending oneself unbidden into the presence of the Almighty, Lee moved toward a climax by addressing those who spread heretical teachings such as had just been heard. If the other preacher was correct, then all those "fallen, the downtrodden, the friendless, the homeless, the sorrowful, and the wretched of earth" who linger to endure such a miserable existence, ought to avail themselves of the "lead pill, a grain of arsenic, or three feet of rope [with which] they can transport themselves to realms of eternal joy." He finished by counseling that if his listeners really believed the nonsense espoused by the other preacher, that the deceased at that time really enjoyed the bliss of heaven, then all would do well to imitate his actions and likewise commit suicide. He urged them to apply the logic of his opponent to the text in Psalms. The result would be:

> "The Lord reigneth," as may be seen in the fact that this man hanged himself. "Let the earth rejoice," for we see the result of God's reign: the man is dead before our eyes! "Let the multitude of the isles be glad thereof," for this man has, by the purpose of his heart and the skill of his hands, choked himself to death![34]

Having firmly made his theological point, and that by appealing to simple logic, Lee ended his sermon by urging the crowd to prepare to meet God. That ended any further debate with the Universalist preacher.[35]

Lee's first year on the Heuvelton Circuit passed with no significant problems or achievements. His observations on the results of that year reveal "no general revival, but a steady increase of numbers . . . less Sabbath-breaking, and much more church-going." He reports several conversions and the addition of many church members. A camp meeting in a grove near the edge of the hamlet produced solid results for the town in general and the Methodists in particular. During one of the critical meetings at that camp, Lee provided insight about his philosophy of preaching.

Nathan O. Hatch has written extensively on the ungenteel ranting of most camp meeting pulpiteers. He depicts the methodology of such religious upstarts and the colloquial sermons that they created. "These loud and unrestrained exhorters honed the sermon into a razor-sharp recruiting device, drummed out theological subtlety and complication, and incorporated personal idiosyncrasies and dramatic flair."[36] Certainly many unlettered men were an embarrassment to their college-educated colleagues. Cross, in *The Burned-over District*, casts the majority of the evangelists of the day as imitators of Finney and Nash who "must throw himself back and forward just as far as they did; and must if strong enough, smite as hard upon his chair, besides imitating their wonderful drawl and familiarity with God. . . . Hand clapping, wild gesticulation, and the shift of voice from shout to whisper added visual and auditory sensation to a theatrical performance."[37] Lee, the self-made cleric, probably came as close to such extravagant actions at the camp in Heuvelton as at any point in his career; but even at his most radical moment, he cannot be viewed as a wild-eyed ranter. His art of persuasion evidenced a logical appeal to his hearers' power of choice.

Years later, commenting on that sermon from a detached setting, Lee declared that his aim was not "to make a show of skill at sermonizing, but to arrest attention, and make a bold attempt to stir the heart." Lee obviously enjoyed full control of his faculties and knew the point at which he was taking aim. An altar (the "mourner's bench"), according to standard procedure, stood in front of the speaker's platform. Lee invited his audience to respond to his urgings by coming forward for prayers. His invitation focused on human volition: "This 'will not,' of which the text speaks, is all that has heretofore kept you from being saved; and this 'will not' is all that keeps you from being saved now, this moment." He declared his intention to try and persuade them to come forward. At that precise moment he observed that a strange impulse seized him, and he found himself saying words that he on other occasions would not speak. Never one to be impulsive or extravagant, he seemed struck by the urgency of his own words even as he spoke them:

> My only object is to persuade you to come to this altar. When this altar is full of seekers my object in preaching will be secured and I will close. I can break off anywhere when the object is secured. To save time, then, you would better come at once, that we may have more time to pray; for you will come, and, God being my helper, I shall not close this sermon until I see the altar full! Come, then, without waiting; fill up the altar, and I will stop preaching, and we will come down and meet you there.[38]

In this altar call, which a reading of Lee's extant sermons indicates to be his strongest urging for his hearers to yield, his style is not a rabidly emotional scare tactic, but rather the almost lawyer-like style of Finney. Lee's appeal could be interpreted by some historians as coercive, but that is a matter of perspective. Compared to most camp meeting doggerel, Lee's message and methods appear rational, persuasive, and reasonable. In any event, the result on that occasion must have pleased the preacher: folk began to stream forward for prayer, many claimed to be converted, and a significant addition to the church membership resulted.[39]

While Lee served at Heuvelton, he was engaged for his "last and greatest" debate with the Universalists. Actually, the affair developed out of a challenge that had been issued to a younger Methodist colleague of Lee's who served on the Antwerp Circuit in Jefferson County, the adjacent county to the south of St. Lawrence. The Universalists enjoyed their greatest numerical strength in northern New York in the town of Antwerp. Their influence enabled them to boast the only church structure in the town, an imposing brick building situated on a prominent rise of land. No other denominations had been able to construct a regular meeting place and, consequently, they shared the schoolhouse for worship.

Lee's comrade-in-arms managed to get himself into an argument over religion with a medical doctor in Antwerp. The man was a strong Universalist who challenged the young preacher to a public debate. The physician bragged: "We have challenged the Presbyterians and the Baptists, and they dare not meet us, and we now challenge the Methodists." Unwilling to get involved, but just as unwilling to let the taunt pass, the preacher accepted with the understanding that each would locate a man to debate in their place. The doctor chose a Universalist, Pitt Morse, the acknowledged champion debater from Watertown; the cleric selected Luther Lee. The affair would take place on the enemy's turf, the Universalist church in Antwerp. As word spread, the whole countryside managed to get worked into a fever pitch of excitement. Such events made an excellent social outing for everyone. Lee, once contacted by the Methodists, indicated that he enjoyed his pastoral labors well enough without getting involved and would have been happy to be released from any such obligation. His mind kept busy enough with his routine studies without getting involved with a man of the stature of Morse. At least that is what Lee would have us believe. One arrives at the distinct impression that, by this point in his life, Lee loved to perform in the public arena; like a boxer, he could not wait to get into the debating ring. Somehow on these occasions he managed to maneuver his opponents into issuing the challenge that he anxiously wanted to accept, as he left the impression that he accepted the challenge with reluctance. Thus at Antwerp Lee probably permitted himself to be talked into something he wanted to do all along. The stage was set and an eager David agreed to meet Goliath.[40]

Lee received further encouragement for the coming contest from a totally unexpected quarter. Bishop Elijah Hedding had left Manlius near Syracuse at the close of the 1832 Oneida Conference. Lee, who had also attended the conference, had returned home to finish preparation for the coming debate. Hedding traveled toward Canada by way of Watertown. News of the showdown reached him as he spent time in the area with friends. Upon hearing that Lee was to represent the orthodox side, the venerable bishop asserted that his friends need not fear the outcome:

> You need have no fears for Brother Lee on that subject. I have heard it preached upon by our strongest men from the St. Lawrence to the Gulf of Mexico, and at the camp meeting in Canton, a year ago, Brother Lee preached upon it by the request of the preachers, and he went beyond any thing I ever heard before. He had argument enough to overturn all the Universalism in the world.[41]

With such a ringing endorsement from the chief spokesman of Methodism, Lee moved with alacrity to polish his weapons of debate.[42]

When the great contest day arrived, people assembled from as far away as Boonville, Oneida County, some sixty-six miles to the south. Each debater chose a representative who together agreed upon a third person. Those three composed a "board of moderators" that presumably oversaw the fairness of matters and kept the speakers on the assigned question: "Will all men be finally holy and happy?" Morse and Lee would speak alternately for fifteen minute periods.

Morse, having the affirmative, led off on the first night. Rather than use his time effectively by laying down a specific argument to which Lee must confine his response, Morse wasted his first round on a "sensational declamation over a Methodist hell." Lee seized the initiative in his allotted time and began his "chain of logic-linked arguments on the negative proof that all men will not be finally holy and happy."[43]

By keeping his rejoinders condensed, and then spending the balance of his time in advancing new material to which Morse must respond, he kept the initiative and forced his opponent to "follow in [Lee's] wake." After a period of frustration, Morse challenged Lee to settle the argument by selecting one scriptural text for his position, and then the Universalist would respond with one verse, and thus the matter would be settled. Lee, well aware that he had been scoring heavily for orthodoxy, refused such an easy out for Morse. But Morse insisted by forging ahead on his own and quoted Psalm 145:9, "The Lord is good to all: and his tender mercies are over all his works." Lee refused to rise to the bait, knowing that the audience might be swayed by an overly simplistic approach. He replied that since Morse had cited that text, Lee would assume that Morse's passage must be his strongest text in scripture. If, therefore, Lee could show that the text did not support the affirmative to the main question, his opponent, by default, was admitting that no other text could sustain the question either. Morse immediately saw his error and tried to reverse his ill-advised tactic but Lee refused to let him wiggle off the hook.[44]

In each of his allotted time periods, Lee unleashed his full barrage against Universalism in general and Morse's untenable position in particular. Using two main points, underscored by no less than twenty-eight subpoints, and a total of 203 verses of Scripture, Lee pounded away unmercifully until he had flummoxed his floundering adversary. By the third day of debating, everyone seemed ready to end the contest. It was mutually agreed to set a time for closing. Unable to decide who should speak last, a rather unconventional approach seemed to satisfy all. Each man spoke for ten minutes followed by a round of five minutes, then each would conclude with one minute; Lee would speak last. The results for unorthodox Christianity in Antwerp are the best indicator as to who won the debate: The Universalists ceased to use their own church building in that place, so severely did their support erode. After standing unoccupied for a period of years, their church passed into the hands of the Roman Catholics in the area.[45]

As for Lee, his reputation grew immensely. Morse, proving to be a hard loser, submitted articles to the Universalist periodical, *The Magazine*, published in Utica, in which he claimed a huge victory for himself. He challenged Lee to meet him in further debate within the columns of the paper. Lee at first submitted his articles to the *Christian Advocate*, the official Methodist organ in New York. Eventually he sent them directly to the editors of *The Magazine*, only to have them refuse to print his material after a column or two. Lee wrote the editor to express his chagrin at such shabby treatment. After all, he had only submitted the articles to that paper in response to the challenge of his opponent. The exchange of letters with the editor dragged on until late in the summer. Eventually Lee dismissed the entire affair, seeing that he had no chance for an unbiased hearing. The best response to the whole matter, he concluded, was to write a book in refutation of Universalism. In 1836 he published *Universalism Examined and Refuted* and quickly assured his place as a polemical debater within the ranks of the Methodist Episcopal church.[46]

Lest one assume that Lee's successes had utterly put his theological foes on the route to extinction, the editor the *Trumpet and Universalist*, the official organ of Universalism, wrote that contrary to rumors in the nation, Universalism was alive and well. By 1840, their numbers had increased from 654 societies and 245 meeting houses in America, to 853 societies and 513 meeting houses. New York by far had more than the rest, with 214 societies, 119 meeting houses, and 109 preachers. Lee, it appeared, had not killed the foe after all.[47]

The balance of Lee's second year at Heuvelton Circuit proved to be anticlimactic after the excitement of the Morse-Lee debates had subsided. Soon it was time to pack the family belongings in anticipation of another move. The Oneida Conference met that year at Cazenovia, Madison County, with Bishop Hedding presiding over business. Lee received further approbation from a powerful new acquaintance during the session, the Reverend Wilbur Fisk, D.D., then the president of Middletown University. At the time of his introduction, Fisk, who had been following Lee's articles on Universalism, lauded Lee's efforts: "I thank you that you have taken up that controversy against Universalism, and I thank you for having done so well." As Lee basked in the glow of such warm praise, he had no idea that Fisk would prove to be his nemesis in the antislavery controversy a few years hence.[48]

When the time for pastoral appointments came, Reverend Josiah Keyes, Presiding Elder, gave Lee, for the first time since entering the ministry, his choice of any circuit within the Black River District. Lee must have recognized the offer to be a kind of promotion. Any one of those circuits was an advancement over the districts of northern New York, where Lee had been since entering the ministry in 1827. Understanding that Lowville in Lewis County suffered the reputation for being a difficult assignment for previous pastors, Lee commented that he would gladly accept any circuit in the Black River District with one exception; he preferred not to be sent to Lowville. For reasons never known to Lee, that is precisely the place to which he was sent. Had he either not been consulted, or at least been given a sympathetic warning of what awaited him, Lee would not have objected to the assignment. What particularly piqued him, however, was the crude way the matter was handled. Happily, to his utter amazement, he jubilantly claimed in later years that Lowville turned out to be one of the best circuits in the entire Oneida Conference. The two years he spent there were the best years of his life. So much for the appointing powers of benevolent presiding elders! Lee was not unmindful, however, of the unfairness of such arbitrary actions by church leaders when he reached his decision for secession in 1843.[49]

The Black River District of the Methodist Episcopal church received its name from the river that flows northwesterly throughout most of the length of Lewis County. It was a land of heavily forested uplands and ridges laying just to the west of the Adirondack Mountains. In addition to typical logging and grazing enterprises, the area boasted a substantial mining business for iron, lead, and in 1828, even silver mines. Iron furnaces dotted the countryside since 1800. Numerous turnpike companies received charters to build plank turnpikes in the early decades of the century, but few of them completed their ambitious projects. The only significant internal improvement in the county was the Black River Canal that connected the Black River below Lyons Falls with the Erie Canal at Rome. That enabled Lee to make easy canal boat connections with Utica, some fifty miles to the south—a place which became prominent in the life of the Lees in the days ahead.[50]

The Black River Circuit encompassed most of the country that lay west of the Adirondack Mountains as far as Lake Ontario. The first building used by the Methodists at Lowville had been erected immediately west of the village in 1823. It was a brick church edifice which must have been a novelty for Lee during his two years as the pastor. Again he had no parsonage provided.[51]

Lee spent a satisfying year at Lowville. He shared his circuit duties with a young colleague, Rufus Stoddard, who lived in the Lee household as a boarder. Martinsburgh, a hamlet about five miles to the south, was part of the circuit. That preaching point had been assigned to Stoddard by Reverend John Dempster, the new presiding elder. Dempster proved to be a close friend and confidant of Lee in the decades to come. Unfortunately, young Stoddard had failing health and Lee preached his funeral sermon in 1837. Lee reported two productive revivals during his first year at Lowville.[52]

Lee was returned to the same place for a second year and the results proved to be about the same as the first year. In 1835 he began writing his book on Universalism. Most of his writing took place between four o'clock in the morning and breakfast. Unfortunately, just as the conference year came to a close, typhoid fever stalked the town. A next-door neighbor was stricken and quickly died. That person's mother also fell ill, and a girl living with the Lees tended to the elderly woman until she expired. At that juncture, Lee had to leave for Oswego where the annual conference would be seated. No sooner had he arrived at his destination than he received word from his wife that the girl had also died, and that Mrs. Lee and all five of their children had fallen ill with typhoid. Jumping into his buggy, he raced to cover the ninety miles to Lowville. Upon his arrival he discovered that some had already begun to recover, but Mrs. Lee had reached a critical point in her illness. Contrary to the doctor's advice, Lee sat up with her through the night. On Saturday word arrived from the conference that he had been stationed at Watertown, twenty-five miles to the north. Knowing that the congregation must have a preacher for the following day, Lee harnessed up and drove off, aware that the symptoms of typhoid fever had steadily advanced in his own body. Upon reaching the home of a member of his new congregation, Lee asked for a bed, took a large dose of "Dr. Lee's Pills" and retired to a feverish night of tossing. On the morrow he rode with the family to church where he somehow managed to preach. The next day, by exerting his indomitable willpower, he managed to arrive at home. Mary Lee recovered and the family moved to Watertown in Jefferson County.[53]

Everyone agreed that the Watertown church was one of the choicest in the Oneida Conference. Lee, for the first time, had a taste of a more settled pastorate. The Methodist Episcopal church enjoyed a pleasant year under his leadership, and a revival provided growth in the church membership. In the following spring, Lee secured the services of a local printer to publish his *Universalism Examined*. The Methodist Episcopal official organ, *Zion's Herald,* carried numerous notices of the availability of Lee's book, along with several glowing endorsements by the editor.[54] Interestingly, the editor of the *Trumpet*, the official organ of the Universalists, also offered a quantity of *Universalism Examined* from their bookroom!

At the Oneida Conference of the preceding year, the Black River Conference had been drawn up as a new organization. Its first annual session was to be held at Watertown, and to the Lees fell the task of securing entertainment for the clergy. Bishop Beverly Waugh presided over the business sessions, his first in that episcopal capacity. Two incidents punctuated the events. Due to sickness in the Lee family in the preceding year, they had steadily fallen behind in finances. Lee owed an outstanding debt of thirty dollars to the Methodist Book Room in New York City. The agent pressed Lee for a payment. A friend overheard the bill collector's insistence and due to the gracious intervention of his friend Dempster, the conference raised an offering to pay the balance due in full. But Lee's close colleague did even more.[55]

During the course of routine business, Dempster introduced a resolution that lauded Lee's recently published book and urged all of the clergy to avail themselves of it. Bishop Waugh refused to put forth the motion, claiming that the book had not been issued by the Methodist Episcopal Book Room, but was a private enterprise. Lee's champion did not let the matter drop. He had another tack he could try.

When a preacher gave his yearly report the presiding elder stood and gave his opinion of the man whose report was about to be passed as his name was called by the chair. After the one whose character was being examined left the room, the presiding elder spoke concerning him. When Lee's name came up he left the room. Unable to hear him but informed later, Lee learned what his friend had said. In a magnanimous gesture, Dempster lauded Lee's character, his industry, his powers of endurance, and his new book: "That book is as remarkable as its author; it is a masterly production; it is like himself, and every thing he lays his hand upon bears the stamp of greatness." The eulogy may have been somewhat overdrawn, but it does permit one a sampling of what Lee's friends thought of him by the time he was thirty-eight. When the session closed, Lee had been appointed to Fulton, another prosperous church. It was during his service in that place that Luther Lee encountered the issue of antislavery, a controversy that changed the course of his life.[56]

To that point in his life and ministry Lee appears to have operated in a small world with a narrow focus of issues that lay beyond his ken. Lee had not left his native state of New York by the age of thirty-six. If there were problems brewing in the nation, he provides us with no hint that he knew or cared about them. His aim in life by that point had focused on spreading the gospel as Methodists perceived it, only stopping along the way to involve himself in a good debate with the unorthodox of Christianity. When he moved to his next assignment in Fulton, however, he caught the vision of a world that was much larger than the one in which he had been functioning. In that realm he would form lasting friendships while he reaped undying hatred from those who disagreed with his views of society and the problems that confronted him.

NOTES

1. Harry R. Landon, *The North Country: A History Embracing Jefferson, St. Lawrence, Oswego, Lewis and Franklin Counties, New York* (Indianapolis, Ind.: Historical Publishing Co., 1932), 133.

2. Landon, *North Country*, 134.

3. Franklin B. Hough, *A History of St. Lawrence and Franklin Counties, New York from the Earliest Period to the Present Time* (Albany, N.Y.: Little & Co., 1853), 507. Lee wrote in an article "Our Centenary Year," for the Methodist Episcopal *Northern Christian Advocate,* January 1, 1885, that the country around the Malone Circuit had but few roads that were passable through the entire year. He wrote that were he to return to the Malone area in 1885, "I should find a railroad where I used to wade through mud to my horse's knees; I should find beautiful dwellings where I used to be entertained

in a log cabin."

4. Cf. Whitney R. Cross, *The Burned-over District: The Social and Intellectual History of Enthusiastic Religion in Western New York, 1800-1850* (Ithaca, N.Y.: Cornell University Press), 161-64; Keith J. Hardman, *Charles Grandison Finney, 1792-1875: Revivalist and Reformer* (Grand Rapids, Mich.: Baker Book House, 1990), 133-49.

5. Donald G. Mathews, "The Second Great Awakening as an Organizing Process, 1780-1830," *American Quarterly* 21 (Spring 1969): 36.

6. William Ralph Ward Jr., *Faith in Action: A History of Methodism in the Empire State, 1784-1984* (Rutland, Vt.: Academy Books, 1984), 14-15.

7. Luther Lee, *Autobiography of the Rev. Luther Lee, D.D.* (New York: Phillips & Hunt; Cincinnati: Walden & Stowe, 1882), 39-40.

8. Lee to Rev. Ralph W. Allen, corresponding secretary of the New-England Methodist Historical Society, information by Lee on a questionnaire submitted to all "corresponding members of that society"; ca., 1880, since Lee indicated in it that his "autobiography" was in manuscript form and was not published until 1882.

9. Charles E. Cunningham, *Timothy Dwight, 1752-1817: A Biography* (New York: Macmillan, 1942), 84-98; Nathan O. Hatch, *The Democratization of American Christianity* (New Haven, Conn.: Yale University Press, 1989), 133-35; *Autobiography*, 43.

10. See James Mudge, *History of the New England Conference of the Methodist Episcopal Church, 1796-1910* (Boston: Published by the Conference, 1910), 386-87, for an overview of how Methodists ran their camp meetings during the era; cf., Hatch, *Democratization of American Christianity*.

11. See William Sargant, *Battle for the Mind: A Physiology of Conversion and Brain-Washing* (New York: Doubleday, 1957; paperback edition, Baltimore: Penguin Books Inc, 1961), for an excellent discussion of bizarre camp meeting phenomena. Sargant, a British psychiatrist, did much research and analysis on shell-shocked British troops after their harrowing experience in the escape from Dunkirk in 1940. He argues for a common link between revivalist techniques, especially those of the Second Great Awakening and continuing to the snake handlers of rural Appalachia, among voodoo practitioners of Haiti, and, interestingly, he includes rock and roll dancers and musicians of his era. Building upon I. P. Pavlov's classical and operant conditioning in his laboratory dogs, Sargant argues that evangelists develop skills in arousing the emotions of their rapt congregations until such a fervor pitch is attained that bizarre manifestations frequently occur; cf., William James, *Varieties of Religious Experiences* (New York, 1902; repr., New York: The Modern Library, 1929); *Autobiography*, 44.

12. *Autobiography*, 61-65.

13. *Autobiography*, 73-74.

14. *Autobiography*, 78.

15. Francis Asbury, *The Journal and Letters of Francis Asbury*, ed.

Elmer C. Clark, J. Manning Potts, and Jacob S. Payton, 3 vols. (Nashville, Tenn.: Abingdon, 1958), 3: 341-45, 453; Hatch, *Democratization of American Christianity*, 49-56.

16. George Hughes, *Days of Power in the Forest Temple: A Review of the Wonderful Work of God at Fourteen National Camp-Meetings, From 1867 to 1872* (Boston: John Bent & Co, 1873; repr., Salem, Ohio: Allegheny Publications, 1975); B. G. Paddock, writing from Potsdam in 1826, claimed that over six thousand had been converted in the previous six months, which indicates that Lee should reap some benefits from the earlier revivals, in F. W. Conable, *History of the Genesee Annual Conference of the Methodist Episcopal Church* (New York: Nelson & Phillips, 1876), 254.

17. *Autobiography*, 76-77.

18. John Allen Krout, *The Origins of Prohibition* (New York: Alfred A. Knopf, Inc., 1925; repr., New York: Russell & Russell, 1967), 66, 67, 104, 108. In citing the rule, Krout gives the wording as it existed when he was writing. Actually the word "extreme" was the focus of the Utica debate of the 1828 Oneida Annual Conference; see Douglas J. Williamson, "The Rise of the New England Methodist Temperance Movement, 1823-1836," *Methodist History* 21 (October, 1982): 3-28, for an extensive overview of Methodist treatment of temperance.

19. Krout, *Origins of Prohibition,* 112, 113; *Autobiography*, 80-81.

20. See F. P. Tracy, "Historical View of Universalism in the United States," *The Methodist Magazine and Quarterly Review* 19, no. 4 (October 1837): 390-404, for an excellent overview of Universalism as perceived by the orthodox churches in antebellum America; *Autobiography*, 83.

21. *Autobiography*, 84, 85.

22. Ernest Cassara, ed., *Universalism in America: A Documentary History* (Boston: Beacon Press, 1971); Elmo Arnold Robinson, *American Universalism: Its Origins, Organization and Heritage* (New York: Exposition Press, 1970); R. P. Hesselgrave, "Universalism," in *Dictionary of Christianity in America*; cf., Hatch, *Democratization of American Christianity*, 41-42 for an overview of the shift in Winchester's theology from classical Calvinism to Universal Restoration.

23. Richard Whately, *Elements of Rhetoric: Comprising an Analysis of the Laws of Moral Evidence and of Persuasion, with Rules for Argumentative Composition and Elocution* (n.p., 1828; repr., ed. Douglas Ehninger, foreword by David Potter, Carbondale, Ill.: Southern University Press, 1962); George Campbell, *Philosophy of Rhetoric*, (n.d, n.p.); Ernest G. Bormann, *The Force of Fantasy: Restoring the American Dream* (Carbondale, Ill.: Southern University Press, 1985), 168, 180, 183, 191; cf. *Christian Advocate and Journal*, May 10, 1833 for a complete list of the books required for those being ordained into the ministry within the Methodist Episcopal church; cf., *True Wesleyan*, August 10, 1844; December 28, 1844; April 18, 1846; wherein Whately is listed as the standard text for Wesleyans studying for ordination examinations.

24. Lester Thonssen and A. C. Baird, *Speech Criticism* (New York: The Ronald Press, 1948), 139; see *Zion's Herald*, July 6, 1842 and July 25, 1843, where are listed the texts of Whately as requirements for both rhetoric and logic on the Course of Study for those preparing for ordination examinations.

25. Bormann, *Force of Fantasy*, 180-83.

26. *Autobiography*, 86-87.

27. *Autobiography*, 88.

28. Luther Lee, *Universalism Examined and Refuted, and the Doctrine of the Endless Punishment of Such as Do Not Comply with the Conditions of the Gospel in This Life, Established* (Watertown, N.Y.: Knowlton & Rice for the author, 1836).

29. *Autobiography*, 88-91.

30. The town's current name is Heuvelton.

31. Franklin B. Hough, *History of St. Lawrence and Franklin Counties*, 293-97; Cortland F. Smithers, *History of Heuvelton and Vicinity* (n.p.: published by the author, 1971), 6-18; Persis E. Boyeson, "Early History of Heuvelton Methodist Church," unpublished essay, 1993.

32. *Autobiography*, 92-97.

33. Hatch, *Democratization of American Christianity*, 41-42.

34. *Autobiography*, 97.

35. *Autobiography*, 92-97.

36. Hatch, *Democratization of American Christianity*, 133.

37. Cross, *Burned-over District*, 175.

38. *Autobiography*, 101.

39. Cf., Richard Carwardine, "The Second Great Awakening in the Urban Centers: An Examination of Methodism and the 'New Measures,'" *Journal of American History* 52 (February 1972): 327-40, for an analysis of evangelist's techniques in the business of getting sinners to seek publicly for a religious conversion.

40. *Autobiography*, 102-103.

41. *Autobiography*, 103.

42. D. W. Clark, *Life and Times of Rev. Elijah Hedding, D.D.* (N.Y.: Carlton & Phillips, 1856), 420-21.

43. *Autobiography*, 106.

44. *Autobiography*, 106-119.

45. *Autobiography*, 106-119.

46. Luther Lee, *Universalism Examined and Refuted*.

47. *Trumpet and Universalist Magazine*, December 19, 1840.

48. *Autobiography*, 121.

49. *Autobiography*, 120-23.

50. Franklin B. Hough, *A History of Lewis County in the State of New York from the Beginning of Its Settlement to the Present Time* (Merrick, N.Y.: Richwood Publishing Co., n.d.), 255-57; J. H. French, *Gazetteer of the State of New York: Embracing a Comprehensive View of the Geography, Geology, and General History of the State, and a Complete History and Description of*

Every County, City, Town, Village, and Locality (Syracuse, N.Y.: R. Pearsall Smith, 1860), 374-79.

51. G. Byron Bowen, ed., *History of Lewis County New York, 1880-1965* (n.p., Board of Legislators of Lewis County, 1970), 352-53; Hough, *History of Lewis County*, 282-83.

52. *Autobiography*, 123-24.

53. *Autobiography*, 126-29.

54. *Zion's Herald*, June 6, December 5, and December 19, 1838.

55. *Autobiography*, 128-29.

56. *Autobiography*, 128-30.

Chapter Three

1836-1837: Becoming an Abolitionist

The issue of why people became abolitionists has occupied historians for years. Of course, writers who dislike the methodology and abrasiveness of the more outspoken enemies of slavery see them as troublemakers—professional agitators. Avery O. Craven began writing history from the Southern prospective in the late 1930s. His utter contempt for abolitionists led him to describe them as irresponsible fanatics who must shoulder the blame for the secession of the Confederate States and even for the Civil War. Craven argued that the war was a "needless conflict" that came about as the result of the extreme antisouthern rhetoric of shrill, hateful fanatics who would not permit the South to be left alone with its "peculiar institution." In the next decade T. Harry Williams described abolitionists as radical, fiery, scornful, revolutionary, Jacobins, vindictive, bitter, sputtering, fanatical, and extreme. Other historians, rather than simply heaping vituperation on those who would free the slaves, sought a common motive that propelled abolitionists into their unpopular enterprise.[1]

David Donald attempted to solve the "problem of why people enlisted in the antislavery fray" by presenting a different approach. Denying that reformers got involved for the reasons that they stated in their many memoirs and autobiographies, he sought a deeper motivation. Donald disagreed with historians James Ford Rhodes and Gilbert Barnes, who argued that reformers simply had fallen under the persuasive influence of William Lloyd Garrison and Theodore Dwight Weld. In his revisionistic analysis Donald sees abolitionists, at least the leaders of the movement, as a "displaced social elite" who came from old socially prominent New England families. Those clans had fallen victim to industrialization and modernization, losing their accustomed role as leaders in society. He maintains that the sons and daughters of these social elites entered reform movements of all kinds in an attempt to recoup their lost status. Robert A. Skotheim responded to Donald's thesis with a revisionist conclusion of his own, arguing that Donald's research had been drawn from too small a sample and that too many abolitionists did not conform to Donald's profile.[2] In defense of Skotheim's argument, we can safely assert that Luther Lee did not descend from wealthy, displaced, social elites of New England!

Historians in the school of interpretation that view abolitionists as farsighted reformers can appeal to men such as Luther Lee for a good example of their thesis. Russell B. Nye, Martin B. Duberman, and Donald G. Mathews generally agree that abolitionists entered into social reform because they genuinely believed in the cause. Most of these social reformers paid heavily for their efforts. As we will see in the following chapters, Lee's relatively peaceful life as a Methodist minister at times took on the dimension of a pursued victim as he hurried from one antislavery speech to another. Obviously people did not become abolitionists for personal aggrandizement. In the case of Lee, we must admit that he did enjoy a good fight, but his life bears out the fact that he entered because it was morally right for him to do so.[3]

It was in upstate New York, in the little town of Fulton, that Lee's literary record reveals his first contact with the slavery issue. How he got involved, and the first steps that he took as a result, is the topic of this chapter.

The move to Fulton took the Lee family around to the south shore of Lake Ontario, to a village in Oswego County, about twelve miles up the Oswego River from the port city of Oswego. Reverend Isaac Teller, a Methodist circuit rider, had preached occasionally in the area since 1809. Four years later the Methodist Episcopal church organized its first class in this hamlet and enjoyed solid growth in the ensuing years. Most of the services were held in schoolhouses or in portage warehouses near the river. The membership reached sufficient size and resources to construct a brick edifice in 1828, and the next year, the Fulton group was organized as a separate congregation within the circuit. Lee had further opportunity to utilize his growing debating skills while serving at Fulton. In addition to writing temperance articles for the press, Lee managed to get himself pulled into a theological dispute by a friend. It developed into a classical case of "lets you and him fight."[4]

A local preacher in the circuit had managed to involve himself in a conversation with a minister from a nonorthodox Christian church. The local folk referred to its members as "Christ-ians" [sic], placing a sarcastic emphasis on the final syllable. Lee described them as a "kind of Unitarian-Baptists."[5] To a plea for help from the young preacher, Lee agreed to meet for a confrontation in the form of a sermon by himself and the adversary. On that occasion, Lee ascertained that the real doctrinal issue revolved around the divinity of Christ. With customary measured steps, he built a "chain of closely-connected arguments" that served to confuse the inexperienced debater-foe. Rather than answer Lee's points, the other chose to spend most of his allotted time calling the sinners in the audience to repentance. No doubt existed in anyone's mind that Lee had bested his opponent, who found it best to stop badgering Lee's young preacher-friend in the future.[6]

On another occasion, Hiram Mattison, who traveled the Lysander Circuit, just to the west of Fulton, got into a similar scrape with another of the Unitarian-Baptists. The two debated for two days and declared it a draw. To settle the issue, the two combatants decided to call in heavier theological artillery. Mattison summoned Lee; the other fellow staked his hope for winning upon Elder Moral, a fairly well-known debater in the area. On the appointed day the two met to settle the question as to the divinity of Christ. Lee stated his premises: either Christ was essential divinity, or else he was not. Simply stated, if Christ was divine; the argument was over. Or if Christ was not essential divinity, what was he? Lee then asserted that only three possibilities of intellectual and moral natures are possible to all: divine, angelic, or human. Since his opponent had not opted for the first, that Christ was of a divine nature, he must choose one of the latter options: Christ had to be either angelic or human. When Lee's opponent replied that he was neither of those, but "all divine; but not eternal God. . . . He is the Son of God, and, of course, has the same nature of the Father, but is not as old. . . . I have a son; he possesses the nature that I do, but he is not as old as I am,"[7] attempting to create a theological impossibility.

Lee then rebutted, moving in for the kill:

> You hear my opponent deny the humanity of Christ, and affirm that he is all divine, of the same nature of the Father, only not so old. Waiving all other objection to this theory, I will state but one, which must be fatal [to his opponent]. The Son of God died, and as the Father and the Son are of the same nature, and as the Son died, so may the Father die, and we have no certain assurance that there will be a God on the throne to-morrow. To-morrow God may be dead.[8]

His opponent knew the game was up. After receiving the full force of Lee's logical deduction, the audience had identified the obvious winner. The other preacher attempted a brief but futile response. Failing miserably, Lee's hapless victim of sound logic picked up his theological books and headed for home. Lee basked in the sweetness of victory; orthodoxy had once again triumphed over heterodoxy in the Fulton area. In the flush of winning, however, he had little idea of what lay ahead for him.[9]

An issue freighted with enormous consequences for him had been forming on his life's horizon, the matter of human bondage—the South's· "peculiar institution." It was about to draw the Methodist preacher into its maelstrom. The problem of slavery had long bedeviled both the nation and the churches. In 1787, the Founding Fathers had hoped that the new Constitution would sufficiently bury the issue of black bondage for the new nation. The Methodist Episcopal Church, at its famous "Christmas Conference" of 1784, was just as hopeful that its actions would lay the matter to rest for American Methodism. In fact, success eluded both institutions.[10]

The Methodists certainly could not claim ignorance as far as the desires of its founder, John Wesley, were known. His opposition to human bondage originated with his labors as an Anglican missionary to South Carolina and Georgia in the 1730s. Unfortunately, George Whitefield, his old colleague in the "Holy Club" at Oxford, manifested fewer scruples on the matter of slavery than Wesley. Whitefield had been the first to import slaves into the colony of Georgia, by buying a coffle of blacks for his beloved orphanage project.[11] Wesley, however, never reconciled himself to human bondage.

In 1774, sixty years before the abolition of slavery in the West Indies, Wesley had written an essay entitled, "Thoughts on Slavery," in which he asserted that he "absolutely den[ied] all slave-holding to be consistent with any degree of natural justice, mercy, and truth. . . .You first acted the villain in making them slaves, whether you stole them or bought them. . . . And this equally concerns every gentleman that has an estate in our American plantations; yea, all slave-holders of whatever rank or degree—seeing men-buyers are exactly on a level with men-stealers."[12]

In a letter to Thomas Funnel in 1787, he spoke further of his opposition. Wesley deplored the "execrable [slave] trade" and acknowledged that response to his earlier tract of slavery would produce "vehement opposition made by both slave-merchants and slave-holders."[13] Wesley's last blast at the institution of slavery was delivered on February 26, 1791, just four days prior to his death in a letter to William Wilberforce: "Go on in the name of God, and in the power of his might, till even American slavery, the vilest that ever saw the sun, shall vanish away before it."[14]

Methodism, subsequently, came to the shores of America and by the early 1760s, societies had been organized in New York and Maryland. In 1773 the first official meeting that could be construed as a conference met at Philadelphia. At that time no action developed on the issue of slavery. Early leaders of American Methodism spoke frequently of their opposition to the institution. Freeborn Garrettson, the childhood hero of Luther Lee, voiced his sentiments on the matter the day after his religious conversion. As was the practice in family worship he called his family together for prayer. Just as he stood to begin the devotional exercises, the thought suddenly dawned upon his mind, "It is not right for you to keep your fellow creatures in bondage. . . . You must let the oppressed go free." Until that moment the idea that slavery was wrong had never occurred to him. He determined at that instant: "Lord, the oppressed shall go free."[15]

The "Christmas Conference" at the Lovely Lane Chapel in Baltimore (1784) organized the itinerant Methodist missionaries into an official body soon to be the Methodist Episcopal church. Events that transpired at that epochal meeting defined the shape that the church would assume on many issues for decades to come. On the matter of slavery, its delegates' position was not ambivalent:

> We view it as contrary to the golden law of God, on which hang all the law and the prophets, and the inalienable rights of mankind, as well as every principle of the Revolution, to hold in the deepest abasement . . . so many souls that are all capable of the image of God. We therefore think it our most bounden duty to take immediately some effectual method to extirpate this abomination from among us.[16]

Not content to merely insert a rule in the *Discipline*, these erstwhile spiritual sons of Wesley charged all slave holding members, within a period of one year, to draw legal instruments that provided a time table for the manumission of all their slaves. Anyone failing to comply faced being summarily excommunicated, a policy not unlike that of the Quakers.

A sticking point, however, remained in this well-intentioned rule: it was to be carried out in accordance with the laws of the individual states. That presented a problem since numerous state slave codes prohibited the manumission of slaves. Thus, a wedge remained in the door that otherwise might have been slammed shut on Methodist slave holding. Although the Conference of 1780 had gone on record asserting that slavery violated both the laws of God and man, when confronted with the necessity of choosing between God and man, it yielded to the latter. Within six months of passing the above rule, opposition overwhelmed the clergy's best intentions; the rule was greatly diluted to suit those who insisted on keeping their slaves. Bishop Francis Asbury and Dr. Thomas Coke, the two most powerful voices in Methodism, recognized the futility of trying to hold the line. In June, 1785, they agreed to suspend the newly-enacted rules, "until the deliberations of a future Conference. . . .We do hold in deepest abhorrence the practice of slavery; and shall not cease to seek its destruction by all wise and prudent means." The second General Conference in 1796 began its slavery deliberations with these words: "We declare that we are more than ever convinced of the great evil of the African slavery which still exists in these United States." Three rules enacted that: (1) no slaveholder *in the future* could occupy an official station in the church until he had given security for manumitting his slaves, (2) no new slaveholding members could join without being spoken to "freely and faithfully" on slavery, and (3) any person selling a slave was to be excommunicated. One can imagine how little influence such weak rules had. For all practical purposes and intents, the General Conference of 1808 ended any hope of eliminating slavery in the church as the last remaining rules were struck from the *Discipline.*[17]

While the Methodist Episcopal church had seemingly reached a truce within it ranks on the issue of slavery, the same could not be said for the nation. Slaveholders could not quiet their troubled consciences for holding humans in perpetual bondage. By 1816, the ideal plan took shape in the institution of the American Colonization Society. Its concepts were broad enough and appealed to many because it gave to the general population the appearance that something tangible was being done to solve the problem of holding humanity in bondage. It likewise appealed to the slave owner, because in all probability he would not be forced to forego his part of the "peculiar institution," since the effects of such gradualism impacted the institution only slightly. Rooted in a gradualistic approach to emancipation, the American Colonization Society sprang into life. Significant names appear on the first subscription lists and membership rolls: Henry Clay, John Randolph, Andrew Jackson, Francis Scott Key, John Taylor of Carolne, and other powerful slaveholding political figures from the upper South. Judge Bushrod Washington, nephew of the sage of Mt. Vernon, presided over the initial Board of Managers. While the final verdict on that enterprise reveals that, at best, it proved to be a negligible force against the tide of slavery proponents, it nonetheless served as an excellent salve to the nation's troubled conscience.

The concept of gradualism fitted the needs of the Methodist Episcopal church especially well. As time went on, it swung its support in an ever-increasing fashion behind the Society; by the early 1830s, its bishops regularly appointed members of their own clergy as agents for the gradualist organization. Traditionally, Methodism had made it standard procedure not to support non-Methodist organizations. With that high level of commitment to coexistence with the forces of gradual emancipation, it is little wonder the church would some day react to the concept of immediatism as violently as it did.[18]

Just when it appeared that the giant forces of slavery had been lulled into a sound slumber, the Missouri statehood issue broke in 1819 like a clap of thunder out of a clear sky. For the first time in its history, the nation found itself divided along the sectional line. For nearly two years the Tallmadge Amendment held political forces in a state of suspended animation. Only the manipulations of the Great Compromiser, Henry Clay, managed to get the wheels of political progress moving forward again in 1820. In actuality, however, only a truce had been declared in the political and philosophical war over slavery. Given the strategic spark, the conflagration could, and would, erupt at any point. That spark, in the form of a dynamic agitator who totally rejected the gradual emancipation of slaves, broke into open combustion in the early 1830s.

William Lloyd Garrison was a career in search of an issue. He could not decide at what place in the world to apply his youthful idealism. Born in Newburyport, Massachusetts, in 1805, he initially flirted with the idea of going to Europe to assist the Greeks in their fight for independence. Or he might lend his voice and pen to the cause of temperance. He finally decided upon the field of journalism, at least for the moment, watching for some issue to surface in which he might involve himself. By the late 1820s, about the same time that Luther Lee was preparing for his ordination examination, Garrison linked up with Benjamin Lundy, the Quaker abolitionist. Lundy, a saddle-maker, had been chased hither and yon throughout the 1820s by slaveholders who despised both him and his antislavery paper, the *Genius of Universal Emancipation.* On several occasions he had narrowly escaped with his life, only to move to another place, secure another press, and continue his antislavery efforts. By the end of the decade Lundy invited Garrison to work with him in Baltimore, the site of his most recent antislavery publishing efforts.[19]

The youthful Garrison had finally found his true calling in life—as an abolitionist journalist. Lundy, however, showed a degree of moderation toward the slave holder that Garrison, the young ideologue, simply could not abide. Lundy's articles lacked verve and dynamism—

and they subscribed to gradualism. Garrison soon took up his pen and launched out mightily against the institution of slavery in general, and the white masters, in particular. For his literary vituperation, he found himself in a Baltimore jail on the charge of slandering a slave owner in the area. Philanthropist Arthur Tappan, the acknowledged king of the benevolent empire, was only too happy to provide bail to the restive captive.[20]

Once free of slavery's immediate grasp, Garrison set up shop in Boston, the safest place in the nation for the kind of activities he had in mind. By January 1, 1831, he was ready to issue the first number of the *Liberator*. Rejecting the gradualist concept of the American Colonization Society, he trumpeted his shrill demands for the immediate emancipation of all slaves.[21] Any persons who advocated a gradualist plan, he asserted, were not genuine emancipationists. All they were managing to accomplish was the riddance of the country of undesirable free blacks. His demand for freedom and citizenship for all blacks carried to the corners of the nation. The tone of his first volume could not be overlooked:

> I am aware that many object to the severity of my language; but is there not cause for severity? I *will* be as harsh as truth, and as uncompromising as justice. . . . I am in earnest—I will not equivocate—I will not excuse—I will not retreat a single inch—AND I WILL BE HEARD.[22]

Garrison built a significant cadre of converts to immediatism throughout the North. In the following year he had enlisted enough followers to enable him to form the New England Anti-Slavery Society.[23] The message of his paper and his unceasing efforts at organization culminated in December, 1833. The American Anti-Slavery Society came into existence in Philadelphia at that time. Once organized on a national level the membership rolls of abolitionism continued to burgeon. By 1835 Garrison learned, however, that abolition activities came with a steep price.

In October Garrison was to deliver an address to the Boston Female Anti-Slavery Society. Before the meeting had progressed very far, a crowd of anti-abolitionists stormed the hall, forcing him to flee for his life. After a desperate chase through several rooms of the hall, the unfortunate editor of the *Liberator* surrendered to the howling mob. His ruffian captors seized him, tied a rope around his neck, tore off his clothes, and led him through the streets of Boston in a parade of triumph, demonstrating their contempt for abolitionism in general and Garrison in particular. The mobsters probably would have killed him except that the mayor intervened and had him locked in the jail for his own safety. He sarcastically penned his emotions on the jail cell wall: "Wm. Lloyd Garrison was put into this cell on Wednesday afternoon, October 21, 1835, to save him from the violence of a 'respectable and influential' mob, who sought to destroy him for preaching the abominable and dangerous doctrine, that 'all men are created equal'. . . ."[24]

Undaunted, Garrison pressed on. As the result of his arduous organizational activities, he gloated that over four hundred local societies had been formed by the end of the year. Within a few years membership had reached 250,000 abolitionists in 1,350 societies. Soon the ranks of the Methodist Episcopal membership would feel the waves of his rapidly expanding enterprise. The first thrust of abolitionism centered in the New England Conference in response to the agitation of Reverend Orange Scott, the presiding elder at Springfield, Massachusetts. Scott's unceasing efforts in behalf of the slaves did more to influence the Methodist Episcopal church than those of any other single person. Scott's influence on Lee became significant after 1839.[25]

Scott, the eldest of eight children and, like Luther Lee, the son of a poverty-stricken day laborer, was born in the year 1800, at Brookfield, Vermont—the same year as Lee's birth. Enjoying very limited educational opportunities, he too was practically a self-made man. In 1820 Scott underwent a religious conversion at a camp meeting in Barre, Vermont. Later he stated: "I felt that my name was written in Heaven, and [I] could shout aloud the praises of God with my whole heart."[26] He entered the ministry of the Methodist Episcopal church in 1822, taking his first appointment in the New England Conference. Being a man of excellent leadership skills and possessing strong public speaking abilities, Scott rapidly progressed to the position of presiding elder in the Springfield District. In 1831 he enjoyed further prestige when his colleagues elected him as a delegate to the General Conference of 1832. Soon, however, his life, also, was radically changed when confronted by the polarizing issue of slavery.[27]

In the summer of 1833, Scott met Hiram H. White, a preacher in the Springfield area. The two had a lengthy discussion of the merits of the American Colonization Society and the "Garrison Society," meaning the American Anti-Slavery Society. Scott at first expressed surprise that Garrison had been writing and living within a hundred miles of him, and he had never heard of him, much less read his *Liberator*.[28] Within a few weeks of that conversation, Scott visited Boston where he subscribed to Garrison's paper. He also purchased the writings of Lydia Maria Child, Amos A. Phelps, George Bourne, and Garrison's book against colonization. For the next year he immersed himself in studying the contrasting views of slavery and pondered how to deal with the issue of emancipation.[29]

By April of 1835, Scott reached a decision; he declared himself a modern abolitionist. He subsequently viewed his task to be the conversion of his ministerial brethren to the cause of the slaves. In that month, from his meager funds he sent money to Garrison to pay for 100 three-month subscriptions, to be sent to Methodist preachers in New England. His efforts yielded handsome dividends. By the time of the 1836 General Conference many of his conference colleagues had been abolitionized. Scott was further rewarded for his efforts by again being elected as a delegate to the conference. As the events of that tumultuous General Conference trickled back to the northern states, men like Luther Lee were soon to be forced to decide on the matter of slavery. In the meantime, Scott prepared to travel to Cincinnati where an epochal session was about to begin.[30]

Cincinnati, located across the Ohio River from slave holding Kentucky, had a long history of tolerance toward the institution of slavery. Abolitionists in that area had learned as early as the Lane Debates of 1833-34 that their efforts at freeing the slaves were met with hostility. James G. Birney, a former agent of the American Colonization Society and editor of the *Philanthropist*, covered the business sessions of the Methodist's General Conference. Birney, recently converted from gradualism to immediatism under the influence of Theodore Dwight Weld, observed and wrote editorial notes from the gallery as the delegates censured two of their own for antislavery activities during the session.[31] During the heated exchanges of the sessions, two of the New England delegates had attended one of the weekly meetings of the Cincinnati Anti-Slavery Society, each giving a brief address. For that, resolutions of censure were introduced against the men. Scott stood solidly in support of the two, making numerous speeches in their behalf. Birney witnessed the formidable attitude of the delegates from Dixie when resolutions were offered by Scott and others to denounce slave-holding bishops and preachers. Speaking for two hours, Scott declared that abolitionism could not be crushed:

> When you can put your foot on one of the burning mountains and smother its fires—when you can roll back the current of the thundering fall of Niagara—or stop the sun in its course, you may then begin to think about "crushing abolitionism." *Sir, the die is cast*—the days of the captivity of our country are numbered! ITS REDEMPTION IS WRITTEN IN HEAVEN!![32]

When the voting took place, however, Scott's warning went unheeded. Reverend William A. Smith of Virginia gave vent to his outrage that some Yankee had the audacity to challenge slavery. Venting his spleen on Scott, he vowed, "I have no more to do with that brother, than if he did not exist. I wish to God he were in heaven."[33]

After two days of animated debate, the forces opposing abolitionism won the passage of the censure resolutions. The conference ended on a sour note for the defeated antislavery delegates. Their ardor, however, continued to burn brightly; they intended to stay the course. Their task in the days ahead would become increasingly difficult due to the "bishop's rule." The bishops had determined to employ an unwritten policy to enforce within the annual conferences what the abolitionists in derision referred to as the "gag rule." The bishops, Robert R. Roberts, Joshua Soule, Elijah Hedding, and James O. Andrew, determined to apply heavy-handed tactics to restrict debate on "this agitating subject."[34]

By determining such an arbitrary course, the bishops reflected the repressive measures being employed within the federal government. First, President Andrew Jackson had insulted the antislavery pamphleteers by ordering southern postmasters to stop accepting for delivery what they deemed to be incendiary literature. Adding insult to injury, the pro-slavery forces in the United States House of Representatives passed the "gag-rule" that effectively closed all debate of slavery matters by laying on the table all such resolutions as soon as they were read. Now the episcopal strong-arm tactics of the Methodist bishops denied resolutions from being presented in the annual conferences. Orange Scott, utterly disillusioned by the arbitrary manner in which he had been handled by bishops and presiding elders subsequent to the General Conference, resigned his ministry (then termed taking a "location"), and in June, 1837, he accepted an agency with the American Anti-Slavery Society for a period of two years. Such was the state of affairs as Lee moved toward his decision.[35]

The Methodist Episcopal church at Fulton, New York had already begun to respond to the message of freeing fellow humans in bondage.[36] By 1836 several men of the Fulton church had sided with forces of abolition. Lee could not have been uninformed of details of the noisy Cincinnati conference. While he may never before have heard of Orange Scott, Lee did perceive the unfairness of the bishops' gag policies. Lee, at the age of thirty-six, stood at a crossroads in his ministry.

The thrust of his preaching until then had been to win souls through the power of the gospel. He should have enjoyed a measure of satisfaction at his accomplishments. His greatly enhanced debating skills had enabled him to stand forth as a champion of nineteenth-century Christian orthodoxy against all heterodox challengers. His book against Universalism had been quite well received by his colleagues. Now as a father of five children, he was confronted by a strange new phenomenon. Much like a startled deer staring, perfectly frozen, into the bright light, so Lee peered into the chasm of abolitionism. The issues of slavery were totally new to him.[37] To get involved meant certain trouble. Antislavery had been such a divisive issue everywhere. It bore the potential of polarizing his church and could even threaten his career. In a state of relative suspended animation, he pondered the issue and weighed the evidence. He was not like the youthful Garrison, casting about for something to do with his life—Lee had a calling, and had enjoyed considerable success until that juncture. What was needed to push undecided men such as Lee off the fence had been prophesied by William Ellery Channing in the previous year: "One kidnapped, murdered abolitionist, would do more for the violent destruction of slavery than a thousand societies." In November of 1837, just such a martyr, Elijah Lovejoy, stepped forward, and the backwash of it swept Lee out of his stultifying reverie and catapulted him into action.[38]

Lovejoy had first moved to St. Louis in 1827, looking to make his fortune in the world. The influence of the Second Great Awakening had been sweeping the nation in waves. Soon, Lovejoy, the son of a New England Congregational minister, fell under conviction for his sins and shortly thereafter experienced a religious conversion. Feeling the call to prepare for the ministry, he headed back east to Princeton for theological training. By 1833 the Second Presbytery of Philadelphia licensed him to preach under the authority of the American Missionary Society. Soon, Lovejoy found himself, as had Lee and others, confronted with the slavery issue. During the next three years he moved from gradualism to outright abolitionism. He eventually located in St. Louis as the publisher of an antislavery paper *The Observer.*

On several occasions he had suffered the destruction of his press at the hands of angry pro-slavery mobs. Moving to Alton, Illinois, hoping for a climate more amenable to his work, he stood the loss of yet another press thrown into the Mississippi River before he could put it into operation. By November 7, 1837, he had taken shipment of another press on which he determined to continue his efforts against human bondage. On that night, defending his press in a warehouse in Alton, Lovejoy suffered martyrdom, shot down in cold blood at the hands of the mob, which finally quieted his voice forever. That violent action by the mob in Illinois, however, jolted Lee into taking up the torch for freedom of the slaves just as Lovejoy fell. He intended to lend his voice to the cause for which the martyr at Alton had died.[39]

For several years Lee had been standing, otherwise occupied, on the side lines when the American Anti-Slavery Society came to birth. He observed in a reflective mood the news that the New York mob had broken into the home of Arthur Tappan and burned his furniture to punish him for supporting abolitionism. Lee frankly admitted that his mind had been poisoned by the slanderous attacks by the religious press that cared more for the unity of the church body politic than for the freedom of the slaves or for the freedom of speech of those who assayed to speak for the blacks. At that point Lee became outraged at the ongoing process of mob rule, the bishops' rule, and gag rules. For Lee, to continue to temporize and vacillate would be morally wrong; he determined that he could be silent no longer. He drew his abolitionist sword, threw away his scabbard of uncertainty, and charged into the fray from the pulpit of his own church in Fulton.[40]

On Sunday evening, December 3, 1837, Lee preached a funeral sermon on the murder of Elijah Lovejoy.[41] The address, surprisingly, did not focus initially on abolitionism, but rather, on mob violence. Lee took his text from Acts 19:38: "Wherefore if Demetrius, and the craftsmen that are with him, have a matter against any man, the law is open, and there are deputies: let them implead one another."

For an introduction, Lee presented the analogous case that had taken place in the ancient city of Ephesus. In that instance the mob, upset that the conversion of many in the city would lead to the end of the purchase of idols from the local craftsmen, had rioted and ranted for two hours against St. Paul and his companions. The town clerk spoke the words of Lee's text to remind the mob that offenders must only be prosecuted using the due process of law, not by mobocracy: "the law is open . . . and there are deputies" who deal in such matters. Lee then proceeded to make his application to antebellum America in general and to the murder of Lovejoy in particular. The application of principles of logic can be easily recognized. Like an attorney building a case, Lee stated that he intended to prove:

> I. That no circumstances or pretense . . . can justify any illegal proceedings against a supposed criminal;
>
> II. That in the case of Reverend Mr. Lovejoy there was no offense or provocation on his part . . . which is not the constitutional right of every American citizen.[42]

The logical deductions of the sermon could not be misunderstood. Lee made his most telling point: If there could be one case that would justify mob law, then there could be more, many more. How can society determine a safe line beyond which a mob may not pass? The answer was too obvious for his audience to miss. Lee proceeded to castigate mob actions: those who had burned the Ursuline Convent in Boston, the mob that had shed blood over a national bank issue in Philadelphia, and the rioters who had seized the United States mail in Charleston, South Carolina. Curiously, he revealed no knowledge of the mob that had humiliated Garrison in Boston.[43]

In the middle section of the sermon, Lee began to deal with the evils of slavery. He used the words "Chattel," "Property," "Merchandize" [*sic*] as he denounced the institution of slavery. He also cited lengthy quotations by Thomas Jefferson and John Wesley against the bondage of blacks, even though Jefferson was a slaveholder who believed that blacks were innately inferior to whites. He concluded the sermon by predicting that the blood of Lovejoy would be as "the seed of martyrs, that his death . . . [would be as] a signal of the success of the cause in which he fell."[44] Without any equivocation, Lee had thrown himself into the fight against slavery, which would take him far from his initial purpose solely to preach the gospel.

NOTES

1. Avery O. Craven, *The Coming of the Civil War* (Chicago: University of Chicago Press, 1957), 134-50; T. Harry Williams, *Lincoln and the Radicals* (Madison: University of Wisconsin Press, 1941), 3-6.

2. David Donald, *Lincoln Reconsidered* (New York: Alfred A. Knopf, 1956), 21-36; Robert A. Skotheim, "A Note on Historical Method: David Donald's 'Toward a Reconsideration of Abolitionists,'" *Journal of Southern History* 24 (August 1959), 356-65.

3. Russell B. Nye, "The Slave Power Conspiracy, 1830-1860," *Science and Society* 10 (Summer, 1946): 262-74; Martin B. Duberman, "The Abolitionists and Psychology," *The Journal of Negro History* 47 (July 1962): 183-92; Donald G. Mathews, *Slavery and Methodism: A Chapter in American Morality 1780-1845* (Princeton, N.J.: Princeton University Press, 1965).

4. *Landmarks of Oswego County* (n.p., n.d.), 52-53, 824-25; *History of Oswego County, New York* (Philadelphia: L. H. Everts & Co., 1877); *Fulton, New York: An Illustrated Sketch of Local History from the Birch Bark Canoe to the Automobile* (Fulton, N.Y.: Morrill Press, 1901), 52; John C. Churchill, ed., *Land Marks of Oswego County, New York* (Syracuse, N.Y.: D. Mason & Co., 1895), 25.

5. In *Landmarks of Oswego County,* 53, one observes that the Unitarians

and the Baptists shared the same building in the 1830s. If such an arrangement was commonplace, that might account for the curious theological blend that Lee described; *Autobiography*, 131.

6. *Autobiography*, 131-32.

7. *Autobiography*, 131-32.

8. *Autobiography*, 132-33.

9. *Autobiography*, 132-33.

10. *Autobiography*, 133.

11. Harry S. Stout, *The Divine Dramatist: George Whitefield and the Rise of Modern Evangelicalism* (Grand Rapids, Mich.: William B. Eerdmans Publishing Company, 1991), 198-99.

12. John Wesley, "Thoughts Upon Slavery," *The Works of John Wesley*, 14 vols. (Grand Rapids, Mich: Zondervan Publishing House, n.d.), 11: 59-79.

13. Wesley, *Works*, 12: 507.

14. Wesley, *Works*, 13: 153.

15. L. C. Matlack, *The Anti-Slavery Struggle and Triumph in the Methodist Episcopal Church* (New York: Phillips & Hunt, 1881; repr., New York: Negro University Press, 1969), 47-48.

16. Abel Stevens, *History of the Methodist Episcopal Church in the United States of America*, 4 vols. (New York: Carlton and Porter, 1864), 2: 199-200.

17. Richard M. Cameron, *Methodism and Society in Historical Perspective*, vol. I of *Methodism and Society*, ed. by Board of Social and Economic Relations of the Methodist Church (Nashville, Tenn.: Abingdon Press, 1961), 1: 99-100; Lewis M. Purifoy, "The Methodist Anti-Slavery Tradition, 1784-1844," *Methodist History* 4 (July 1966): 3-15.

18. Ronald G. Walters, *American Reformers, 1815-1860* (New York: Hill & Wang, 1978), 78-79.

19. Merton L. Dillon, *Benjamin Lundy and the Struggle for Negro Freedom* (Urbana: University of Illinois Press, 1966), 57-59; Aileen S. Kraditor, *Means and Ends in American Abolitionism: Garrison and His Critics on Strategy and Tactics, 1834-1850* (New York: Pantheon Books, 1969), 1-2; Richard H. Sewell, *Ballots for Freedom: Antislavery Politics in the United States, 1837-1860* (New York: W. W. Norton & Co., 1976), 3-5.

20. Bertram Wyatt-Brown, *Lewis Tappan and the Evangelical War against Slavery* (New York: Atheneum, 1971), 78-79; Mathews, *Slavery and Methodism*, 57-60.

21. See David Brion Davis, "The Emergence of Immediatism in British and American Antislavery Thought," *The Mississippi Valley Historical Review* 49 (September 1962): 209-30, for a link between Enlightenment thought and gradualism. The problem for the *philosophes* and their heirs revolved around the fact that slaves were property—property that natural law mandated must be protected by legitimate government. Racism placed them on the horns of a dilemma from which they could not extricate themselves. That is why blacks were passed over in the aftermath of both the American and French

Revolutions.

22. *Liberator,* January 1, 1831; Walters, *American Reformers,* 77-79.

23. See Elaine Brooks, "Massachusetts Anti-Slavery Society," *Journal of Negro History* 30 (July 1945): 311-30, for a discussion of the aims for civil and political equality of Garrison's first organizational efforts; Roman J. Zorn, "The New England Anti-Slavery Society: Pioneer Abolition Organization," *Journal of Negro History* 47 (July 1957): 157-76, points out that the Massachusetts Anti-Slavery Society was the new name given to the original New England Anti-Slavery Society in 1835. Mathews, *Slavery and Methodism.*

24. Merton L. Dillon, *Elijah P. Lovejoy, Abolitionist Editor* (Urbana, Ill.: University of Illinois Press, 1961); Hazel Catherine Wolf, *On Freedom's Altar: The Martyr Complex in the Abolition Movement* (Madison: University of Wisconsin Press, 1952), 26-27; David Dorchester, "The Relations of the Churches and Mr. Garrison to the American Anti-Slavery Movement," *Methodist Quarterly Review* 63 (July 1881): 478.

25. See Donald G. Mathews, "Orange Scott: The Methodist Evangelist as Revolutionary," in Martin Duberman, ed., *The Antislavery Vanguard: New Essays on the Abolitionists* (Princeton, N.J.: Princeton University Press, 1965), 71-101, for an excellent analysis of Scott's antislavery activities as a member of Garrison's organization, and as a later critic of Garrison's "no-human government theories."

26. Lucius C. Matlack, *The Life of Rev. Orange Scott, In Two Parts* (New York: Snowden & Prall, 1848; repr., Freeport, N.Y.: Books for Libraries Press, 1971), 5-11; James Mudge, *History of the New England Conference of the Methodist Episcopal Church, 1796-1919* (Boston: Published by the Conference, 1910), 278-79.

27. Matlack, *Life of Orange Scott,* 25-33; Mudge, *History of the New England Conference,* 278-79.

28. It is curious that Garrison's influence had not yet penetrated his own state. The New England Anti-Slavery Society had been in operation for at least two years by 1834, and the *Liberator* had a continuous run since its first issue in January 1, 1831.

29. Matlack, *Life of Orange Scott,* 25-33.

30. Orange Scott to William Lloyd Garrison, December 30, 1834, Garrison Papers, Boston Public Library; Matlack, *Life of Orange Scott,* 32-33; Mathews, *Slavery and Methodism,* 122.

31. See "Mr. Birney and Mr. Clay," *True Wesleyan,* in which Birney is taken to task by the *Herkimer Journal* for selling one slave, even though he manumitted the rest. That eventually was held against him by the Whig supporters of Clay, who had freed his personal valet, Charles, January 18, 1845.

32. Charles Baumer Swaney, *Episcopal Methodism with Sidelights on Ecclesiastical Politics* (Boston: The Gorham Press, 1926), 61; James M. Buckley, *A History of Methodism in the United States* 2 vols., (New York: Christian Literature Co., 1897) II: 18-19; cf., Mathews, "Orange Scott: The

Methodist Evangelist as Revolutionary," 86, in which he claims that the Cincinnati affair cast Scott in the role of symbolic leadership of Methodist abolitionism.

33. James Gillespie Birney, *Debate on "Modern Methodism," in the General Conference of the Methodist Episcopal Church, May, 1836* (Cincinnati: Ohio Anti-Slavery Society, 1836); Lucius C. Matlack, *The Anti-Slavery Struggle and Triumph in the Methodist Episcopal Church* (New York: Phillips and Hunt, 1881); Matlack, *Life of Orange Scott*, 32-33; Mathews, *Slavery and Methodism*, 99.

34. Luther Lee, *Wesleyan Manual: A Defense of the Organization of the Wesleyan Methodist Connection* (Syracuse, N.Y.: Samuel Lee, Publisher, 1862), 16; Mathews, *Slavery and Methodism*, 148.

35. Walters, *American Reformers*, 84-85; Lucius C. Matlack, *The Life of Rev. Orange Scott, In Two Parts* (New York: Snowden & Prall, 1848; repr., Freeport, N.Y.: Books for Libraries Press, 1971), 121; Arthur Tappan to Orange Scott, May 18, 1837, Scott Papers, Boston Public Library; Swaney, *Episcopal Methodism with Sidelights* 60-65; Bertram Wyatt-Brown, *Lewis Tappan and the Evangelical War against Slavery* (New York: Atheneum, 1971), 149-67.

36. Cf., Gilbert Hobbs Barnes, *The Antislavery Impulse 1830-1844* (New York, 1933; repr., New York: Harcourt, Brace & World, Inc, 1964), 33-69; see Whitney R. Cross, *The Burned-over District: The Social and Intellectual History of Enthusiastic Religion in Western New York, 1800-1850* (Ithaca, N.Y.: Cornell University Press), 220-24, wherein Cross states that Scott deserted Garrison when the latter abandon orthodox religion, subsequently enlisting as one of Weld's "seventy" antislavery disciples. While that is true, it must be noted that Scott continued to attend, participate, and hold office in Garrison's organization as late as 1840 when Lewis Tappan formed the American and Foreign Anti-Slavery Society in protest to the appointment of Abby Kelly to a committee. It is impossible to determine from sources available to me which of these men's disciples or writings influenced the Fulton church first.

37. It is possible that Luther and Mary Lee discussed an incident that involved slavery in the home of Dr. Joseph Bellamy, where she was reared. Dr. Samuel Hopkins, an ardent foe of slavery and the slave trade in Newport, Rhode Island, had visited the home of Bellamy in Litchfield, Connecticut, where he discovered the family owned a single household slave. Hopkins pressed Bellamy to free him; Bellamy assured him the slave was well treated and happy. Hopkins challenged Bellamy to bring the slave in and put the issue to him. The slave came into the room and Hopkins quizzed him as to his treatment, work, happiness with his life, et cetera. Affirming that everything was fine, Hopkins asked him if he would be more happy if he were free. He responded, "O yes, massa, me would be much more happy." Bellamy responded, "You may have your desire, from this time you are free," in "Dr. Bellamy's Slave," *Wesleyan,* November 21, 1860.

38. *Autobiography,* 137-38.

39. Wolf, *On Freedom's Altar,* 32-43; Barnes, *Antislavery Impulse,* 162-63.

40. See Ronald G. Walters, *The Antislavery Appeal: American Abolitionism after 1830* (New York: W. W. Norton & Co., 1978), 78, for an excellent analysis of the interval of time that often transpired between one's religious conversion and the subsequent conversion to social reform; see Timothy L. Smith, *Revivalism and Social Reform in Mid-Nineteenth-Century America* (New York and Nashville: Abingdon Press, 1957), 7, for an insightful statement about the vitality of evangelical religion and its role of importance in spawning social reforms in antebellum America: "Religious doctrines which Paine, in his book, *Age of Reason,* had discarded as the tattered vestment of an outworn aristocracy, became the wedding garb of a democratized church, bent on preparing men and institutions for a kind of proletarian marriage supper of the lamb"; also cited in Sydney E. Ahlstrom, *A Religious History of the American People* (New Haven, Conn., and London: Yale University Press, 1972), 638; *Autobiography,* 133-34.

41. Luther Lee, *A Sermon Preached in the Methodist Episcopal Church, in the Village of Fulton, N.Y., Sabbath Evening, December 3d, 1837, On the Occasion of the Death of The Rev. E. P. Lovejoy Who Was Murdered by a Mob at Alton, Ill., November 7th, 1837* (Fulton, N.Y.: T. Johnson, 1838; repr., Donald W. Dayton, ed., *Five Sermons and a Tract by Luther Lee,* Chicago: Holrad House, 1975), 25-42.

42. *Lovejoy Sermon,* 26.

43. Wyatt-Brown, *Lewis Tappan and the Evangelical War,* 149-150; Swaney, *Episcopal Methodism with Sidelights,* 50; Lee, *Lovejoy Sermon,* 38-42; see Russell B. Nye, "Day of the Mob," *Fettered Freedom: Civil Liberties and the Slavery Controversy, 1830-1860* (Urbana: University of Illinois Press, 1972), 174-218, for an excellent overview of the implications of mob action in Jacksonian America.

44. Lee, *Lovejoy Sermon,* 38-39.

Chapter Four

1838-1839: New York Antislavery Struggles

Once Lee charted his course on antislavery, he never hesitated or looked back. After he delivered the sermon at Fulton, he announced, "For this declaration I may be denounced as an abolitionist. . . . If this is abolitionism, then am I an abolitionist, and I would be glad, were it possible, to give my abolitionism a thousand tongues, and write it in letters of flame on the wings of every wind, to be seen and read of all men."[1] Perhaps "all men" would never hear of Lee, much less of his abolitionist stance, but once his sermon was published and began to circulate in Methodist circles, Lee achieved both fame and notoriety, depending upon one's perspective. The first altercation with his superiors came in the form of a literary debate with the leader of the Methodist Episcopal church's own Wesleyan University.

President Wilbur Fisk had aligned himself with the pro-slavery faction out of a desire for unity within the church rather than for any love for the institution of slavery. His true position manifested itself when he refused in 1835 to sign a petition for the abolition of slavery in the District of Columbia. Fisk proved to be one of the most prominent spokesmen for the American Colonization Society in Methodism at that time.[2] He also seemed to reserve his strongest venom for radical reformers of the day. One such victim, La Roy Sunderland, Fisk had attempted to have censured in the New England Conference for his abolition activities.[3] Meanwhile, Fisk regularly published articles supporting colonization. But his article on the death of Lovejoy lured Lee into direct conflict with Fisk. After that event, he would prove to be much less laudatory of Lee than he had on the

69

earlier occasion of Lee's defeat of the Universalists, when Fisk had commended him earlier in the Black River Conference.[4]

Shortly after Lee's sermon on Lovejoy was published, Fisk ran an article on Lovejoy in the *Christian Advocate and Journal*, the official organ of the Methodist Episcopal church. In it he managed barely to stop short of justifying mob rule. As Lee interpreted it, ". . . if [Fisk] did not justify the mob . . . [he, at a minimum] censured the murdered man more than [he] did the murderers, and threw the responsibility of his death largely on himself [Lovejoy]."[5] Fisk continued in the ensuing weeks to submit articles that correctly predicted that the antislavery issue had the potential of dividing the whole church. Lee endured Fisk's position as long as possible, and then felt he must respond to them in print. Thus, a newspaper war developed between Lee and his former booster.[6]

Fisk's aim, of course, was to head off a schism in the church. In so doing, he impugned the motives and methods of every antislavery preacher in the organization. Any member of the clergy foolish enough to put antislavery ahead of the unity of the bride of Christ deserved the opprobrium that would cling to them. Men with impeccable character of the caliber of Lee stood to lose sterling reputations that a lifetime in the ministry had earned them. Lee did not intend to stand idly by and permit Fisk's volleys to pass unanswered. The problem that confronted Lee centered on the church's official paper. It refused to run his articles. What to do? Another periodical, albeit one of a dubious reputation, did circulate throughout the church in much of New York and New England and to it Lee resorted.

The paper's editor was La Roy Sunderland, the Methodist Episcopal minister at Andover, Massachusetts. A feisty abolitionist possessing a critical pen and dynamic speaking abilities, he had won his entire congregation to the antislavery cause in 1831. Shut out of the official organ of the church, he had resorted to publishing *Zion's Watchman*. While the paper stopped short of what later came to be known as "yellow-sheet journalism," its enemies probably would have perceived it as such. Sunderland was no stranger to controversy. Constantly in trouble with the bishops for his incendiary views and writings, in the years that followed he answered charges in the annual conferences no less than seven times.[7] His name and that of George Storrs, a Methodist abolitionist preacher from New Hampshire, and just as radical as Sunderland, had become anathema to the officials. Before many years elapsed, Lee and this notorious publisher would join forces in the secessionist movement. In 1838, however, it was enough that Sunderland happily consented to run any article that would cast pro-slavery bishops and college presidents in a bad light. Coincidentally, Orange Scott's responses to Fisk's articles ran in the same issues as Lee's.[8]

Lee's articles appealed to thinking men. In balanced, logical arguments, he pointed out that antislavery men possessed no inherent principles or methods that would of necessity force a schism in the church. If a split resulted it must come as a result of the intolerance of the anti-abolitionists. He predicted that oppressive measures, taken by unyielding bishops, probably would eventually produce a hiatus within the membership. The real problem for Lee, however, came when men sacrificed purity only to preserve unity. If cohesion could only be accomplished with the cement of slavery, then schism was not the worst case scenario. It is impossible to quantify how many men Lee actually won over to antislavery, or even to ascertain the number of opposers who paused to consider their gradualist course in dealing with slavery as a result of his efforts. What we do know, however, is that Lee won for himself the undying enmity of Fisk and his cohorts. Lee's destiny was sealed at that juncture; only time was needed to reveal the process of his ouster. It was not a question of "if" but "when."[9]

Having taken the steps of challenging a prominent church leader, Lee found the subsequent steps easier to take. An antislavery convention had been scheduled for May 2 and 3, 1838 in Utica, New York, and Lee determined to attend. On the first night, Lee met and heard Scott speak for the first time. The two became solid comrades-in-arms.[10] As the keynote speaker, Scott preached an antislavery sermon from Isaiah 58:1, "Cry aloud, spare not; lift up thy voice like a trumpet." On the second night, Lee delivered a lecture entitled "The Sinfulness of Slave-holding." In the business sessions that followed, Lee found himself appointed to serve on several committees: the nominating committee, a committee to prepare a Declaration of Sentiments, the finance committee, and a committee empowered to "call another General Anti-Slavery Convention in the M.E. church."[11]

Among the resolutions adopted was one that read, "Resolved, That the thanks of this convention be presented to the Reverend Luther Lee for his very able and interesting discourse, delivered before the Convention, and that he be requested to furnish a copy for publication."[12] Lee, whether by default or design, was by that point firmly ensconced in the forefront of Methodist abolitionism. The will of the convention mandated that Lee travel to Canada as a delegate to the sister church to present the cause of abolitionism. At the same time, Scott would represent the convention in the English Wesleyan Conference in London.[13]

Early in July, Lee traveled to Kingston, Ontario, as a fraternal delegate from the Utica Convention to the Canada Wesleyan Conference. The president, however, informed him privately that while he was sympathetic to abolitionism, he could only recognize representatives from *official* bodies. The real reason for his refusal was the influence of Jessie T. Peck, C. W. Leet, and A. J. Phelps, three of Lee's colleagues who opposed his position on slavery, who had warned that to recognize Lee would offend the Methodists of America.[14]

After returning to Fulton, Lee discovered that Peck had submitted the results of the proceedings in the *Christian Advocate and Journal,* referring to Lee as a delegate of an "illegitimate and revolutionary" organization that could only be "schismatical and highly dangerous." Peck made a point in his article of putting Lee at the conference two days before Peck and friends arrived, apparently wanting to distance himself from their influence in keeping Lee from being received.[15]

Never one to let such errors pass, Lee responded in a lengthy article in *Zion's Watchman,* which was entitled, "The Canada Conference." His article directly challenged Peck, asserting that Lee had not arrived until well after the body had begun deliberations. Lee then added a lengthy explanation of his version of events. He declared that the Canadians had assured him of their sympathy and prayers for the abolitionists, and that Peck had completely missed the ethos of that body, if he assumed that it supported the enemies of antislavery, President Fisk, Bishop Hedding, and the Reverend Nathan Bangs. Lee was not about to permit his adversaries to gather the Canadians into their camp on the issue of antislavery![16] In their own paper, *Christian Guardian,* the Canadian Wesleyans printed a report of the conference which lends strong support to Lee's interpretation of the proceedings.[17]

Soon the Black River Conference of 1838 was to meet at Fulton, New York. Lee faced not only the task of preparing for the entertainment of the delegates; he must prepare himself for the charges that he knew would be raised against him during the session. Coming so soon on the heels of the Canadian affair, Lee's antislavery activities had placed him in harm's way. The conference business appeared to proceed without a problem until Lee's name was called for his character to be passed. Jessie Peck stood and preferred charges against Lee. The charges stemmed from the Canadian affair and Lee's article in the paper. The presiding officer, Bishop Morris, supported by cranky old Bishop Hedding, asked Lee if he was ready to defend himself in a trial. Lee stated that he was not. The bishop agreed to postpone the hearing until the next day at Lee's request. Fearing for his future usefulness in the church, should the result go against him, Lee fretted and planned for his own defense through the intervening hours. At ten o'clock the next morning, all expected the affair to commence. To everyone's surprise—and Lee's delight—Peck stood and withdrew his charges, stating that he had instituted them only in response to official pressure. Lee heaved a sigh of relief.[18]

His happy reverie, however, proved to be premature. Someone friendly to Lee informed him during the session that he had been tapped to pastor the Oswego Circuit, one that everyone knew was the poorest circuit in the district. The Panic of 1837 had ruined the economy of many of the nation's towns and Lee doubted that the place could support a minister. Rather than accept punishment for his abolitionism, Lee determined a bold course of action; he sought and received a location, meaning that he was free to pursue his own employment. By the time the Black River Conference had adjourned, Lee had accepted an agency with the New York Anti-Slavery Society. The Oneida Conference to the west would soon be in session. With his certificate of location, Lee could expect a reasonably good assignment in that conference should he so desire. Instead of accepting the advice of his friends, however, Lee prepared to preach his last sermon in Fulton on the next Sunday. On the following day he packed his meager belongings and loaded them all onto the canal boat that passed through Fulton in the middle of the night. His family then consisted of six children, ranging from twelve years to eighteen months. At the age of thirty-seven, his decision was epochal. His life would never be the same and there was no turning back. In the next several years, Lee would travel all of New York and the New England states as an abolition lecturer. In the summer of 1838, the Lees moved to Utica, a city that boasted the reputation of being a focal point of change.[19]

Utica had a somewhat distinguished history as the center of religious and political dissent. Located in Oneida County along both the Mohawk River and the Erie Canal, it sat squarely astride the main east-west highway of travel, and was a terminus for traffic moving north along the western foothills of the Adirondack Mountains. Because of its easy accessibility to travelers, it had hosted some of Finney's early revivals, was the state headquarters of the New York Anti-Slavery Society, and later, was the headquarters for the Liberty Party. In nearby Whitesboro was located the Oneida Institue, the only college-level institution in New York State to accept black students. The institute was a manual arts college begun by George Gale (Charles G. Finney's pastor), a place where poor men could work their way through college, something akin to cooperative colleges of our day. Under Beriah Green, the school's second president, it had become a hotbed of abolitionism. Of course its students attended most social reform conventions that met at Utica. Later, in 1843, the Wesleyan Methodists assembled in Utica for the formation of their secessionist church. By the middle of the nineteenth century, any religious or political conservative in America might rightly ask: Can anything *good* come out of Utica? In 1838 that was the place where Lee chose to live.[20]

Being in harmony with the town's innovative position on such issues, Lee settled his family in Utica, while he traveled as an antislavery agent during the next year. The family found a house at 72 Washington Street in the main section of the city. As it turned out, William Goodell, Lee's colleague in political reform, lived close by. The Methodist church in Utica probably presented another reason for Lee's choice of Utica. Its membership had been "thoroughly abolitionized." That meant that his ministerial license would be secure from those who might seek to defrock him. Lee chose to give one of his earliest antislavery speeches in that place. At its close, 130 names were added to the membership role of the Wesleyan Anti-Slavery Society of Utica. With such an auspicious beginning, Lee looked forward with optimism to the coming year. Unfortunately for many Methodist preachers, the bishops started cleaning the antislavery rats out of the Methodist Episcopal henhouse.[21]

The Methodist preachers who had recently attended the Utica Convention were marked men. The bishops determined to single out each of the leaders in their respective annual conferences for charges of insubordination or any other charge that stood a chance of passing a vote by the conferences. Lee's debating skills by then were generally well known in the northern conferences. As the men singled out for expulsion faced charges, Lee was enlisted by several of these to assist in their defense before the unfriendly conferences.[22]

The storm first hit in New York City where the New York Conference gathered in May of 1838, soon after the close of the Utica Convention. Lee had not left for Canada by that time, so Reverend C. K. True sent to Fulton enlisting his presence in New York as his spokesman and counsel. Lee agreed but warned him that a defense, no matter how sound and well presented, probably would not save True. The outcome had already been pre-determined. Lee reasoned, however, that in speaking in their defense he would have an opportunity also to present his antislavery arguments. Perhaps some of the hearers would see the validity of abolitionism. Lee, accordingly, traveled to New York City to assist True.

The charges against the abolition preacher consisted of only two: "contumacy and insubordination." True had allegedly pledged with all the others at the previous annual conference not to agitate over the slavery issue. He had, however, written tracts and attended the stigmatized Utica antislavery convention just weeks before. Lee argued that most of the charges came down to mere semantics and the interpretation of the pledge, not of True's character and conduct. Testifying in his own behalf, True claimed that he had not understood the pledge to be as narrow as the bishops now interpreted it. While this was taking place, Lee suffered the angry glances of many of the leaders and delegates. When his turn to speak came, Lee exhibited a flair for diverting the focus of the argument, in the hope of gaining time and sympathy. In a typical *argumentum ad hominum,* employing excellent courtroom tactics, he began:

> Bishop and brethren: I appear before you as the advocate of an accused brother whose innocence I am anxious to maintain, and regret that I can bring to the aid of my argument no personal prestige, having been denied the common civilities in your body usually accorded to members of a sister Conference.[23]

Presiding at the session, Bishop Hedding leaped to his feet and demanded an explanation for such an outrageous claim that had nothing to do with the case against True. Lee knew that Methodist Episcopal protocol dictated that whenever outside members of another conference visited a conference in session, the chairman introduced such visitors as a gesture of courtesy to the delegates and the visitor. Lee, a known agitator from the Black River Conference, had not been afforded the usual civilities. As a result the bishop appeared foolish and embarrassed. The visitors in the galleries cheered and whooped for Lee. Dr. Nathan Bangs demanded that the galleries be cleared, but to avoid further embarrassment they continued without such a rash step. At that point in the proceedings, Lee put away his lawyer tactics of Saul's armor and took up his own stones of logic, with which he was immeasurably more comfortable.[24]

In his argument Lee maintained that the vaguely-written pledge of 1837 was either morally right or wrong. If it really was what the prosecution claimed it to be, it was wrong. Since God commands that men speak on behalf of the "dumb" and that they "remember those in bonds as bound with them," to demand a pledge that violated scriptural commands must necessarily be wrong. Therefore, the accused preacher must be acquitted. Before being stopped by the bishop, Lee, as he earlier had hoped to do, managed to interweave some strong abolition arguments, before being ruled out of order for introducing material that had nothing to do with the immediate charges against the defendant, True. The bishop ended the charade when Lee declared that any vows taken for ordination that required obedience to a pro-slavery bishop were just as morally wrong. All of Lee's efforts proved to be unavailing. In the final outcome of the proceedings, True was convicted and suspended from the ministry.[25]

The other ministers, James Floy, Paul R. Brown, and David Plumb, subsequently were charged for the same crimes. All of these were convicted and suspended by the conference. Floy took a pledge not to agitate the slavery issue and was reinstated. Plumb limited his pledge to his membership in the New York Conference, planning to request a location, after which he meant to leave that conference. He was denied the location and summarily sent to a poor circuit instead. At the next conference he was expelled for not going to his appointment. Lee was marked as a troublemaker; he could expect problems from the bishops at the next session of the annual conference.[26]

Lee, in the meantime, had located another editor in Utica who eagerly published anything Lee submitted to him. William Goodell edited the *Friend of Man*, the official organ of the New York Anti-Slavery Society, in Utica, and he and Lee developed a strong friend-ship in the cause of reform. Lee submitted articles to him as he traveled through New York as an antislavery lecturer. Most of the material gave detailed reports of many of the towns that he visited, as well as a report on the number of societies organized and other similar information. In the years ahead, the two men not only fought for the rights of the slaves, they were among the earliest founders of the Liberty Party.[27]

Toward the end of the year, Methodist Episcopal ministers all over the northern sector of the nation were feeling the pressure of a determined group of bishops. All efforts to turn the ecclesiastical structure toward the plight of the slave had been steadily repulsed by an increasingly intolerant leadership. But antislavery men all over the North were just as determined. Their efforts would need to shift pragmatically as each new contingency in the battle arose. By Novem-ber of 1838 the storm center of antislavery forces in Methodism had shifted to Lowell, Massachusetts. Since the New England Conference had proved to be the most open to antislavery rhetoric, it is easy to understand why abolitionists in the Methodist Episcopal church were drawn to the area.

In November Lee journeyed to the textile-mill town located on the Merrimac River, north and west of Boston, to assist Scott, Sunderland, and Storrs. The acknowledged leaders of Methodism's revolt against their church's official position of slavery conducted a Methodist antislavery convention at Lowell. Feeling the utter hopelessness of

converting society or their church to abolitionism, these men entertained the notion of turning to politics to advance their beliefs. They, of
course, were not claiming to be the first to consider the political arena.
That event signaled the beginning of a final split within the ranks of the
national antislavery cause, since Garrison had loudly endorsed a "no
human government" position that denounced the use of politics for
pushing any reform. During these and other discussions and conventions for societies, Lee kept up his lectureship as an agent of the New
York Anti-Slavery Society.[28]

During 1838 and 1839 Lee traveled throughout New York on
behalf on the state society. He met with great opposition in some
places; in others, the message of abolitionism fell on sympathetic ears
and societies sprang into existence. In Cedarville the Methodist Episcopal pastor of the village refused Lee the use of his pulpit.[29] Interestingly, the Universalist congregation offered him theirs. The antislavery
movement produced strange bedfellows, indeed! First, Lee had beat
them down in theological debates; now he unabashedly used their
church for his purposes! As usually happened whenever he was denied
the use of his own denomination's church in a place, when the time
arrived for his lecture in another friendly church, the Methodist Episcopal church was virtually empty—they had all come to hear him at the
other location.[30]

Near Cedarville at a place known as "Smith's Pond," his support
proved to be less than unanimous. A large stone schoolhouse had been
filled to capacity to hear the speech. A drunken mob attempted to ruin
the lecture. Only two or three successfully stormed the building, and
their efforts failed when several large gentlemen sympathetic to Lee
impeded their charge to the platform. One fellow, attempting to climb
in the window, received a trip through the air for his efforts. Another
deposited a pile of some sulfurous powder around Lee's feet; his
attempt to light the powder produced nothing but the odor of his
smoking matches. To the ones who progressed to the front of the room,
Lee let loose a verbal barrage, shouting above the din:

> Back, you cowardly miscreants! Do you come to disturb me in
> the exercise of my right of free speech! I am the son of a revolution-
> ary [*sic*] soldier, who fought through seven bloody years to win this

right for me, and do you think I will resign at the clamor of a mob?
No, never! when I do it, let my tongue cleave to the roof of my
mouth; when I do it, let the ashes of that venerable father awake
from the dead to reprove a recreant son![31]

In Crane's Corners, in the town of Litchfield, Lee endured another
attack as he lectured in the Methodist Episcopal church. At midpoint
he heard the shout, "Shoot him right in his eyes." Expecting to soon
meet his Maker, he happily discovered that the ammunition on this
occasion was whiskey and lampblack. Remarking that he was not as
prejudiced against the color black as some were, he continued speaking
with the black concoction on his face and clothing. Not until nearly
midnight did he manage to remove the last of the liquid ammunition
from his body and clothes. Writing later of this incident he declared
that when the ruffians charged, he had not run, although the timeless
lines advise that:

> He that fights and runs away, may live to fight another day—but
> he that is in battle slain, can never live to fight again. . . . However,
> . . . it reminded me of the cowardly sailor, who hid himself at the
> commencement of a battle among some casks; but soon a cannon
> ball struck a tub of butter near him, and covered him with its
> contents, whereupon he rushed into the scene of action, crying,
> "there is no danger, they shoot nothing but butter"—and so, they
> have got to shoot something at me worse than whiskey and lamp
> black, before I shall be conquered or discouraged. I do not know but
> some would contend that this mob was got up under the "golden
> rule," for the mob, no doubt, would, all of them, like to have
> whiskey put into their faces, and most of them, rather than not to
> have the whiskey, would be willing to take a little lamp black with
> it!
>
>   Yours, for God and the oppressed,
>   Luther Lee[32]

One assumes that his indomitable spirit reflected the determination—and trials—of antislavery lecturers of the period.
His autumn and early winter lectures took him through Albany,

Troy, Schenectady, and as far north as lower Canada. In some towns he remained for an entire week; in almost all places, he usually formed new antislavery societies or added members to those that already were in existence. As 1838 drew to a close, Lee planned to spend a few days at home with the family in Utica. Soon thereafter, he took up his travels again.[33]

Lee continued on his way, visiting villages, hamlets, and cities all over the western part of the state. He then returned to points along the upper Hudson and visited many of the villages in which he had formerly preached the gospel along the St. Lawrence River. He never knew what to expect at each stop. On one occasion a gun was fired at the door of the church in which he was speaking. On another, a stone was flung through a window. At Albany he received the following letter from a "friend":

Albany, Jan. 14, 1839.

Mr. Luther Lee,

Sir:—I would advise you as a friend to leave the city as soon as possible, or you will lose your life. Such conduct as you are pursuing will not do; you must not try to blind people's eyes with false stories. You had not better deliver another lecture in the city; if you do you will surely lose your life. It may not be in the church, but the remedy is sure.

A Friend.[34]

So went the life of an antislavery agent in the late 1830s.

At the outset of the new year Lee had learned of a layman in the Methodist Episcopal church in Auburn who faced abolition charges. Actually the main charges against "Brother Brown" consisted of attending antislavery prayer meetings and slander against the bishops whom Brown had claimed would be glad to have a sword in their hands. Brown contacted Lee to serve as his defense counsel and, of course, Lee agreed. Lee planned an itinerary that would take him through Auburn. On February 15, 1839, the trial began. The pastor who presided over the ecclesiastical trial excluded as jurors all church members who had attended antislavery prayer meetings. Lee focused his defense arguments on the vague charges of attending the antislavery prayer meeting. Appealing to logic, he reasoned that such attendance, at most, could only denote a very general commitment to abolitionism. To assume that all men who pray for the slaves cannot qualify as fair arbiters of slander was outrageous. He lost the point. He next objected to a trial that was to be decided only by those who already had gone on record as opposing antislavery principles and men, but again to no avail. The trial proceeded in the same tenor. Lee argued that the *Discipline* had not been followed in many instances throughout the charade.[35]

At the conclusion the jurors found the defendant guilty of about half the charges and not guilty of the rest. He might well have been guilty of all; the result was the same. The hapless victim of anti-abolitionism was expelled from the church. The process of expelling members for activities that the bishops found to be counterproductive to national unity within the church became common, ending only when the Methodist Episcopal church split in the next decade. Lee continued his travels from Auburn. The culmination of a long series of developments that had been festering throughout the decade took place in the spring of 1839. Lee and his Methodist colleagues, just as they had been forced into making difficult choices when they entered the ranks of abolitionism, now became involved in polarizing reform issues that focused on what methods to employ and who could participate in the process.[36]

Garrison and his followers had been sparring over several matters throughout the previous years. Some of their problems revolved around the issues of "no human government" and whether or not to remain in the churches that supported slavery. Also there was debate over whether or not to turn to politics in their quest to end slavery. Overshadowing these issues was the matter of permitting women to enter fully into the reform movement on the same par with men. All of these had the potential for producing division within the supporters of the American Anti-Slavery Society, and indeed, their combined effect pushed the society toward a showdown.[37]

While Garrison alone cannot be faulted for the radical ideas that began to develop within the New England ranks of antislavery, he was the catalyst and chief proponent. Everything appeared black or white to him. The concept of compromising never occurred to him. All of his followers were either for him or against him. He viewed institutions of the period in the same light.[38]

The Constitution became the focus of Garrison's vituperation since it contained several concessions to the institution of slavery: it legalized the slave trade until 1808, and it agreed to count slaves as three-fifths of a white man for purposes of taxation and representation. For Garrison, that proved that the Constitution comprised "a covenant with death and an agreement with hell." He subsequently publicly burned a copy of that revered document to demonstrate his feelings toward such a government. That philosophy made it easier for him to oppose those within the ranks of antislavery who advocated the use of the ballot and politics. In the age of Jacksonian America the use of the ballot box was allegedly the expedient to all issues. Garrison and many of his supporters insisted, to the contrary, that "truth is not ascertained by public-opinion polls."[39]

The matter of whether or not to utilize force against slave holders presented grist for another battle within antislavery circles. As early as 1809, David Low Dodge, a wealthy Presbyterian minister of New York City, had published a pamphlet against the use of violence and war in maintaining peace. In 1828 the American Peace Society was born and its influence grew steadily thereafter. It is evident that Garrison did not develop his anti-political stance until later in his career. In his earliest years as a New England editor, he certainly exhibited no reluctance about resorting to politics to accomplish desired goals. He had demanded in one of his articles that Massachusetts be reimbursed for militia expenses incurred in the War of 1812. On another occasion he gave a speech in support of a local nominee for the United States Congress. By 1835, however, Garrison refused an appeal to any political influence in general, and the use of force in particular. He argued that "it is the duty of the followers of Christ to suffer themselves to be defrauded, calumniated and barbarously treated, without resorting either to their own physical energies, or to the force of human law, for restitution or punishment."[40] Lee could not have disagreed more on the use of law to defend free speech.

Garrison had been influenced by John Humphrey Noyes, a convert of Finney and the exponent of a radical form of perfectionism. Noyes had even signed a "declaration," symbolically severing all connection with the government of the United States. Garrison eventually came to endorse such radicalism. On the occasion of Lovejoy's murder, the abolitionist leader held the curious position that Lovejoy had committed a serious mistake when he resorted to force in defending his press against the pro-slavery mob at Alton, as though he should be blamed for his own death. That was almost the same argument that Fisk had used, one for which Luther Lee had taken him to task.[41] The logical outcome for Garrison was a burning hatred for the Constitution and, ultimately, the view that all human government was sinful. Orange Scott answered some of Garrison's ideas, which smacked of religious anarchy, in the columns of the *The Liberator*. Arguing that God himself had instituted human governments, Scott wrote that Garrison "as well might . . . trust God to edit and print your paper, without human agency" as to expect our world to function without government.[42]

Another matter bothered Garrison. He took a dim view of any religious organization that tolerated slavery within its ranks. Knowing that most of the mainline churches had either refused to deal with the matter or else, as the Methodists had chosen to do, gag the troublemakers, Garrison opted simply to turn on all ecclesiastical organizations. His next step was to question the veracity of Scripture, a concept that earlier would have been abhorrent to him. Soon he printed articles in the *Liberator* that took issue with such basic teachings of Scripture as observing the Sabbath. His denunciations of all churches became increasingly more shrill as the decade progressed. Of course, Garrison's clerical followers could not support him in such outlandish actions. Men such as Josiah Bissell, a Presbyterian reform-minded layman at Rochester, had spent most of his financial resources to operate a stage line that strictly adhered to Scriptural injunctions concerning the Sabbath. He also staunchly opposed Sunday delivery of the mail and canal traffic through the town on the Lord's day. Orthodox Christians such as Bissell (and there were thousands of them) could never support Garrison on those issues. But he was willing to live with those defections from his ranks. The most volatile issue that confronted the Garrisonians, however, proved to be the debate over permitting women to engage in antislavery activities alongside men.[43]

It was the "woman question" that proved to be the shoals on which abolitionism foundered and subsequently fell apart. One of the greatest anomalies in the entire course of abolitionism can be seen in the ambivalence toward women. The Second Great Awakening proved to be the epochal event that released women from their restraining "cult of domesticity" and placed them in the spotlight of the public gaze.

The forces of egalitarianism that were let loose upon the nation in the early decades of the nineteenth century did not "forget the women." Finney's "New Measures" included "promiscuous prayer" by the women during the revival services. While almost all of these reformers were willing to stake their fame and fortune in defense of the rights of the slaves, they somehow overlooked the fact that the same logic could be applied to the rights of women. That fact, however, had not escaped the northern women of antebellum America.[44]

Sarah and Angelina Grimké, Quaker sisters from Charleston, South Carolina, came north and in 1837 began lecturing on the evils of slavery to audiences comprising both men and women.[45] One year earlier Angelina captured public interest, both male and female, with her *An Appeal to the Christian Women of the South* in an effort to engage women in efforts to end slavery.[46] Little could they have predicted that their actions would produce such explosive results. Once the opposition developed, Angelina Grimké argued that all human beings have the same rights because they are all moral beings. On the opposing side of the issue, men such as Amos A. Phelps argued that women were unfit for public life by physiological nature and divine command. Wives had been ordered in Scripture to remain in submission to their husbands. That left no place for the women taking to the lecture circuit, because they would be in a position of authority over the men who sat in their audience. Thus, the ranks of antislavery polarized into two factions on the issue of women. In 1838, at the annual New England Anti-Slavery Convention, women had taken part in the proceedings. Outraged male members had asked that their names be expunged from the roll of the convention, rather than let them appear on the same roll with women. Between December and January, the New England abolitionists almost came to a parting of the ideological ways.[47]

On January 23, 1839, the state society packed Marlboro Chapel in Boston to conduct its business. Reverend Charles T. Torrey led an unsuccessful attempt to stop women from taking part in the meeting. The majority that opposed Garrison on the issue of women were members of the clergy—men who also feared Garrison's radical statements against organized religion. In protest against the allowing women, Amos A. Phelps resigned as corresponding secretary and as a member of the board of managers of the Massachusetts Anti-Slavery Society. But that was not the end of the uneasy situation.[48]

On May 27, 1839, the antifemale faction withdrew and formed the Massachusetts Abolition Society.[49] Splits soon developed in other local societies. Some thought the woman question was being overplayed. Elizur Wright Sr. in a letter to Phelps declared: "I think the tom-turkeys [*sic*] ought to do the gobbling, I am opposed to hens' crowing, and surely, as a general rule, to female-preaching," adding that for those women who insisted on playing the role of a man, his advice was to let them alone, eventually nature would weed them out. They simply were too delicate to stand up in the long struggle of reform.[50] At the American Anti-Slavery Society meeting on May 7, the organization faced a critical moment, but the real showdown on the main question within the national organization would not come until the next year. Luther Lee unwittingly found himself in the vortex of the convention; he had been asked to deliver the keynote address.[51]

Throughout the spring and early summer of 1839, Lee had faithfully continued his work as an agent of the New York Anti-Slavery Society. His travels took him all the way to the extreme western counties. Later in the spring he traveled to New York City where he attended the convention of the American Anti-Slavery Society that met on May 7-10. Arthur Tappan convened the first session at which Lee delivered a rousing antislavery speech. His assignment called for him to present an oration in support of a resolution that had been put for consideration:

> Resolved, That the system of American slavery usurps the prerogatives of God, tends to blot the divine image from the soul of man, degrades him below the rank his Maker assigned him in the scale of creation, and subverts all the social relations which God and nature have made essential.[52]

Some of Lee's salient points dealt with social conditions that black slaves endured. Appealing to his audience's sense of logic, Lee employed a highly stylized but effective conclusion by utilizing the caricature of an imaginary marriage ceremony for two slaves:

Question. "Wilt thou have this woman to be thy wedded wife?"

Answer. "Master says I may, or must, as the case may be."

Quest. "Wilt thou love her and keep her?"

Ans. "Master keeps her for me; I cannot keep myself; master keeps us both."

Quest. "Wilt thou keep thee only unto her so long as ye both shall live?"

Ans. "I will if master does not separate us by selling us apart."

Quest. "Wilt thou have this man to be thy wedded husband? Wilt thou keep thee only unto him so long as ye both shall live?"

Ans. "I will if master, some of his boys, his overseer, or some other white man does not step in between us and force me to break my promise, as I have no right to resist or lift my hand against any white man."[53]

Building on his make-believe wedding ceremony, Lee hammered with oratorical blows that logically defied the morality of the conditions under which American slaves were forced to live. By so doing Lee appealed to his audience's conscience and reason. In the above case he appeared humorous or probably ironical. At any rate, Lee ended his oration with a ringing cry for his audience to take up the cause of the slave. That speech propelled him into the highest levels of influence within the American Anti-Slavery Society. He might have remained among the ranks of the leadership, but he subsequently parted company with Garrison on key issues.

Also during that convention, those who favored the use of political action had made their presence felt. Various pro-political resolutions were offered, amended, and then tabled. John G. Whittier's proposal forced the issue; he reaffirmed the Society's position that voting "so as to promote the abolition of slavery, is of high obligation—a duty which, as abolitionist, we owe to our enslaved fellow-countrymen, groaning under legal oppression." Garrison opposed the resolution, but it passed by a vote of eighty-four to seventy-seven. Of course, Lee, Sunderland, and Scott all supported the resolution, even though Lee quite probably would have preferred even stronger language. Immediately following that vote, James G. Birney presented a Protest of 123 members against the admission of women, signed by Sunderland and Scott but not Lee.[54]

The convention ultimately came to a showdown between Garrison and his pro-women forces against the conservatives. His supporters had not shown up unprepared. Nearly a hundred delegates from New England, both men and women, had helped to pack the hall to the rafters. Opposition forces appeared to be quite numerous also. The control of the national society came down to the "woman question." For a day and a half the convention debated the issue of permitting women to be admitted. When put to a vote, Garrison's side polled 180 yeas, and the conservative side, led by the clergy, voted 140 nays. Lee, again, voted for the women and his close friend Scott voted against them. What really complicated the matter, however, was the fact that many who supported political action had voted for the women. Thus, the issue would drag on until the next year when the split finally took place. Lee headed back to Utica to conclude the last of his work in the New York agency. He also kept his eyes on political developments in anislavery circles. He strongly supported taking the cause of the slaves to the American people by use of the ballot box and elected officials.[55]

Lee does not indicate with certainty the time or circumstances at which he consented to take reformism into politics. It is probable that in the early months of 1839, Lee had become involved in the formation of the Liberty Party. Living in Utica put him precisely in the center of the movement. Goodell, his neighbor and fellow reformer, had been pushing the idea of a third political party in his *Friend of Man.* Upon the insistence of the Executive Committee of the New York Anti-

Slavery Society, and personally by Alvin Stewart, Beriah Green, and Theodore D. Weld, Goodell moved to Utica and commenced publication of that paper.[56]

Goodell represented a number of reformers that had been particularly disillusioned with the presidential candidates presented to the nation in 1836. For a period of time they employed a stopgap procedure of questioning candidates about their position on slavery. Candidates, however, usually proved unreliable. Once ensconced in Washington, they had a way of forgetting about the politically correct answers that they had given to their antislavery questioners during the election campaign. Coupled with that was the fact that the tactics of moral suasion seemed not to be producing much of a result across the nation. Actually it would not be respectable to be identified with abolitionism until after the Fugitive Slave Law of 1850 began to reveal to the North some of the horrid ramifications of the alleged slave conspiracy. Slowly, more and more reformers saw that it would take nothing less than political action to challenge the indomitable forces of slavery. Thus, Alvin Stewart in January had come out strong for a political party, and Lee joined him, Goodell, and others in their stance. Lee wrote that he "had strongly committed . . . [himself] to political action against slavery."[57]

Lee understood only too well that Garrison, just as adamantly, opposed the use of political parties. On June 28, Garrison's *The Liberator* carried an article in which he took James G. Birney to task for promoting political action. On July 10, Lee submitted an article from Utica to the editor of *Zion's Herald* for the purpose of defending Birney against Garrison on the issue. His lengthy article argued that political action was indirectly prescribed in the United States Constitution. Since it clearly stated that "All legislative powers shall be vested in a Congress" and that such a body "shall be chosen every second year by the people of the several states," Lee reasoned that surely Garrison could understand that the very act of selecting U.S. representatives constituted political action. How could that be condemned? Garrison was only too happy to reply, and did so by printing the entire article from *Zion's Herald* in the columns of *The Liberator*.[58]

Garrison attacked Lee as a man who came into abolitionism "at the eleventh hour." He lambasted him for justifying bloodshed and political action in the cause of America's liberation from England. Resorting to ridicule in his *argumentum ad hominum* he jeered,

> Mr. Lee aspires to be a logician. . . . He is fond of manufacturing syllogisms, and commonly exclaims at the close of each deduction, "This is as plain as logic can make it"—of which he has no doubt, whatever his hearers may think of the soundness of his argument.[59]

In other sections of his article Garrison castigated "Mr. Lee's logical curiosity," claimed that Lee's ground was a "sandy foundation," and accused him of being a "politically rampant" clergyman. Obviously, Lee and Garrison could never be collaborators. Nor did Lee escape abuse by others of Garrison's persuasion. Wendell Phillips, the patrician abolitionist who agreed with Garrison on most issues, also assailed Lee for supporting politics in the cause of reform. Phillips's letter of rebuttal did not appear in *The Liberator* until almost a year later. Even at that late date Garrison was only too happy to print it since it added a significant voice to his position. Undeterred, Lee traveled to the national convention without wavering in his ideas about the use of politics in freeing the slaves.[60]

The National Anti-Slavery Convention met at the city of Albany in the Fourth Presbyterian Church on July 31, 1839. At that meeting Lee delivered a speech in which he strongly urged his colleagues in reform not to hesitate to take their case to the American voters. As he wrote later, ". . . We can [not] secure a right government without right voting."[61] Garrison, who was present, tried to get the convention to admit women as delegates, but his efforts fell short. He attempted to do so by proposing an amendment to a resolution, so that the word "freeman" would be understood to include "all persons," meaning women.[62] Convention leaders such as Scott and Torrey, however, continued firmly to oppose the pro-woman movement. To Lee's chagrin, however, the convention, on the other hand, had not stood squarely for a third party. In fact, the strongest move in that direction was the passage of a resolution that all members should vote only for candidates who favored immediate abolition. That regressed to the old method of interrogation, a method in which no one professed much faith. Of course, Lee voted in the affirmative on the resolution. The entire affair sent Garrison home in a foul mood—more recalcitrant, and less apt to compromise than ever.[63]

Since no national candidate who hoped to win the election could blatantly offend pro-slavery voters even by paying lip service to abolitionism, the resolution proved to be small consolation to men who agreed with Lee. Despite the setback for a third party at the Albany convention Lee joined men such as Myron Holley and Alvin Stewart and continued to press for political action. Slowly, newer and more powerful figures joined the movement. Finally Gerrit Smith ended his indecision and came out solidly for the Liberty Party. Since he was probably the richest man in New York state, his influence proved to be significant.[64]

In the summer of 1839 Lee resigned his agency with the New York Anti-Slavery Society. He had traversed the entire state during the previous year. He refused to accept a pastorate with the stubborn Methodists. Scott influenced the committee of the Massachusetts Abolition Society to tender an offer to Lee to travel their state as general agent for the organization, which was established by those clerics who had opposed the radical direction that Garrison was taking the older state antislavery society. Lee, knowing that his work in the Empire State had reached an end, agreed to discuss the matter with the committee.[65] He had spent his life, a span of thirty-nine years, within the borders of New York. Firmly committed to the sacred cause of freedom for his black brothers, Lee traveled eastward.

NOTES

1. Luther Lee, *Autobiography of the Rev. Luther Lee, D.D.* (New York: Phillips & Hunt; Cincinnati: Walden & Stowe, 1882), 137-38.

2. Cf., Douglas J. Williamson, "Wilbur Fisk and African Colonization: A 'Painful Portion' of American Methodist History," *Methodist History* 23 (January 1985): 79-98.

3. See Edward D. Jervey, "LaRoy Sunderland: *Zion's Watchman*," *Methodist History* 6 (April 1968): 16-32, for background on Sunderland's church and civil trials, and for a prospectus of *Zion's Watchman*.

4. Charles Baumer Swaney, *Episcopal Methodism with Sidelights on Ecclesiastical Politics* (Boston: The Gorham Press, 1926), 48; Donald G.

Mathews, *Slavery and Methodism: A Chapter in American Morality 1780-1845* (Princeton, N.J.: Princeton University Press, 1965), 106, 132.

5. Mathews, *Slavery and Methodism*, 138.

6. Mathews, *Slavery and Methodism*, 138.

7. Sunderland submitted a complete account of all the trials in manuscript form to the New England Methodist Episcopal Historical Society on April 27, 1873. The writer has a copy of the original manuscript, which is located at the Boston University School of Theology Library.

8. *Autobiography*, 144; Matlack, *Life of the Reverend Orange Scott: Compiled from His Personal Narrative, Correspondence, and Other Authentic Sources of Information, In Two Parts* (New York: C. Prindle and L. C. Matlack, 1847; reprint, Freeport, N.Y.: Books for Libraries Press, 1971), 32-33; Mathews, *Slavery and Methodism*, 120.

9. *Zion's Watchman*, February 24, 1838; April 14, 1838; Mathews, *Slavery and Methodism*, 158-59.

10. See *Zion's Herald*, June 6, 1838, for an account of the creation of the Boston Wesleyan Anti-Slavery Society, which Scott was instrumental in founding. Lee and Scott remained close friends until the latter's death in 1847.

11. *Zion's Herald*, May 9, 1838.

12. *Zion's Herald*, May 9, 1838.

13. James M. Buckley, *A History of Methodism in the United States*, 2 vols. (New York: Christian Literature Co., 1897) 2: 9-10; Matlack, *Antislavery Struggle and Triumph in the Methodist Episcopal Church* (New York: Phillips & Hunt, 1881; reprint, New York: Negro Universities Press, 1969), 126.

14. Swaney, *Episcopal Methodism with Sidelights*, 82.

15. *Christian Advocate and Journal*, July 13, 1838.

16. *Zion's Watchman*, July 20, 1838, in a letter to the editor.

17. *Autobiography*, 162.

18. Swaney, *Episcopal Methodism with Sidelights*, 82; *Autobiography*, 162-65.

19. John L. Myers, "The Beginning of Anti-Slavery Agencies in New York State, 1833-1836," *New York History*, 43 (April 1962): 149-81, argues convincingly that "the agency system used by the antislavery societies succeeded in disseminating abolitionist ideas throughout countless small towns and rural areas of the North," 156.

20. One indication of the extent to which Utica supported reform is the fact that five antislavery societies were located there with a conservative number of members at 720; see *Fifth Annual Report of the Executive Committee of the American Anti-Slavery Society* (New York: William S. Dorr, 1838; repr., New York: Kraus Reprint Co., 1972), 144; see Milton C. Sernett, *Abolition's Axe: Beriah Green, Oneida Institute, and the Black Struggle,* (Syracuse, N.Y.: Syracuse University Press, 1986), 97-125, for discussion of the extent to which the leaders of the Oneida Institute at nearby Whitesboro were also involved in the Liberty Party; Carol M. Hunter, *To Set Captives*

Free: Reverend Jermain Wesley Loguen and the Struggle for Freedom in Central New York, 1835-1872 (New York: Garland Publishing, Inc., 1993), 51-53; cf., Mary P. Ryan, "The Power of Women's Networks: A Case Study of Female Moral Reform in Antebellum America," *Feminist Studies* 1 (Spring 1979): 66-83, for an overview of feminism in Utica that began in 1837.

21. A. P. Yates, ed., *The Utica Directory and City Advertiser: Arranged in Five Parts, for 1839-40* (Utica, N.Y.: R. Northway, Jr. Printer, 1899), 68; *Autobiography,* 169; Richard H. Sewell, *Ballots for Freedom: Antislavery Politics in the United States, 1837-1860* (New York: Oxford University Press, 1976), 43-79; Whitney R. Cross, *The Burned-over District: The Social and Intellectual History of Enthusiastic Religion in Western New York, 1800-1850* (Ithaca, N.Y.: Cornell University Press), 11, 84, 129, 152, 221, 266, and 296.

22. *Autobiography,* 141.

23. *Autobiography,* 144.

24. L. C. Matlack, *The Anti-Slavery Struggle and Triumph in the Methodist Episcopal Church* (New York: Phillips & Hunt, 1881; repr., New York: Negro University Press, 1969), 112-13; *Autobiography,* 144-45.

25. *Autobiography,* 144-54.

26. *Autobiography,* 144-54.

27. See for example, *Friend of Man,* October 3, 1838; November 7, 1838, and June 5, 1839; William Goodell, *Slavery and Anti-Slavery* (New York: Wm. Goodell, 1855), 448-56.

28. Mathews, *Slavery and Methodism,* 113-32; cf., Aileen S. Kraditor, *Means and Ends in American Abolitionism: Garrison and His Critics on Strategy and Tactics, 1834-1850* (New York: Pantheon Books, 1969; repr., Chicago: Ivan R. Dee, Inc., 1989), 78-109, for discussion of the process whereby Garrison, influenced by Henry C. Wright and others, moved toward nonresistance, and "no human government" ideas.; cf., *Liberator,* October 26, and November 16, 1838, for Orange Scott's articles written in opposition to the "no human government" ideas of Garrison; Bertram Wyatt-Brown, *Lewis Tappan and the Evangelical War Against Slavery* (New York: Atheneum, 1971), 185-205.

29. According to Lee, this is the place where the scenes of "Ten Nights in a Bar-room" took place, *Autobiography,* 170; cf., Curtis D. Johnson, *Islands of Holiness: Rural Religion in Upstate New York, 1790-1860* (Ithaca, N.Y., and London: Cornell University Press, 1989), 125-26, in which Johnson cites an example of the Courtland Methodist Church refusing its facilities to antislavery speakers in the same year that Lee traveled the area as an agent. By way of compromise between those who supported antislavery meetings and those who did not, the church agreed that on the one occasion their "meeting house doors may be opened on the 21st inst. for the use of the abolitionist, without opposition, calculating that the doors are not to be opened for such meetings again."

30. See *True Wesleyan,* September 14, 1850, for the account of Lee returning to this place twelve years later, riding a train from New York to

conduct a quarterly business meeting for the Wesleyan Methodist Church in Litchfield.

31. *Autobiography*, 170-71.

32. Frederick A. Norwood, ed., *Sourcebook of American Methodism* (Nashville, Tenn.: Abingdon, 1982), 251-52.

33. *Autobiography*, 172-78.

34. *Autobiography*, 176.

35. *Autobiography*, 179.

36. Charles Baumer Swaney, *Episcopal Methodism with Sidelights*, 86, incorrectly states that when Lee passed through Auburn on his lecturing travels that "the Methodist minister refused to permit Luther Lee to preach, although he had formerly been a pastor there." Lee, on one occasion had preached from that pulpit during a session of conference, but never served as pastor in Auburn; cf., *Autobiography*, 189.

37. Lee generally supported the right of women to participate in the reform movements; however, on occasion (cf., Massachusetts Abolition Society's second meeting in Boston) he spoke of women having their own sphere from which to press reform. There he appeared ambivalent; however, it is safe to say that he usually supported the women. When Lee was forced to vote on the matter, he sided with the women.

38. Students of antislavery are aware of three periods that mark off the movement: 1816-1830, the gradualist phase; 1830-1840, the institutional phase; and 1840-1861, the political phase. In the 1830s, one can easily discern how Garrison systematically turned against one institution after another: government, churches, political parties, and ultimately social order; see Stanley Elkins, *Slavery: A Problem in American Institutional and Intellectual Life* (Chicago: University of Chicago Press, 1959), for a classic discussion of the collapse of institutions, and their subsequent inability to lend significant control to society in the pre-Civil War years.

39. Kraditor, *Means and Ends*, 26-27; Ronald G. Walters, *The Antislavery Appeal: American Abolitionism after 1830* (New York: W. W. Norton & Co., 1978), 52.

40. Francis Jackson Garrison and Wendell Phillips Garrison, *Life of William Lloyd Garrison, 1805-1879: The Story of His Life, Told by His Children*, 4 vols. (New York: Houghton Mifflin Co., 1894) 2: 52; Alice Felt Tyler, *Freedom's Ferment: Phases of American Social History from the Colonial Period to the Outbreak of the Civil War* (New York: Harper & Row, Publishers, 1944), 411.

41. Tyler, *Freedom's Ferment*, 411.

42. Kraditor, *Means and Ends*, 88-89; Sewell, *Ballots for Freedom*, 25.

43. *Liberator*, December 2, 1835; December 12, 1835; cf., Paul E. Johnson, *A Shopkeeper's Millennium: Society and Revivals in New York, 1815-1837* (New York: Hill & Wang, 1978), 74-75, 92-94, for a description of Bissell's private crusade against the Sunday mail deliveries, his six-day-only Pioneer Line, and his efforts to stop canal boats from traveling through

Rochester on Sunday.

44. Whitney R. Cross, *The Burned-over District,* 37-38, 84-89, 177, 229.

45. See "Narrative and Testimony of Sarah Grimké," for her own account of leaving the South, *True Wesleyan,* April 19, 1845.

46. Catherine H. Birney, *The Grimké Sisters, Sarah and Angelina Grimké* (Repr. ed., Westport, Conn.: Greenwood Press, 1969), 138.

47. Walters, *American Reformers,* 87-89, 104-105, 109; Kraditor, *Ways and Means,* 41-45, 60-61; Gilbert Hobbs Barnes, *The Antislavery Impulse 1830-1844* (New York, 1933; repr., New York: Harcourt, Brace & World, Inc, 1964), 153-60.

48. See *Liberator,* January 10, 1840, for an abusive review by Garrison of Lee's speech at Marlboro Chapel in 1839; Kraditor, *Means and Ends,* 50-51, 68.

49. Donald Dayton, an otherwise meticulous researcher, in his *Five Sermons and a Tract by Luther Lee,* p. 10, maintains that the Massachusetts Abolition Society "had separated from Garrison and his followers over their refusal to engage in political action." Evidence indicates that the real issue was permitting women to join the old society; cf., *Liberator,* January 10, 1840 and, Kraditor, *Means and Ends,* 50-51, 68.

50. See *Friend of Man,* June 12, 1839, for the Constitution and goals of the new Massachusetts Abolition Society; Elizur Wright Jr. to Amos A. Phelps, July 11, 1838, Phelps Papers, Boston Public Library; Kraditor, *Means and Ends,* 61.

51. See Cross, *Burned-over District,* 177-78 for a discussion supporting the fact that women had been involved in such a manner in church meetings, even before Charles G. Finney and Theodore Dwight Weld had begun the practice. Cross argues that those men received the credit of initiating the practice of women praying publicly, only as a result of the discussions at the Lebanon Conference in 1827. Gilbert H. Barnes, *Antislavery Impulse, 1830-1844* (New York: Harcourt, Brace & World, 1933), 12, argued that Weld was the innovator; Kraditor, *Means and Ends,* 44-45, 49, and 50.

52. *Sixth Annual Report of the Executive Committee of the American Anti-Slavery Society, with the Speeches Delivered at the Anniversary Meeting Held in the City of New York, on the 7th of May, 1839, and the Minutes of the Meetings of the Society for Business, Held on the Evening and the Three Following Days* (New York: William S. Dorr, 1839; repr., New York: Kraus Reprint Co., 1972), 4-9; *Autobiography,* 198-99.

53. Actually the minutes of the society state that, "The Rev. Luther Lee, of Utica, N.Y., offered the following resolution," and then proceeded to give a complete account of the speech. Interestingly, the caricature of the marriage ceremony does not appear, although a lengthy paragraph that takes up the matter of marriage among the slaves is given. It is likely that Lee gave the illustration extemporaneously, and for that reason it is not in the copy of his speech that he gave to the secretary for inclusion in the official proceedings, *Sixth Annual Report,* 4-9; *Autobiography,* 208-209.

54. Sewell, *Ballots for Freedom*, 38-39; *Sixth Annual Report*, 42-44.

55. Sewell, *Ballots for Freedom*, 36-40.

56. William Goodell, *Slavery and Anti-Slavery; A History of the Great Struggle in Both Hemispheres; with a View of The Slavery Question in the United States* (n.p.: William Harned, 1852; repr., New York: Negro Universities Press, 1968), 468-69; *In Memoriam, William Goodell* (Chicago: Guilbert & Winchell, Printers, 1879), 26-27.

57. Wyatt-Brown, *Lewis Tappan*, 269-87; *Autobiography*, 217.

58. *Liberator*, September 6, 1839; October 9, 1840.

59. *Liberator*, September 6, 1839.

60. *Liberator*, September 6, 1839; October 9, 1840. The reason that Phillips's letter was so long in appearing in print was due to the fact that he had written it to a friend who had misplaced it. When the letter was discovered months later, Garrison insisted on printing it, even though it was anachronistic.

61. Sewell, *Ballots for Freedom*, 25, 52-54; *Autobiography*, 217.

62. *The Pennsylvania Freeman*, July 15, 1839.

63. See *The Pennsylvania Freeman*, July 15, 1839, for a list of how each delegate voted on the political issue.

64. See *Friend of Man*, August 7, 1839, in which Lee is listed as one of six agents for the New York Anti-Slavery Society; Sewell, *Ballots for Freedom*, 52-55; Douglas M. Strong, "Partners in Political Abolitionism: The Liberty Party and the Wesleyan Methodist Connection," *Methodist History* (January 1985): 103-104; see *Liberator*, January 10, 1840, for Garrison's scathing response to the speech in which Lee advocated the use of political parties for furthering reform; cf., Reinhard O. Johnson, "The Liberty Party in Massachusetts, 1840-1848: Antislavery Third Party Politics in the Bay State," *Civil War History* 28 (March 1982): 237-65, for an overview of antislavery politics in Massachusetts where most of Lee's Methodist colleagues entered the pro-political phase of abolitionism; Alan M. Kraut, "Partisanship and Principles: The Liberty Party in Antebellum Political Culture," in Alan M. Kraut, ed., *Crusaders and Compromisers: Essays on the Relationship of the Antislavery Struggle to the Antebellum Party System* (Westport, Conn.: Greenwood Press, 1983), 72-73, in which he cites Sewell as arguing that the Liberty Party "was a political party by design rather than a 'religious crusade,'" whereas Walters argues that the Liberty Party reformers were political "in name only and that they adopted the rhetoric and style of partisan politicians only because electioneering was the 'great American sport'" and "little more than a propaganda technique." Sewell's model compares favorably with respect to it being more than a religious crusade. While the founders of the Liberty Party all had strong church ties, they felt driven to a third party since interogation tactics had failed and neither major party was favorably disposed to antislavery platform planks. It was a pragmatic act born out of sheer desperation; see Alan M. Kraut, "The Forgotten Reformers: A Profile of Third Party Abolitionists in Antebellum New York," Lewis Perry and Michael

Fellman, eds., *Antislavery Reconsidered: New Perspectives on the Abolitionists* (Baton Rouge: Louisiana State University Press, 1979): 119-45, where he points out that the Liberty Party was organized on April 1, 1840 in Albany. In 1840 it had no official platform (that came in the 1844 election), but an editorial by Joshua Leavitt in the *New York Emancipator,* July 15, 1841, defined the province of third-party abolitionists.

65. Goodell, *Slavery and Anti-Slavery,* 468.

Chapter Five

1839-1843: Bay State Antislavery Battles

Lee's final three years in the Methodist Episcopal church found him investing an enormous amount of energy in the battle to reform society. Driven by the Methodist doctrine that stressed the perfectibility of man, Lee intended to spend and be spent in that effort. During the years that he lived in Massachusetts he witnessed a rebirth of the temperance cause that had lost much of the impetus it had enjoyed in the previous decade and a half. The debate over moderation versus total abstinence and spirituous liquor versus wine and malt products had distracted temperance people. Their cause developed renewed momentum after the Washingtonians added a new dimension. Lee gave an important address to the citizens of Lowell just as the cause caught its second wind.

Lee managed to get himself involved in politics with the approach of the election of 1840. He provides historians with no record of how he had voted until the year of the "log cabin" campaign. To students of Jacksonian America it is nearly impossible to see Lee as voting anything other than the Whig ticket. Daniel Walker Howe in his magisterial *The Political Culture of the American Whigs* has provided us with a biographical overview of representative Whig politicians. Lee fits the profile of the typical Whig supporter to perfection. His advocacy of harnessing government to bring about social reform is the centerpiece of the politics of such Whigs as Lyman Beecher, Joshua Giddings, Horace Greeley, William Henry Seward, and "old man eloquent," John Quincy Adams. If Lee did not support Whig politicians in the 1830s, it is clear that as a Mason he could hardly support William Wirt or any other candidates of the Anti-Masonic Party. Most frontier Methodists voted for Democrat candidates in the West where antitemperance and pro-slavery sentiment was strong. Since Lee's adult years and the earlier part of his ministry were lived in the burned-over district, it would seem likely that his interests would be with the Whigs. Once the supporters of an antislavery party moved ahead with their plans to nominate a presidential candidate, Lee busied himself in talking up James G. Birney, the Liberty Party nominee, as he talked down slavery and alcohol.[1]

In September, Lee set out for the city of Boston to discuss the offer of the Massachusetts Abolition Society. Along the route to Boston he had been urged to deliver some antislavery speeches wherever it seemed propitious. His first stop was at Middletown, Connecticut, the home of the Methodist's Wesleyan University. Since this place had been greatly influenced by President Wilbur Fisk, Lee's earlier adversary on the issue of colonization, he knew that he could possibly be in for trouble. To his delight, however, a number of the students had been abolitionized and were anxious to hear him speak. The Methodist Episcopal minister there, not surprisingly, had barred men such as Lee. The Congregationalists made their church available, and Lee gave his first lecture.[2]

Even though the Methodists had refused Lee their church, its sexton agreed to ring the bell to call the people to the meeting at the other church, as had been the custom for a long time. Reverend Francis Hodgson, the Methodist Episcopal minister, forbade the sexton to ring the bell again for such nonsense as Lee espoused, and he ended his tirade by challenging Lee to a debate on slavery. At the appointed time the house was packed, but Hodgson failed to appear. Finally a professor from the university came to the place and explained that the faculty had, with difficulty, persuaded Hodgson not to debate, as Lee had the advantage of experience and preparation. After courteously accepting the proffered explanation, Lee proceeded to deliver a series of antislavery lectures in Middletown. Satisfied with the outcome of events in that place, he headed northward.

Lee departed for Boston, only to fall ill on the way. Barely able to continue, he managed to locate a hotel in Boston from which he sent messages to friends, some of whom took him in and cared for him until he was recovered sufficiently to return to Utica, pack his belongings, and then move his family of six to Charlestown. By November as voters listened to candidates' final call for votes, Lee headed out on his antislavery itinerary.[3]

Lee recognized that many social, religious, and political issues cluttered the landscape of reform in the state. His own position on many of the divisive issues in the fall of 1839 can be summed up as follows: on the woman question, he generally favored women having equal influence in reform. On human government, he strongly urged the need for the institution of government and the political process. On the issue of nonresistance, he declared that he had never been utopian enough to give any quarter to it. On the matter of the legitimacy of churches, he claimed never to have "failed to throw [his] . . . whole strength and influence in favor of Church organizations, and defended them on all proper occasions."[4] Thus, he was the target "for all the shafts of pro-slavery politicians, and all non-political, non-voting, non-resistance, non-Church antislavery men."[5] In that context, Lee faced his first challenge at the annual meeting of the Barnstable County Anti-Slavery Society.

Garrison's Massachusetts Anti-Slavery Society agents traveled the same areas as Lee. The result was that Lee sought not only to win converts to the antislavery cause, he had to compete with other hostile abolitionists in the process. The first confrontation involving the two groups shaped up at a meeting in Barnstable County where the older state society had its general agent on hand. Reverend Charles T. Torrey showed up to assist Lee. At Lee's insistence Torrey took the lead in debating their opponent.

After the two debated some issues, Lee stepped up and seemingly had swung the crowd to his side. His opponent recognized that he had lost ground. He tried to stall a vote by stating that the issues were complicated beyond understanding, and seeing he would lose if the vote were taken at that moment, he urged those present to take time to educate themselves further on the issues before any voting took place. Lee, appealing to the crowd's pride, challenged them not to be insulted by his opponent's declaration that the issue was beyond their ability. The issue was put to a vote, and Lee and Torrey won a strong victory. In his triumphant mood, Lee traveled to his next appointment.[6]

Some reformers and evangelists enlisted their wives in the work of revival and reform. Charles G. Finney's wife, Lydia, did much to expand her husband's ministry among the women in revivals. During all the years of his marriage, Lee wrote very little of his wife. In the period of Lee's work in Massachusetts, however, Lee reported that Mary Lee got involved in the Ladies' Anti-Slavery Society of Boston. The contest between Garrison's supporters and the Massachusetts Abolition Society could be expected to be particularly heated in Garrison's home town. Mary Lee did her part in that year to bring about a victory against the forces that opposed all that Lee held as fundamental.[7]

This first year of his labors in the Bay State proved to be a mixed bag for Lee. On one occasion he managed to debate Theodore Parker on the issue of the inspiration of the Scriptures. At another place Lee debated theological liberals in defense of the Christian Sabbath. One of the most bizarre events involved Bronson Alcott. In attendance at a debate concerning the organization of a reform convention, Lee argued that to attempt to conduct business without the benefit of a proper organization would be ruinous. Winning his point, he watched with satisfaction as Josiah Quincy was elected president of the group. Then events took a strange twist.

Alcott, a strong advocate of vegetarianism, rose to set forth his dietary practices as far superior to his opponents:

> Mr. Chairman, I can tell this convention wherein you are all wrong, blind, and carnal. I am as pure and as wise as was Jesus Christ. The reason is, I eat nothing but pure vegetables. You eat cattle's flesh and sheep's flesh and fowl's flesh and swine's flesh. You are just what you eat: you are cattle and sheep and fowl and swine; you are ignorant and blind and carnal.[8]

As soon as Alcott took his seat, Lee rose and secured permission to ask a question of Alcott. His logic was transparent in a farcical question:

> The speaker [Alcott] told us that we are just what we eat; that because we eat cattle's flesh and fowl's flesh and sheep's flesh and swine's flesh, we are cattle and fowl and sheep and swine. He also told us that he eats nothing but vegetables. Now the question is,

Does it not follow, *by parity of reason* [emphasis mine] that he is a potato, a turnip, a pumpkin, or a squash?[9]

The crowd howled at Lee's jest, and throughout the house could be heard the comment, "Too much of the squash!" Logic, apparently, has its humorous applications as well as in formal debate. While the exchange took place on the level of the ridiculous, it does illustrate Lee's familiarity with Aristotelian syllogism. Such levity, however, served only as a temporary respite in the discouraging days of early 1840.

Lee knew that the hope of snuffing slavery out of the ranks of the church had all but vanished. As he traveled from town to town, he waged an uphill battle against the forces of slavery. In the western part of Massachusetts he presented a series of antislavery lectures in Westfield, a small hamlet just to the west of Springfield in the foothills of the Berkshire Mountains. A whip factory provided some of the locals with a place to work—and an excellent stage prop for Lee. Knowing that many of the whips ended up in the cruel hands of slave overseers, Lee cringed when he took the lecture stand on the second night only to find a large whip lying across the stand. Lee chose not to acknowledge the object, assuming that it had been placed there by some pro-slavery fellow, probably as a reminder that Lee might receive a lashing if he continued his speaking. At the right moment of the speech, timed for maximum impact, he illustrated how cruelly slaves received the lash. Lifting the whip and cracking it as loudly as a gun shot, he reminded his hearers that they shared in the guilt of whipping slaves, since they help manufacture the instrument of torture right in their village. Then he made his point by confronting them: "Will you ask again what we have to do with slavery here at the North?"[10] In any event, he managed to conclude his series in Westfield without feeling the whip from his opponents.

Meanwhile to the north, Orange Scott and Jotham Horton, then fellow pastors in Lowell, also were doing their best to stave off discouragement within the antislavery ranks. Scott, returning from his medical leave from active antislavery work, had been elected again by his abolitionist Methodist colleagues as a delegate to the 1840 General Conference of the Methodist Episcopal church to meet in Philadelphia.

In anticipation of that session, on January 1, 1840, they joined efforts to produce a new paper, *The American Wesleyan Observer*.[11] They intended only to run the journal for six months in the hope that other delegates to that Conference might be influenced by their editorial arguments. They also intended to publish the entire proceedings of the Conference, sensing that it would make good antislavery propaganda. Scott also secured the services of Lucius C. Matlack to fill in as editor during his absences, and also as a supply pastor to his pulpit in St. Paul's Methodist Episcopal Church in Lowell. While the group waited for the quadrennial conference to convene, they clung to the hope of a breakthrough in the membership of that body—a hope that would prove to be unfounded. In the meanwhile, each spoke regularly in antislavery meetings whenever opportunity afforded.

In May of 1840, however, their hopes for positive action from the General Conference were dashed. Although over ten thousand signatures to antislavery petitions had been presented from the church membership, in reality, only four out of twenty-eight annual conferences accounted for the petitions. The session proved to be a nightmare for Scott and his fellow abolitionist delegates. The bishops kept a strict hand on business, unless, of course, it was to permit comments such as those from William Smith, a pro-slavery delegate. In one speech he avowed that the southern delegates would oppose any resolutions against "O. Scott and Co." if, at the same time, they "held the same. . . [antislavery] doctrines he contends for."[12] The Southerners were not modest about defending their position. During the session one other issue further illustrated the power of the southern members. The incident also revealed the determination of the bishops to humor the pro-slavery forces within the ranks. The Silas Comfort affair and the resulting Few Amendment appalled antislavery men everywhere.[13]

Silas Comfort, a delegate to the General Conference in 1836, had accepted a pastorate in St. Louis. One of his members there apparently sought a secret affair with a young lady from the church. The would-be paramour sent her a note by a black messenger. The lady, thoroughly outraged, responded ferociously, claiming that the man was "a Villain and if you knew me you would not send such notes to me. I am a Divorced lady and have had trouble enough with a man never to wish to see one as long as I live."[14] She reported the incident to Silas

Comfort, her pastor, who conducted a church trial, and the man was found guilty of "ungentlemanly and unchristian conduct." The testimony of the black man who had carried the note constituted the main evidence. The scoundrel appealed to the quarterly conference of the church on the grounds that black testimony would not be admissable in civil court and must be disallowed in the ecclesiastical realm as well. The Missouri Conference agreed with him, declaring that Comfort had acted erroneously. As though that were not sufficient, the conference proceeded to put him on trial and convicted him of maladministration! Then it was Comfort's turn to appeal to the General Conference of 1840.[15]

Comfort surely predicted accurately that "the testimony of 88,000 Methodists would be automatically voided if the decision of the Missouri Conference were allowed to stand." But stand it did. Ignatius Few, a delegate from Savannah, Georgia, offered the now-famous (infamous?) Few Resolution. It did not equivocate on the standing of blacks in the church, avowing: "That it is inexpedient and unjustifiable for any preachers to permit colored persons to give testimony against white persons, in any state where they are denied that privilege in trials of law."[16] Such actions, passed by a majority of delegates and supported by the bishops, had ominous implications for Lee and his friends.[17]

By the close of the General Conference it was clearer than ever that Lee and his fellow reformers had no chance of converting their church to abolitionism. The thought of turning back in the struggle, however, seemed never to dawn on Lee. He stubbornly continued to press ahead. By the end of May he made his way to Boston for the annual meeting, and first anniversary of the Massachusetts Abolition Society.

The convocation assembled in Boston's Marlboro Chapel on May 28, 1940. A reporter for *The Liberator* was on hand, ready to spot anything negative that he could trumpet in Garrison's columns. Several men had been scheduled to address the delegates, among them a Liberty Party man and close friend of Lee, Reverend Joshua Leavitt. Lee himself was also on the program to give the concluding address. After the reading of Scripture, a congregational hymn, prayer, and a hymn by the choir, the reports and speeches began. Some of Lee's closest friends, however, did not support his performance. Whereas at

New York earlier he had supported the women, he now completely changed positions.[18]

The bulk of his speech focused on persuading women "to form themselves into Societies separate from the men . . . [referring to their] appropriate sphere as pointed out by God, by the Bible, and by the usages of the civilized world." Near the conclusion he urged women to exert strenuous efforts in behalf of the slave. Even though men and women have "different spheres," that should not be construed as meaning women had nothing to do. Waxing eloquent, he boasted: "Give me the nerve of man to stir and put in motion the pulsations of woman's heart, and I will conquer the world!"[19]

Lee may have felt like conquering the world, but he failed sorely at conquering the women with talk like that. Given his usual support of women, such statements sounded hypocritical. Students of Lee must keep in mind that he was an employee of the Massachusetts Abolition Society, a group that opposed females mixing with males in the cause of reform. It also supported the Liberty Party. Here Lee had fashioned his speech to please the pro-political faction, rather than any pro-female people in the audience. Expediency was the better part of valor, at least at that meeting. Undoubtedly Lee would have been better served had he steered clear of discussing women in reform on that occasion. What motivated him there to depart from his regular support of women remains a mystery. Garrison probably ran the article with glee, hoping to cause division in the opposition society. Lee left Boston knowing that matters did not bode well for success for reform. A darkening cloud was settling down on each of the reformers.

By the year's end Lee had begun to plumb the depths of despair. Not only had the General Conference been a disaster for antislavery, the rupture within the antislavery ranks had left the participants fighting each other as much as fighting slavery. The annual meeting of the American Anti-Slavery Society in May of 1840 saw the monolithic organization finally split in two. When the delegates voted to appoint Abby Kelley to the business committee, the inevitable division took place. Whittier called the move the "bomb-shell that *exploded* the society."[20] The seceders, led by Lewis Tappan, formed the American & Foreign Anti-Slavery Society. Garrison disdainfully labeled them the "disorganizers."[21] The timing, however, could not have been worse.

The nation had made little economic recovery since the Panic of 1837. Also, disagreement over the use of politics further complicated matters for the new organization. The dismal election returns hardly encouraged anyone but Garrisonians.[22]

The Liberty party had put up a noble fight in the presidential election of 1840. James G. Birney, their candidate for president, however, made a disastrous showing, winning approximately 6,000 votes. One embittered party worker cried in dismay, "May God forgive the thousands of Abolitionists who . . . by their votes have bolstered up the tottering fabric of slavery."[23] In addition to the loss of the election, Lee watched as his abolitionist friends divided on the concept of the Liberty Party. Men such as Lewis Tappan, a financial bulwark (at least until the Panic of 1837) in the antislavery movement, opposed the third party tactics. William Henry Harrison enjoyed prestige as the hero of the West. The farther west the third party attempted to reach out, the more adamantly men opposed it. In Ohio Gamaliel Bailey, who had given up a life in medicine to succeed Birney as the editor of the *Philanthropist*, had used his influence and his paper to stamp out a third party movement in Ohio. Henry B. Stanton had insisted that by 1840, "19/20ths of abolitionists" were firmly opposed to such a party. No wonder Barnes called the Liberty Party organizers "the most pathetic residue of [the] antislavery organization."[24] The one positive event that transpired in early October proved to be the Methodist Anti-Slavery Convention that met in New York City.[25]

Labeled as "The Great Convention" by an anonymous reporter, the article boasted that despite the Methodist Episcopal church's non-response to the plight of slaves, many of its members had not forgotten them. The convention was to meet in the Baptist Church on McDougal Street. The leaders present included:

> . . . the much abused Scott, the mild and persuasive J. Dodge, from the Genesee Conference; the able and popular Prindle from the Troy Conference, together with the logical Luther Lee.[26]

Approximately 250 abolitionists listened as Lee delivered the main address. When the enclave finally ended, he returned to Lowell, trying desperately to be optimistic in the face of certain defeat.

The final blow to Lee's agency status had been the poor recovery of the national economy following the Panic of 1837. With all the infighting within the reform community in general and the antislavery supporters in particular, the Massachusetts Abolition Society found it impossible to provide a livable salary for Lee. By the time he resigned in 1840, the Society had declared bankruptcy, and Lee was forced to accept a financial settlement that provided only about half the salary due him.[27]

Events over which he had no control propelled Lee toward leaving the church that had been home for more than two decades. In the next two years Lee and his colleagues moved toward the inevitable. They were thinking the unthinkable. Still, the decision did not come easily. The process of time was needed to bring their plan to maturity. By the end of 1842, feeling himself a pariah or at least a *persona non grata*, Lee and several of his closest friends in the cause of the slaves would secede from the Methodist Episcopal Church and establish a seceder, reform denomination—the Wesleyan Methodist Connection.

At the New England Conference of 1840 Scott had been assigned to the church at Lowell, a place where he had strong antislavery support. Once there he began the publication of *The New England Christian Advocate*, a journal aimed to convert more of the New England clergy and laity to abolitionism. Later in 1840, however, Scott's health forced him to relinquish the work at Lowell and retire to Newbury, Vermont. He offered the editorship to Lee, who gladly accepted.[28] With the January 7, 1841 issue, Lee began the masthead with a clean slate, starting over with volume 1, number 1. In a "Prospectus" he wrote that the paper would be published on Thursday of each week, subscriptions to be two dollars per year, payable in advance. Obviously Lee could not support a family from his editor's wages; so he accepted the position of supply pastor of the First Methodist Episcopal Church on Lowell Street in the same town.[29] Reverend A. D. Merrill supplied the St. Paul's Methodist Episcopal church in Lowell when Scott left. Lee ran an article in the February 11, 1841 *Advocate,* on the "State of Religion in Lowell," in which he describes a "protracted meeting now in progress in St. Paul's Church, under the leadership of Reverend O. Scott." Probably Scott was the evangelist for that revival. Lee wrote that services had been conducted for a period of weeks and that fifteen to twenty seekers were at the altar at the close of most of the services. Such glowing reports of revival indicate that antislavery men did not forget their call to evangelize sinners even as they tried to convert slave holders from their evil ways.[30]

The paper, unfortunately, proved to be too little, too late to be effective within the Methodist Episcopal church. The bishop's efforts to quiet agitation within the ranks of the clergy had produced their desired results. Despite the efforts of those who had chosen to defend the slaves, new additions to the ranks of antislavery were slower in coming. Due to a lack of finances and subscribers, *The New England Christian Advocate* ceased publication after the first volume.

In the winter of 1840-41 Lee responded to the invitation of friends to take the banner of abolitionism into the state of Maine. A resolution against slavery was being discussed in a committee of the Maine state legislature. Lee managed to secure a hearing before the committee where he spoke in favor of an antislavery resolution. He also lectured on temperance and antislavery in several places in the area of Augusta. He wrote later of the bitterly cold temperature as he departed the state capital in a stage coach. Stopping occasionally throughout the night, he managed to reach the train depot at Portland just as the train for Boston was pulling out. A red-hot stove in the rail car managed to thaw out the weary lecturer as he made his way home.

Once home in Lowell, he discovered that the city had been stirred to a fever pitch in the cause against alcohol. In 1841 the temperance cause was nothing new to the nation or to Lee. As early as 1836, while a pastor in Fulton, he had written numerous articles against the use of intoxicating drink. The battle on the national level, of course, had begun long before.[31]

As early as 1784, Dr. Benjamin Rush, one of the signers of the Declaration of Independence and an early advocate of temperance, had published his *An Inquiry into the Effects of Spirituous Liquors on the Human Body and Mind.* While he stoutly maintained that beer, cider, and wine had no deleterious effects upon the body (in fact he maintained they were good for health and well-being), he strongly opposed distilled drink as the cause of physical, mental, and moral disaster. America sorely needed rescuing from its love affair with alcohol.

Between 1790 and 1830 "Americans drank more alcoholic beverages per capita than at any time before or since," mainly whiskey and other hard liquor, with each adult male imbibing on the average seventeen gallons per year or more that one-third pint a day.[32]

Except for a very few local temperance societies, nothing of a sweeping nature materialized on the national level until the ubiquitous Reverend Lyman Beecher, who never met a reform he did not like, took up the cause. In 1825 he preached six sermons on temperance and subsequently published them. The result of his efforts initiated a national campaign that culminated in the formation of the American Temperance Society in the next year. Some estimate that as many as five thousand state and local societies had mobilized the public to fight the plague of the nation. Many of the antislavery leaders had first fought demon rum. Following the lead of Rush, the earliest reformers focused on ardent spirits, or distilled products. Recruiting seminary students and unemployed graduates to go on the lecture circuit proved quite successful. Many women active in the churches during the Second Great Awakening moved to get involved in the struggle. People listened to the awful results of the use of alcohol and then signed the pledge card, distributed at the close of the speech, promising never to drink another drop.[33]

As the cause gathered impetus, the issue of using wine at the communion table, manufacturing and selling drink, and the use of beer and cider all added fuel to the fire. By the late 1830s many temperance reformers were "teetotalers." The initial flush of success, however, had subsided. Discouraged by infighting over which methods to pursue, whether or not to permit women in temperance reform, and the lack of funds resulting from the Panic of 1837, many began to drift away from the movement. Temperance, however, received a huge boost with the addition of the Washingtonians in April of 1840. This movement began as a group of six tipplers resolved to reform their drunken ways. They swore off alcohol and promptly formed the Washington Temperance Society in Baltimore. The converts to that movement skyrocketed to six hundred thousand in the succeeding three years. While the two national societies did not merge, together they impacted America in a significant fashion by mid-century. In that context Lee received an invitation to get involved in the fray at Lowell.[34]

Upon arriving home, he read the following announcement in the Lowell *Courier,*

> At a meeting of the Directors of the Lowell Temperance Union, a vote was passed, inviting the several clergymen of this City, to deliver a series of discourses, on Sunday evening, upon Temperance. To this call the ministers responded with great cheerfulness and entire unanimity.[35]

Lee observed that Jotham Horton, his fellow Methodist abolitionist preacher, was to speak ahead of him on the schedule. Horton's topic was "The Want of the Temperance Reform," while his own topic was "Prohibitory Laws."[36] The clerics of the city had met and responded to the invitation, dividing the issue into several topics, each to be addressed in the Lowell city hall by eighteen ministers. Even though Lee had not been present at the discussion, he responded with alacrity. After all, a good challenge might divert his mind from the bleak outlook of the antislavery enterprise. Lee had written on the matter of temperance as early as 1836, while a pastor in Fulton. His ideas on the issue of harnessing governmental agencies in the cause of temperance, however, had not been made known in the Lowell area. By May 16, 1841, he was ready to present his views. Dr. Huntington, a physician and mayor of the town, introduced him.[37]

Lee began by reading the Scripture from Romans 13:3, "For rulers are not a terror to good works, but to the evil." Drawing from the passage the concept that God had ordained government as an instrument to keep evil in check, Lee began on a note of humility, regretting that such an important topic had been assigned to one of so little ability and relatively unknown in Lowell. He then continued on and logically developed his outline to prove the following:

> I. That a prohibitory law is necessary to consummate the temperance reformation;
> II. That the passage of such a law comes perfectly within the design and powers of civil government; and,
> III. That civil government is bound by the strongest moral obligation, to enact and enforce such a law.[38]

Lee put a rhetorical question to his hearers. Did licensing the sale of intoxicating liquors help or hinder the work of reform? He left the obvious answer to them. He argued that licensing liquor sales lent a certain amount of moral suasion in favor of drinking, implying that government approved its consumption. Clearly, moral suasion by the reformers could not accomplish their goal without government's help.

Lee demonstrated that no valid reason existed in the law why government might not enact such laws. To pass such laws would not violate anything in the Constitution; furthermore, government has the right, nay the duty, to suppress vice and immorality. "Is government designed to protect the weak against the strong? . . . No class need that protection more than the drunkard, his abused wife, and hungry and half-naked children—they need the strong arm of the law to protect them against the ravages of the rum-seller."[39]

Lee made reference to Dr. Huntington, who was also the president of the Lowell Temperance Society, reminding the crowd that the civil leaders had the responsibility of suppressing intemperance. Interestingly, he challenged the common error of thinking that the majority should rule in such matters. Lee, no utilitarian on this, insisted that moral obligation takes precedence when confronted by the majority will of the people. He closed on a ringing note, declaring that when all of the evils of the liquor trade had run their full course, "then will all wish there had been enacted and enforced a PROHIBITORY LAW!"[40]

The sermon appeared in printed form and Lee exulted that to his knowledge it was the first of its kind to be published in America. In keeping with his argument for the use of politics in the antislavery cause, he viewed as appropriate a similar course in the battle against intoxicating liquor. By so arguing, Lee, by default or design, was reflecting the classical, antebellum Whig philosophy: Use the levers of government to control the evils of society, the exact opposite of the Democratic position, that government must not meddle with the ills of society. Lee never indicated what parties he supported until the Liberty Party came into existence. While frontier Methodists regularly voted Democrat (a good example is the frontier Methodist preacher, Peter Cartwright, who ran as a Democrat against the Whig candidate, Abraham Lincoln, in the Congressional election of 1846), Lee could hardly vote other than Whig, given his strong proclivity for using government to bring about social reforms. His greatest interest in the realm of reform, however, still lay in the ultimate freedom of the slaves. Antislavery consumed by far his greatest efforts; to that struggle he turned his attention.

As mentioned above, Lee could not keep Scott's *The New England Christian Advocate* afloat for long. At the end of the first volume it had died for lack of a supporting constituency. Still in possession of the subscription list, however, Lee believed that a new periodical that would address other vital issues might be sustainable. Within its columns he intended to oppose the contemporary "wild theological views springing up," as well as other matters.[41] The paper's focus would not be restricted to antislavery alone, as was Scott's paper.

Lee consequently began publishing and editing *The Sword of Truth* on a semi-monthly basis, but the project proved to be dead on arrival. After a short period of time, Lee had to give up his enterprise. Within the ranks of Methodism the abolitionists refused to buy it—it did not attack slavery. Those who opposed abolitionism also turned away from it on the grounds that a hated antislavery fellow was behind it. The pitiful few subscribers outside of Methodism simply could not sustain the expenses. Lee dropped it after a few issues. His personal finances had reached critical proportions. Fortunately for him, in the fall of 1842 the Methodist Episcopal church at Andover, Massachusetts had a vacant pulpit. Due to its strong stance against slavery and a lack of income, the church found itself without a pastor. Lee happily accepted the offer to pastor there, and moved his family to that place, continuing to lecture against slavery wherever he found opportunity. At Andover, a new phenomenon had captured the interest of some Americans and soon summoned forth Lee's debating skills.[42]

The practice of mesmerism had entered the country from Europe. Jacksonian Americans had an insatiable appetite for health reform, spiritualism, forms of the occult, animal magnetism, hydropathy, and phrenology, and they loved such novelties. Each of these isms appeared ultimately to have been driven by the optimistic, perfectionism spirit of the day. To the practitioner of mesmerism, it seemed that the psychological processes could also be perfected by this combination of mental telepathy, autonomic suggestion, and hypnotism. It was never difficult to get an audience to observe the process.[43]

One such practitioner of the new science of mesmerism came to Andover. Lee, typically, had researched the subject to ascertain its methodology as well as its validity and went to observe the performance. He observed many of the students from Andover Seminary in the crowd. When the speaker argued that Christ performed all his miracles through mesmerism, the students, as one, turned to Lee for his reaction. Standing to his feet, Lee inquired whether he had correctly understood him, that the speaker claimed the same power as Christ. Upon an affirmative answer, Lee agreed that if the speaker could feed just one person, he would admit that Christ might have used mesmerism. Obviously hedging, the practitioner responded that he could induce the necessary state on a subject, and cause him to think that he had eaten and was satisfied. Lee countered, "Suppose I allow all that, I must inquire how many baskets full you will have left?"[44] The speaker had more than met his match and the affair ended for him on a sour note.

The abolitionists were finding that their cause had likewise gone sour. The bishops had effectively gagged them; the Liberty Party seemed to be going nowhere and most reform movements had been greatly impacted negatively by the national economy. From his farm in Vermont, Scott wrote an article for *Zion's Watchman* in which he lamented that he had "little hope that the church will ever be reformed in relation to slavery."[45] In June of 1842 he said in *Zion's Herald,* "There is no alternative but to submit to things pretty much as they are, or secede."[46] By the end of the year, that was the course that Lee and others had pursued. They would take the step and form a new denomination, a seceder church built on Scriptural principles. In that enterprise Lee played a significant role as a leader, speaker, editor, church builder, and administrator. They would take the epochal step. They would cross their Rubicon.

NOTES

1. Daniel Walker Howe, *The Political Culture of the American Whigs* (Chicago: University of Chicago Press, 1979).

2. Luther Lee, *Autobiography of the Reverend Luther Lee, D.D.* (New York: Phillips & Hunt; Cincinnati, Ohio: Walden & Stowe, 1882), 212.

3. Charles Baumer Swaney, *Episcopal Methodism with Sidelights on Ecclesiastical Politics* (Boston: The Gorham Press, 1926), 86-87; *Autobiography,* 212-15.

4. *Autobiography,* 216-21.

5. *Autobiography,* 216-21.

6. *Autobiography,* 219-20.

7. Timothy L. Smith, *Revivalism and Social Reform in Mid-Nineteenth-Century America* (New York and Nashville, Tenn.: Abingdon Press, 1957), 81-82, 122-27; Whitney R. Cross, *The Burned-over District: The Social and Intellectual History of Enthusiastic Religion in Western New York, 1800-1850* (Ithaca, N.Y.: Cornell University Press), 176-79; Paul E. Johnson, *A Shopkeeper's Millennium: Society and Revivals in New York, 1815-1837* (New York: Hill & Wang, 1978), 99; *Autobiography,* 220.

8. *Autobiography,* 221.

9. *Autobiography,* 221-22.

10. *Autobiography,* 224-25.

11. *Zion's Herald,* September 9, 1840; Donald G. Mathews, "Orange Scott: The Methodist Evangelist as Revolutionary," in Martin Duberman, ed., *The Antislavery Vanguard: New Essays on the Abolitionists* (Princeton, N.J.: Princeton University Press, 1965), 91-92.

12. L. C. Matlack, *The Anti-Slavery Struggle and Triumph in the Methodist Episcopal Church* (New York: Phillips & Hunt, 1881; repr., New York: Negro University Press, 1969), 135-36.

13. Swaney, *Episcopal Methodism with Sidelights,* 98.

14. Lee himself has an excellent review of the Silas Comfort affair in *Wesleyan Review* 1 (June 1844): 15-16, a small periodical that he published briefly in Lowell; Donald G. Mathews, *Slavery and Methodism: A Chapter in American Morality 1780-1845* (Princeton, N.J.: Princeton University Press, 1965), 200.

15. *Wesleyan Review,* 15; Mathews, *Slavery and Methodism,* 201.

16. Mathews, *Slavery and Methodism,* 201-202.

17. James M. Buckley, *A History of Methodism in the United States,* 2 vols. (New York: Christian Literature Co., 1897) 2: 12-14.

18. See "The Woman Question," *Liberator,* February 1, 1839 for Garrison's ideas on the matter.

19. *Liberator,* June 5, 1840.

20. John B. Pickard, "John Greenleaf Whittier and the Abolitionist Schism of 1840," *New England Quarterly* 37 (June 1964): 250-61; quotation

on 253.

21. Gilbert Hobbs Barnes, *The Antislavery Impulse 1830-1844* (New York, 1933; repr., New York: Harcourt, Brace & World, Inc, 1964), 175, 282.

22. Aileen S. Kraditor, *Means and Ends in American Abolitionism: Garrison and His Critics on Strategy and Tactics, 1834-1850* (New York: Pantheon Books, 1969; repr., Chicago: Ivan R. Dee, Inc., 1989), 53; Richard H. Sewell, *Ballots for Freedom: Antislavery Politics in the United States, 1837-1860* (New York: W. W. Norton & Company, 1976), 74-75; Ronald G. Walters, *The Antislavery Appeal: American Abolitionism after 1830* (New York: W. W. Norton & Co., 1978), 90-91; Barnes, *Antislavery Impulse,* 169.

23. Barnes, *Antislavery Impulse, 176.*

24. Sewell, *Ballots for Freedom,* 45-47; Barnes, *Antislavery Impulse,* 176.

25. Stanley Harrold, *Gamaliel Bailey and Antislavery Union* (Kent, Ohio: Kent State University Press, 1986), 35-40. Actually Bailey dropped total opposition to the Liberty Party on principle and argued only that the third-party movement was not expedient; *New England Christian Advocate,* January 7, 1843.

26. *New England Christian Advocate,* January 7, 1843.

27. *Autobiography,* 226-29.

28. The *New England Christian Advocate,* February 11, 1841, contained a letter from Scott that appeared in an article entitled, "The New Paper." In it Scott wrote, ". . . I am in no wise connected with the paper," indicating that by October 29, 1840, the date of the letter, Lee had taken over the editorship; Matlack, *Life of the Reverend Orange Scott: Compiled from His Personal Narrative, Correspondence, and Other Authentic Sources of Information, In Two Parts* (New York: C. Pindle and L. C. Matlack, 1847; reprint, Freeport, N.Y.: Books for Libraries Press, 1971), 185; *Autobiography,* 230-31.

29. The first Methodists came to Lowell in 1824, not long after the town was founded. In 1827 they built a chapel on Central Street, an area of town which came to be known as Chapel Hill. A strong revival occurred in 1827, one which added 334 members to that church. In 1838 two churches were formed out of the original: St. Paul's, which built the largest Methodist sanctuary on Hurd Street, and the other, the Worthen Street Methodist Church, which built there in 1842, moving from Lowell Street. It has been estimated that sixteen thousand have been converted at its altars and over ten thousand have held membership. Merrill did not secede with the others, James Mudge, *New England History,* 220-21.

30. *The New England Christian Advocate,* February 11, 1841; reports of revivals intermingled simultaneously with reform activities such as those in Lowell cause one to reconsider Ronald Walters' statement, "Even in cases where revivalism did eventually lead to antislavery there was often a long gap between religious awakening and the reform commitment," *Antislavery Appeal,* 39. Evidence exists for both sides of the argument, and one cannot take that as a given, at least in every case.

31. *Autobiography,* 232-33.

32. W. J. Rorabaugh, "Estimated U.S. Alcoholic Beverage Consumption, 1790-1860," *Journal of Studies on Alcohol* 37 (March 1976), 357-64; Edward Pessen, *Jacksonian America: Society, Personality, and Politics* (Urbana: University of Illinois Press, 1985), 20.

33. Walters, *American Reformers, 1815-1860* (New York: Hill & Wang, 1978), 123-31; Cross, *Burned-over District,* 211-215; Alice Felt Tyler, *Freedom's Ferment,* (New York: Harper & Row, Publishers, 1944), 308-50; John Allen Krout, *The Origins of Prohibition* (New York: Alfred A. Knopf, Inc., 1925; repr., New York: Russell & Russell, 1967), 101-53.

34. See the *True Wesleyan,* February 24, 1844, for evidence that the Wesleyans supported this form of reform, even though it was secularly based, and not the result of evangelical reformers; *Autobiography,* 233. Interestingly, the Wesleyans did not understand their rule against intoxicating liquors to apply to communion wine, cf., "Wine for Sacramental Purposes," *The American Wesleyan,* June 12, 1861, in which the editor writes that Mr. William Day of Syracuse "has a quantity of wine of his own make, the pure juice of the grape, suitable for sacramental purposes. . . . We have examined this article, and can recommend it to any church that wishes to use a pure article, instead of a filthy compound, that in most cases would be procured of common venders. The article here commended, will bear two parts of water to one of the wine."

35. *Courier* (Lowell), February 13, 1841.

36. *Courier* (Lowell), February 13, 1841.

37. Luther Lee, *A Sermon for the Times: Prohibitory Laws* (New York: Wesleyan Book Room, 1852; repr., Donald W. Dayton, ed., *Five Sermons and a Tract by Luther Lee* (Chicago: Holrad House, 1975), 60-75.

38. Dayton, *Five Sermons,* 62.

39. Dayton, *Five Sermons,* 67.

40. Dayton, *Five Sermons,* 75.

41. *Autobiography,* 233-34.

42. *Autobiography,* 233-34.

43. See *True Wesleyan,* September 30, 1843, for a description of the book that Sunderland wrote on mesmerism. Horton, a contributing editor at that time wrote, "We recommend it for its clearness of perception, strength of reasoning . . . it strips the subject of 'Animal Magnetism,' so called, . . . a knowledge of its principles may subserve the physical, intellectual, and moral health of man, is alike manifest." The publisher had copies for sale. Later, Sunderland left the Wesleyans and focused upon such "scientific" isms.

44. Walters, *American Reformers,* 156-63; cf., Edward D. Jervis, "LaROY[*sic*] Sunderland: 'Prince of the Sons of Mesmer,'" *Journal of American Studies* 9 (April 1976): 1010-26, for an excellent discussion of these strange mental phenomena, which evolved from the work of Franz Mesmer in Europe; J. R. Jacob, "La Roy Sunderland: The Alienation of an Abolitionist," 6 (April 1972): 1-17; *Autobiography,* 233-34; Tyler, *Freedom's Ferment,* 441.

45. Matlack, *Life of Orange Scott,* 186.
46. *Zion's Herald,* June 15, 1842.

Chapter Six

1843-1852: Wesleyan Methodist Church Planter and Editor

One of the great paradoxes of the nineteenth century that faced abolitionists was the fact that slavery constituted a moral wrong and yet none of the churches was willing to condemn the institution of slavery as a moral evil. Even more frustrating to them were the Scriptural arguments that southern apologists of slavery hurled at the antislavery northerners. How could the book of morality be used to defend such an obviously evil system that condoned human bondage? While the churches generally were willing to live with the status quo, the abolitionists within those "bulwarks of slavery" would not let the issue of slavery alone. Given the provocations of the annexation of Texas, the Mexican War, the Fugitive Slave Law, the Kansas-Nebraska Act, the attack on Senator Charles Sumner in the Senate chamber, and the Dred Scott decision, the North slowly began to perceive the implications of slavocracy. The awakening process received yet another boost with the addition of Harriet Beecher Stowe's *Uncle Tom's Cabin* and other literature that flowed from antislavery newspapers all over the North kept a steady pressure on northern thinking that eventually led to schisms in some of the main denominations.

John C. Calhoun's Senate speech in 1850 observed that "already three great evangelical churches [had] been torn asunder," due to internecine squabbling over the slavery issue. The Presbyterian church took the first step toward separation in 1837 with the Old School-New School split. Of course the main North-South schism did not occur until 1857, when the Southern presbyteries withdrew. The Southern Baptist Convention organized a separate denomination in 1845. In the year preceding that, the Methodists could no longer abide the slave-holding members in the South. Forced out of their mediating position by the secession of thousands of its members in the North, the bishops opened the General Conference of 1844 for debate on slavery and the final split developed by the end of the session. Lee and his colleagues must be credited for much of the agitation that produced the schism. This chapter explores those developments.[1]

The Whig party had little to feel optimistic about on the national level in 1843. Two years into the Whig presidency of John Tyler the Whigs had read their leader out of the party. He had taken the wrong stand on all the issues that defined Whig politicians. On the religious scene, Methodist abolitionist preachers in New England sensed that they, too, might well be read out of their organization. It slowly began to dawn upon them that the best course of action would be to leave their church and start another one, one free of slavery and bishops.

Actually the idea of secession from the Methodist Episcopal church had been discussed between Lee and Scott as early as 1841. For almost two years Scott had reflected on the idea, but his health and other reasons of expediency had kept the matter in check. Lee would not leave by himself. Then precipitously in October of 1842, Scott quit hesitating and called for a meeting at Albany on November 2 and 3. Jotham Horton, Cyrus Prindle, and two others met to lay plans for their withdrawal from the church. Others had left already. George Storrs, complaining of ecclesiastical tyranny, left the church after the General Conference of 1840, seeking a home with the Millerites.[2] Shipley Willson, another abolitionist from the earliest days, had since drifted into Unitarianism. On November 8, 1842, Scott, Sunderland, Horton, and Prindle took the inevitable step.[3]

Lee had not been notified of the Albany meeting. Scott feared that some features of the plan might not win Lee's endorsement, and he did not want to get into potentially abortive arguments early on. Simultaneously, the men agreed that Scott should initiate yet another publication, the *True Wesleyan,* in which they would publish their reasons for seceding from the Methodist Episcopal church. Lee learned of their actions through the press. A series of events quickly followed.[4]

First Lee received a letter from a spokesman for the Boston Preachers' Meeting of the Methodist Episcopal church. Hoping to convince Lee to remain loyal, the writer promised: ". . . you shall have any position in the Church you desire if you will come out and wield your vigorous pen against secession."[5] Lee dashed off a reply in a letter stating that his services were not for sale. He finally met up with Scott and confronted him for not notifying him of his intentions. Scott frankly admitted to him: "I was afraid of you; I did not know that you would agree with me, and I knew if you did not . . . you would sound the alarm before I could get a document before the people."[6]

Lee was first and foremost a Methodist. While offers from other denominations appeared tempting, he knew he must remain in a Methodist milieu. The thought of a new denomination intrigued him. While he had no reason to question the sincerity of the offer of the brethren in Boston, Lee could never bring himself to turn on his abolitionist colleagues. To remain in a church that tolerated slavehold-ing bishops while it prohibited the free discussion of slavery issues made no sense to Lee. Thus, he took the only logical step; he also seceded.

The *True Wesleyan* of January 7, 1843, contained the reasons for the withdrawal of the first secessionists. It also published the an-nouncement of an antislavery convention to be held in Andover on February 1 for the purpose of "the ultimate formation of a Wesleyan Methodist Church, free from Episcopacy and Slavery."[7] That call was issued over the signatures of Horton, Lee, Scott, and Sunderland. The second number contained the new address of the publication: 66 Cornhill Street in Boston. It also contained Lee's reasons for seceding from the Methodist Episcopal church. Slavery headed the list. He called attention to recent pro-slavery statements by Reverend J. C. Postell of South Carolina: (1) slavery is a judicial visitation, (2) slavery is not a moral evil, (3) slavery is supported by the Bible, and (4) slavery has existed in all ages. Lee also complained of the "principles" of government that had developed since abolitionism surfaced in the church, and he concluded his reasons citing the "uncharitable and bitter spirit" of the church leaders, editors, and others. His article closed with a defense of Scott, Horton, and Sunderland, arguing that those men should not be held as traitors, but as men with vision having no other option but to secede.[8] The third number of the paper contained the secession notice of one who became one of the strong leaders of the new church, Lucius C. Matlack.[9] Upon leaving the Boston area, Matlack took the Fountain Street church in Providence, Rhode Island. That same issue also contained a striking poem, "The Slave's Prayer," the first of many written by Lee, and also, "The Quadroon Girl," by Henry Wadsworth Longfellow. The editors clearly meant for their publication to have certain literary and cultural appeal—at least for the abolitionist readership![10]

While the leaders of the new "Scottite" movement awaited the Andover meeting, they received word of individuals and entire congregations that also had voted to secede. Several churches in Michigan, numbering an aggregate membership above six hundred, had been reported to Scott as early as December 26, 1842. Then the large Methodist Episcopal church at Providence served notice, by a vote taken on December 25, 1842 that it, too, had severed relations and wanted the distinction of being the first Wesleyan Church in New England.[11] Out in the West, Edward Smith of Pittsburgh had endured the ignominy of suspension from the old church, and his formal secession was only days away. The *True Wesleyan* urged each seceder to notify the editor so proper promotional advantage could be secured. Finally the day of the Andover convention arrived.[12]

The Methodist Episcopal church in Andover, Massachusetts had been selected as the location for the auspicious Wesleyan Anti-Slavery Convention. Coincidentally, Lee just happened to be pastor of that church.[13] Matlack, soon to be elected secretary, prayed an invocation. Horton of Boston called the session to order. After the "Call" was formally read, a discussion of their business transpired in a spirit of harmony. In the elections the Honorable Seth Sprague Jr. of Duxbury was chosen president. A committee to organize the business was formed; Lee found himself on it along with eight others. Once business recommenced they passed several resolutions about the purpose of the convention. The convention unanimously agreed that the episcopal form of government proved to be "anti-republican, . . . an encroachment upon human rights," and "subversive." Resolutions establishing a committee of correspondence between the newly-formed societies, and a committee to form and publish a *Discipline*, passed easily. Curiously, in a move that reflected badly on the old church, the group also approved a resolution stating that Wesley never intended to establish an episcopal form of government when he appointed Asbury and Coke as superintendents in America.[14] The final resolution invited the Michigan brethren and all others interested to send delegates to a "General Convention" to be held in Utica, on May 31 of that year.[15]

From Andover the delegates returned to their place of labor. Lee remained at his church in Andover while he wrote articles for the *True Wesleyan.* He and Horton served as assistant editors to Scott whose name appeared on the masthead as the editor and proprietor. In the issue of March 4, Lee wrote an article entitled "Are Deacons an Order of Ministry?" His position opposed that of the mother church, which essentially constituted the office of the deacon as a mere doorway to the office of elder. He faulted those who used the deaconate as a probationary step that placed persons halfway between the laity and the ministry. The problem, wrote Lee, was their misunderstanding of the New Testament context. Deacons were not ministers, and as will be seen below, the new church did not provide for such an office.[16]

Lee did not pass up opportunities to employ principles of logic—especially if he could put the Methodist Episcopal church in a bad light in the process. On the matter of temperance, an issue that still lay near to his heart, Lee found just such an issue. The mother church's *Discipline* prohibited its clergy from distilling and vending spirituous liquors; however, it said nothing about the laity's responsibility. Lee proposed to make his former leaders look bad and he had the bonus of applying rules of logic as he did so. Since the rule stated only who may *not* use or sell drink, it *implied* that laity may. Then, in the political realm, he made an analogy: a state constitution states that every *white* male *may* vote. The implication is that all colored persons are prohibited from voting, just as surely as if the Constitution stated it that way. The reasoning is, perhaps, forced. It shows, however, that Lee loved to apply logic to any situation, especially if it promoted the cause of blacks.[17]

In the April 22 issue, the *True Wesleyan* announced the convening of a General Convention for the purpose of organizing the Wesleyan Methodist Church on May 31, 1843. The selection of Utica, New York, as its place of meeting appears appropriate, given its past interest in reform movements, both social and political. Reverend George Pegler, host pastor of the recently formed Wesleyan Church at

Utica, had instructions in an announcement for all delegates.[18] Upon arrival in the city each should call at Andrew Hanna's store, 50 Genesee Street, where the entertainment committee would assign lodging. In addition to the above information, the paper carried a notice "To the Liberty Party Abolitionists throughout the United States," in which it announced a United States Anti-Slavery Convention at Buffalo. Due to the thick ice on the Great Lakes, the event had been postponed until June. Ostensibly this convention would meet to nominate a presidential candidate. Lee was responsible for the political announcements appearing in the paper.[19]

In addition to political articles Lee wrote about the "factory girls" at the Lowell textile mills. No evidence establishes an indisputable link between Lee's feminism and the female workers in the city where he lived in the early 1840s. That notwithstanding, he manifested a growing interest in female working conditions. This was consistent with his general support of feminism. The article lamented that Lowell mill hands must "devote fifteen twenty-fourths of every working day to the corporations; being thirteen hours of incessant toil, and two hours devoted to meals and preparations. . . . Is not this fact a shameful and a painful one?" Lee supported the women's efforts to gain a ten-hour system. But more pressing for him at the moment were preparations for Utica.[20]

The long-awaited convention of all seceders, Methodist Episcopal and otherwise, finally commenced in the Blecker Street church in Utica on May 31, 1843.[21] Most of the delegates had arrived on time; others straggled in, as one later wrote, "owing to the arrangements of the railroad companies. . . . Every seventy or eighty miles . . . they stop the cheap cars and lay over for twenty-four hours . . . to gouge the travelers who prefer the cheap cars."[22] Approximately 150 delegates had arrived; almost twice that many, including a number of blacks, crowded into the galleries. A youthful looking Irish preacher, recently arrived in America as a missionary to Irish immigrants, appeared as a delegate from Ireland. The eclectic group included delegates from sixteen states and about half that number of denominations.[23]

Jotham Horton called the session to order. Orange Scott was appointed chairman and La Roy Sunderland secretary. After Cyrus Prindle led in prayer, a nominating committee that included Lee was formed. To no one's surprise, Scott was elected president. Edward Smith from Pittsburgh, along with Horton, were vice-presidents. The elections completed, the session moved to the business of organizing a new church.[24]

The most important discussion focused on the adoption of a *Discipline* that contained doctrinal views, moral principles, and rules of government. The new denomination would be Methodist in theology. Wesley's Twenty-Five Articles of Religion, a carryover from the Anglican church, formed the nexus of the new organization. Some articles were slightly revised; others that had only faulted Roman practices, but said nothing positive, were deleted.[25]

The delegates spent considerable time debating the form of church government. Smith advocated a "High-Church" approach, meaning a strong episcopacy; Scott leaned toward a modified episcopacy with limited and "well-guarded" powers; others leaned toward a congregational form. Lee's influence pushed the convention toward a mixture of presbyterian and congregational organization. Then, also influenced by Lee, the delegates agreed to use the term "Methodist" in the name because it expressed a principle. They opted for the term, "Connection," to establish that "All these Christian congregations, collectively, are not a Church, but being connected by a central organization they are a connection of churches." In truth, this is one of the most revealing aspects of the mind of the delegates and their leaders. In opting for a system of church government that placed sovereignty at the level of the laity, the Wesleyan Methodists, in fact as well as theory, defined the culmination of an egalitarian process in society that originated with the American Revolution. By so doing, they institutionalized a social movement built around social reform and antielitism.[26]

In actuality, the Utica delegates were organizing a church with which to shape their society.[27] Wesleyan Methodism delineates the process by which popular culture became Christianized and institutionalized, and gave new meaning to *novus ordo seclorum* in freeing itself from the authoritarian episcopacy. Lee, as chairman of the committee that produced the Pastoral Address and the chief architect of the new church's polity, must be viewed as a leader of the *avant garde* of Jacksonian social reform. Therein is his significance. He represented much more than an antislavery agitator, a spokesman for women, and an opposer of drink: He was the personification of all that his father fought for in the American Revolution![28]

The strength of the connection lay with the local church. These were to meet in a quarterly conference as the means for each congregation to conduct business on the local level. Each church elected its own pastor and no power at the conference level could impose a pastor on a congregation without its concurrence. The churches elected their own officers and received their own church members, according to the rules of the *Discipline*. There was no appeal on such local issues.[29] In this system, then, the republicanism of America is mirrored; sovereignty resided in the people.[30]

The annual conference was the next higher level above the local church. Every elder and stationed preacher under appointment had a duty to attend. Lay delegates were selected at the local level. At the annual conference equal representation must be strictly observed: one layman delegate for each elder. This would not be a clergy dominated church! Each conference elected a president and other officers according to the *Discipline*. At these sessions, men who had completed the prescribed course of study were ordained to the office of elder. A stationing committee reviewed all pastor-church agreements that had been agreed upon at each local church. While it might make recomendations to local churches, it had no legal authority to negate the local church's wishes concerning its pastor. There would be no more arbitrary appointments at the whim of the bishop or the presiding elder. The annual conferences also conducted trials involving elders or churches when needed.[31]

General conferences met every four years and were made up of one ministerial and one lay delegate for every five hundred members. The annual conferences elected those delegates. The president of the general conference, elected by its delegates, presided over the business sessions and remained in office for the following four years although he virtually had nothing to do unless a general conference was in session. The general conference had full power to make rules and regulations for the churches, so long as no Article of Faith or General Rule was violated.[32]

By organizing their new church in that fashion, the Wesleyans rejected *in toto* the episcopacy of the old denomination. While not enacting a presbyterian polity, the delegates utilized some of its concepts. It could not, on the other hand, be identified as pure congregationalism, since rules did come down from the general conference, although the delegates who formulated the rules were elected at the local level. At Utica the delegates mirrored the republicanism of the federal government in which sovereignty resided with the laity.

On the second day of the proceedings an aged mulatto with white locks, known only as "Reverend Dungy," who had left the Methodist Episcopal church in 1838, addressed the convention. While his manner of speech lacked polish, his bearing conveyed sincerity, enough to move most of his hearers to tears. After he learned of the 1838 church trials of True, Floy, and Plumb, Dungy feared that he would be next to be charged with abolitionism. After all, he had queried of his presiding elder, "Who will be security for old Dungy?" Recently quite ill, he forced himself to come to the convention that he might look "upon the face of Orange Scott and Luther Lee: O, how my heart rejoiced to see these men that have been so slandered and abused!" The audience sat transfixed as he spoke; Lee later observed that the eloquent address so influenced him that although he had intended to take notes, "our pencil soon fell from our fingers, and our vacant page caught nothing but our tears. . . [and] the whole convention was overwhelmed by the address of Br. Dungy."[33]

Following that speech, a delegate read a letter to the convention from a black preacher who pastored a black church in Dayton, Ohio. The communicaton spoke of his paying several thousand dollars for the freedom of his wife and himself, and the sum of two hundred dollars for his mother's. The crowd reacted strongly, some crying "Shame!" In the afternoon five fugitive slaves had been presented to the convention, just to remind them of the major *raison d'être* for the new organization.[34]

Other matters necessary in forming a denomination were addressed, such as accepting the *True Wesleyan* as its official organ.[35] The delegates agreed to observe only two sacraments: baptism and holy communion. After discussion, infant baptism was retained, although many argued that the adult believer's baptism was the only one authorized by Scripture. In keeping with Wesley's practices in England, all three modes of baptism, sprinkling, affusion, and immersion, were retained; the candidate for the rite could choose his or her desired mode.[36]

The General Rules reflected the Wesleyan position toward social reforms of the era. Two of the most obvious rules prohibited

> drunkenness, or the manufacturing, buying, selling or using intoxi-cating liquors, unless for mechanical, chemical, or medicinal pur-poses; on, in any way, intentionally and knowingly, aiding others so to do. . . . The buying or selling of men, women or children, with an intention to enslave them; or holding them as slaves; or claiming that it is right so to do.[37]

The only requirement for membership for those desiring to join the new church was "a desire to flee from the wrath to come, and to be saved from their sins." Those applicants manifested their "desire" by keeping the general rules. After admission had been granted, members must continue to observe the rules or face expulsion by the quarterly conference.

Business went well and a general spirit of unity was present until Smith raised an issue that would prove to be divisive until the end of the century: the issue of secret societies in general, and the Masons in particular. It is necessary to look closer at this issue.[38]

Masons tended to define theirs as a system of morality that operates independently of any organized religion. Heavy in the use of allegory and symbolism, it roots itself in antiquity, as far back as Hiram, the builder of Solomon's temple. According to legend, this person had been assassinated and brought back to life. Since his Scriptural de-scription involves craftsmanship, he somehow evolves into stonema-son. The cathedral building guild of medieval times kept the tradition alive, but gave it a useful function of protecting its workers from roaming "scab laborers." The essential tools of masonry—the square, the trowel, and the compass—became stylized symbols in modern Masonry.

In 1717, speculative free masonry came into being as several craft lodges met at a tavern in London and drew up a Constitution for Free and Accepted Masons. Earliest members of that lodge were old retired

or unemployed men; before long, however, a knowledge of stonema-
sonry and bricklaying counted for nothing. The membership evolved
into a type of middle class club for those who had the time and the
financial means to join. It could be argued that the concept of the lodge
had its ideological roots in the Enlightenment, and arrived in America
about the same time, and with the same impact. Many of the prominent
leaders in the late colonial and early national periods illustrate how
pervasive Masonry had become. Roman Catholics and Eastern Orthodox adherents had been forbidden to join. Methodists, Baptists, Presbyterians, Congregationalists, and Episcopalians had no rules concerning lodge membership.[39]

Whitney Cross observed that Masonry in the burned-over district
tended to center in the larger towns and cities. Evidence of rural
jealousy toward urban superiority and the controlling classes can be
delineated. The lower reaches had reason to oppose Masonry. Most
could not afford the membership fees. Its rituals and oath-taking were
performed in secrecy. That alone forced adversaries to deem membership morally wrong. Even more dangerous to the opposers of the lodge
was the issue of taking an oath to show partiality to fellow lodge
members in matters of law. That subverted justice in society and
smacked of class and privilege. In addition, its oaths took the Lord's
name in vain and its titles and rituals had the appearance of monarchy
and infidelity. Charles G. Finney, a former member of the Masons who
left as a result of the Morgan affair, wrote a lengthy treatise against
true Christians holding membership in secret societies. He claimed that
the membership was sworn to persecute its opponents, used profanity
in its oaths, profaned the Scriptures, had a false appeal to antiquity,
boasted a benevolence that was a sham, constituted a false religion,
and in general was to be avoided by all true believers in Christ.[40]

In antebellum America, Cross observed that about a fourth of all
Protestant clerics and only a twentieth of the laity belonged to Masonic
lodges in central New York. Many clerics could not afford entry fees;
Dorothy Lipson's research into a Connecticut lodge has found that
membership fees had frequently been waived for the clergy. Why? If
charges of immorality and other unchristian activities allegedly transpired within the masonic lodges, what better way to refute the charges
than by admitting preachers to its ranks![41]

In an era when an egalitarian wave was rolling across the social landscape, however, Masonry had the potential of being divisive. Then in 1826, the supposed murder of William Morgan in western New York unleashed all the social forces that had been kept submerged. Morgan had threatened to expose all the Masonic secrets. After being arrested on questionable charges, he was mysteriously freed from the jail at Canandaigua and subsequently disappeared. Stories and half-truths have obscured the facts, but not the results. A wave of antimasonry sentiment swept across the nation, forming the Antimason Party, and putting many otherwise obscure men into places of leadership within the state houses and federal offices. All this was well known to the deliberating body at Utica.[42]

Edward Smith of Pittsburgh asked the convention what it planned to do regarding the Masonic question. Such a question might otherwise appear innocuous enough, until it became known to the delegates that Scott, Lee, Horton, and Sunderland belonged to the Masons.[43] The effect was electrifying. Several men threatened to withdraw on the spot. How could men of such stature be involved in such a nefarious organization? Had not Charles G. Finney, the ex-Mason, left the "foul" establishment and written pamphlets and books against its teachings?[44] Smith, a large man and a ferocious debater, bore the sobriquet "The Lion of the West." He insisted on a rule in the *Discipline* that would forbid membership to any belonging to a secret society. The Easterners, Scott, Horton, and Sunderland, had significant support, along with the prestige that they carried as leaders in the movement. Smith had his support as well, and he was adamant. Lee had been a Mason since 1821, but as he later wrote: "I was a Mason, but did not feel myself under a masonic obligation to make myself its champion on that occasion."[45] He chose not to reveal his position during the debate, maintaining that it was better to remain neutral so he could offer a compromise. When an impasse developed, Lee offered a mediating rule:

> Question. Have we any advice to give respecting secret oath-bound societies?
>
> Ans.   We leave that matter with the several Annual Conferences and individual churches.[46]

Even though a compromise had been effected, everyone knew that the issue would raise its head again at the next General Conference.[47]

Before concluding business, it only remained to establish the boundaries of the annual conferences. Other than attempts to send missionaries into North Carolina in the middle forties, the new denomination focused on New England, the Middle States, and the Old Northwest.[48]

During the Utica Convention a Pastoral Address, prepared by Lee and several members of a committee, conveyed to the delegates a general description of the character, condition, and prospects of the organization.[49] Within the body of the lengthy document were references to benevolence, Sabbath-schools, Missions, Temperance, and an exhortation for all to seek holiness of heart, one of the peculiar doctrines of the followers of Wesley. The delegates were urged ". . . above all, brethren, we exhort you to make holiness your motto." Also known as the doctrine of Christian perfection, it fit well in the context of the Second Great Awakening, and the postmillennial desires of many of its leaders to seek to live holy lives, a process that had the potential of bringing the Kingdom of God to Earth. The emphasis at Utica presaged the Oberlin Perfectionism of Finney and Asa Mahan. Wesleyan Methodists were leaving Utica with the clarion call to lead holy lives.[50]

An *ad hoc* committee assigned conference presidents and pastoral assignments until duly elected delegates could meet in their respective annual conferences. Lee was appointed president of the New York Conference and assigned to pastor in Syracuse. When the convention adjourned in the second week of June, Lee hurried back to Andover, and once again packed his belongings and moved his family to Syracuse.[51]

When he reached Syracuse, he discovered that the little band of seceders had no place of worship. For the first few weeks, the group used the facilities of the Congregational church. In time they located a hall that could be used until a permanent solution was found. As things worked out, the Unitarians were just completing a new house of worship. As soon as they moved into their new building, the Wesleyans purchased the old one. Thus, Lee and his congregation felt ready to face the world in general, and certain Methodist Episcopal opposition in Syracuse in particular. Lee's new church enjoyed steady growth as long as the antislavery issue appealed to people in the area.[52] In addition to building up the Wesleyan congregation in Syracuse, Lee traveled into the surrounding area where he organized other churches.

The Methodist Episcopal church at Clay, a few miles north of Syracuse, had recently seceded and joined the Wesleyans with twenty-one members. Only three of the old congregation chose not to leave. On Sunday, July 9, Lee rode up to visit the fledgling church. During the summer months the Methodist papers charged Lee and his preachers with stealing "sheep" from the old church. Such charges must be based solely upon one's perspective. As the appointed president of the New York Conference, Lee constantly recruited new preachers to lead the small congregations that were proliferating in the state. The *True Wesleyan* of July 29 contained an announcement, "Fifty Preachers Wanted, . . . [men] of suitable qualifications . . . can find immediate employment," signed by Lee and each of the other five conference presidents.[53]

Ten days later the Black River Conference of the Methodist Episcopal church, Lee's old organization, met in Syracuse for an eight-day session. In their deliberations, the delegates adopted resolutions that began to tighten the noose on slaveholding. Already passed by other conferences, these would be presented to the 1844 Methodist Episcopal General Conference. This action followed events in the New England Methodist Episcopal conferences where the bishops reversed their gag rules and permitted antislavery resolutions to be introduced and debated. Those positive steps, however, came too late to stop Wesleyans from secession in 1843, and too late to avoid a split with the slaveholding Methodists. One wonders how long it would have taken for them to move against the institution of slavery, if Lee and his friends had not agitated the matter and subsequently formed a competing church.[54]

Lee continued to write articles for the *True Wesleyan* on a variety of topics. One, entitled "Colorphobia," describes the symptoms of the malignant disease: "a haughty demeanor towards others, a disregard to character and talents when enveloped in a skin tinged by the Creator a little darker than is agreeable to certain tastes."[55] Lee, despite all of his faults, was no racist. In that same issue, he noted that his old nemesis, the editor of the *Universalist Trumpet,* attacked the Wesleyans because the new *Discipline* supported the concept of eternal punishment. Lee wrote a column setting him straight.

All the while Lee pastored and wrote articles, he kept at a feverish pace in church organizing. On August 12 and 13, he presided over the quarterly conference at his church in Syracuse. He preached a sermon on Saturday evening, twice on Sunday, and conducted a communion service on Sunday afternoon. The next day he rode forty-three miles in an open carriage in the rain to Solon, where he preached "and administered the sacrament for the benefit of a sick family." On Tuesday he did the same in East Solon; on Wednesday he preached an afternoon sermon in a schoolhouse after which he organized a Wesleyan class. In the evening he rode sixteen miles and delivered an antislavery lecture in Cincinnati from the Presbyterian pulpit.[56] On Thursday he returned to East Solon where he preached in the Methodist Episcopal church in the afternoon, also organizing it into a Wesleyan Methodist Church. Lee observed that a venerable old "Father Wire" would hold the new group together claiming that "if the old church was wired together . . . it would fall to pieces, for we had taken all the Wires out."[57] Feeling satisfied with his work, on Friday he enjoyed the long ride back to Syracuse in an open lumber wagon with no springs. On Saturday he traveled to Fulton where he had agreed to exchange pulpits on Sunday. He preached three times that day, once on antislavery.

On Monday and Tuesday he gave antislavery lectures for which he received a barrel of flour as payment. On Wednesday he took a canal boat home where he devoted time to correspondence and articles for the paper. The next Sunday at his church he taught the adult class and preached the morning sermon. That afternoon he rode twelve miles away to New Bridge for a sermon, and by evening he traveled eight miles to preach at Little Utica. In that place the minister urged his congregation not to attend Lee's speeches or sermons—the result being Lee had a full house! On Wednesday he traveled by rail to Canastota where he lectured against slavery to a Dutch Reformed congregation. Six years earlier, he had dedicated the Methodist Episcopal meeting house; now it was closed to him. Lee commented that he had consecrated it "a little too thoroughly, seeing they now regard it as too holy to admit the claims of the slave."[58] On Thursday he lectured in

Wampsville. This time the Presbyterians refused use of their church so he resorted to a school house. He traveled home on "a little line boat . . . [that] made such tardy progress that we did not reach home until about 9 on Friday morning." The following Sunday he spoke at Onondaga, ten miles south of Syracuse. At that time he exchanged pulpits with the Congregational minister who had seceded with his entire church over the slavery issue. Back in Syracuse he met with men returning from the National Liberty Convention, which Lee had been unable to attend. And so it went. Thus, Lee kept at the task of organizing new churches in central New York. Of course, the Methodist Episcopal leaders and clergy made life as difficult as possible for him.[59]

Once secession had taken place, relations with the old church were less than cordial. The two denominations tended to meet in conflict in two formats: In the columns of their respective papers, which Lee seemed to delight in doing, or in public debates. Edward Smith submitted a lengthy article describing his debate in Leesville, Carroll County, Ohio, with a Methodist preacher on whether or not the old church was pro-slavery. The other favorite debate topic focused on Methodism's arbitrary episcopal government. Lee managed to get himself into a series of such debates in the western borders of the state.

In the fall of 1843, Lee received a letter from members of the Methodist Episcopal church in Jamestown, Chautauqua County. Trouble over the matter of musical instruments threatened to destroy the congregation. Some opposed using instruments in worship, others did not. While the matter awaited a business meeting for a full airing, their preacher arbitrarily removed it, claiming sole authority for such decisions. Subsequent appeals to the presiding elder and to the bishops were equally unavailing. Someone suggested that the aggrieved members, now thoroughly beaten down by the "overbearing and insulting" preacher, might turn to the Wesleyans. Knowing nothing about Wesleyans, they sent a spokesman to Syracuse to consult with Lee, the president of the New York conference. He responded that he would consider such a lengthy trip, only if antislavery lectures could also be arranged in that area. The delegate cheerfully agreed to arrange for a series of antislavery lectures in the Jamestown area. Shortly thereafter, Lee headed west in the cause of antislavery and church recruitment.

On September 21 Lee departed by rail at one o'clock in the morning for Jamestown. The first leg of his trip would take him to Buffalo, fourteen hours from Syracuse by rail. Lee had scheduled a speech there for Friday evening. Unfortunately the train did not arrive until two o'clock on Saturday morning. The congregation would have to wait for another trip. Lee finally reached Jamestown, covering the last miles with a horse and carriage. The entire area had been expecting him; folk came from twenty-five miles away to hear the travel-weary speaker.

Lee began his efforts with his standard exposé of slavery and slaveholding churches in the Presbyterian church in the afternoon. That night he moved on to the Congregational Church on the Lake Shore Road in Salem. Before ascending the platform he received a tip: a dozen or more Methodist Episcopal preachers, led by Reverend Josiah Flower, preacher in charge there, made up part of his audience. Also present was Professor Calvin Kingsley from Allegheny College.

Obviously those ministers had not come to support Lee. He gave his lecture, ending with a rousing denunciation of the gag policies of the bishops. The enraged clerics demanded rebuttal time. They accused Lee of slander, and challenged him to a public debate, fully intending to send him packing back to Syracuse. Lee had a schedule to keep until he left for home, but he agreed to return to accept the challenge if done by rules of debate. They agreed to meet on January 2, 1844, the topic to center on whether their church justified slavery and whether their church government was arbitrary and unscriptural. Each side would choose one man and those two would choose a third. These would preside and keep order, but would not decide the winner. After speaking thirteen times in eight days, and organizing several Wesleyan Methodist classes in Napoli and Centreville, and other towns in the area, Lee departed.[60]

Working his way back to Buffalo, he spoke in that city, and after a sightseeing trip past Niagara Falls, he lectured in Lockport.[61] On October 14, he preached the dedication sermon for the new Wesleyan Chapel in Seneca Falls. George Pegler, the pastor, had been at the Utica Convention, where he formed a lasting friendship with Lee. As his Conference President, he had invited Lee to be present for the occasion. Made of brick, forty-four by sixty-four feet, with a gallery on three sides, that same building housed the Woman's Rights Convention which convened there in 1848.[62] Lee returned to Syracuse where he continued writing editorials in between his frenetic travels on behalf of the new organization.

On December 27, Lee started for the debates in Jamestown. He stopped in Canandaigua where he preached before moving on. A railroad accident occurred five miles east of Batavia. The engine and freight cars were derailed, but the passenger cars were safe. The passengers were detained four hours until they could secure a ride on the train from Buffalo which had to return due to the wreck. As a consequence, Lee missed the Western Stage to Jamestown, and was forced to lay over in Buffalo. Due to the extreme weather, Lee and his fellow travelers had to ride in an open wagon, since a taller enclosed one could not be kept upright. The first lap to Centreville took them through mud one to two feet deep; they averaged two miles per hour. The arduous journey finally ended. Lee was glad to be among friends. After preaching twice on Sunday, he was ready for the debate on Tuesday at ten o'clock. The house was packed. His three debating opponents were ripe for the affair. Actually, the Congregational church could not accommodate those trying to enter; they moved to the Baptist church two miles distant, because the Methodists thought it unfair to host the debate having issued the challenge.

J. J. Steadman, Professor Calvin Kingsley, and Thomas Graham had everything their way. It was three against one. Lee had half of the time, but had to rebut three men. Such work was not new to Lee; he loved this kind of thing. Having the affirmative, Lee attacked the Methodist's justification of slavery. His opponents could not deny that their church permitted slave holders to be members and ordained elders. The Methodist Episcopal church made no effort to remove slavery, and had actively pursued those who attempted to remove it, and suppressed discussion on the matter. If the church did not justify slavery, then it did not justify its own conduct. Slavery was either right or wrong, and if the church did not justify it as right, it must condemn it as wrong. Using such logic to demonstrate that the Methodists could not have it both ways, Lee applied steady pressure on his opponents. The crowd could see it, if his opponents could not. When Lee raised the Few Amendment, his opponents denied that any such resolution had ever been passed by their general conference. Lee appeared in error on the accusation of the three. His integrity stood in jeopardy. Finally, the committee agreed to get the minutes and had the entire Few episode read. The crowd loved it; the tables had turned and the Methodist Episcopal preachers were embarrassed. After three days, the whole debating affair wound down with no formal declaration of a winner. By earlier agreement no formal decision was to be rendered; the debate ostensibly had taken place only for the public's information. One man, however, seizing the moment, jumped up and called for a voice vote. The people shouted their vote that Lee had won. His opponents, unwilling to let things rest as they were, insisted on another round in four weeks. By then they would be free from the worst of winter and Lee agreed to return.[63]

In February, Lee conducted a revival in his Syracuse church in which he served as his own evangelist. He reported in the church paper that his church was experiencing a glorious meeting, usually fifteen were going forward for prayers each night, and "dozens were being converted."[64]

On April 6, Lee wrote to the editor of the *True Wesleyan* that he had just arrived at Jamestown for the last of the debates. He had traveled from Buffalo in an old open lumber wagon that boasted no springs. It took three hours to travel the forty-three miles to Fredonia. A stage brought him the balance of his journey. Edward Smith, his co-debater, had just arrived from Pittsburgh. On Tuesday morning the debate began; it ended at noon on Saturday.[65]

The Methodists had used the intervening weeks to prepare themselves. Lee and Smith were not new to debate, and they relished the fight.[66] When Kingsley resorted to history to defend slavery, he appeared quite knowledgeable. He read from a Roman history in Latin, translating as he read, to prove that slavery existed in the time of St. Paul. Lee, in his turn, focused not on the ancient situation, but on whether the Methodists currently justified slavery. If Kingsley admitted that his denomination did justify slavery, he conceded the question. If he denied, however, that Methodists justified slavery, he admitted that they condemned what he just claimed to have proved St. Paul had justified.

The charge by Lee momentarily stunned his opponents. All they could do was to defend the church, rather than try to prove that it did not justify slavery, as the question required them to do. Apparently convinced they had a problem, the Methodists resorted to *argumentum ad hominum,* focusing on Smith. Graham ridiculed Smith's argument (same argument as Lee's), claiming he could see no reason for such a position, unless Smith meant it only "as a cabbage-leaf that he might stick his head under it and get out of sight." Lee countered that ridicule was not argument, and that "good debaters never resort to it while they have good arguments to offer."[67]

An awkward situation developed for the crowd. Many who disagreed with the Methodists retired from the room when they spoke; then they returned when Lee and Smith countered. In later years, Lee and Kingsley (later elected bishop) became close friends; the other two men Lee never saw after that episode. As for the debate, the final arbiter of the outcome was the people. They did not vote, but all except one member of the Methodist Episcopal church in the town seceded and joined the Wesleyan Methodists.[68] Lee left Jamestown on Monday, preaching and lecturing in Dayton and Buffalo, where he dedicated the spacious hall built by "friends of freedom" in the city. He arrived home after being gone for two weeks. The satisfaction he enjoyed as a result of his apparent successes produced a feeling of vindication. He, of course, could not know what would happen at the 1844 General Conference of the Methodist Episcopal Church that convened in May 2, at New York City. At that epochal session, Methodism split over the slavery issue.[69]

On the national scene, the depression since 1837 had run its economic course and the outlook of the nation was optimistic. The annexation of Oregon and Texas consumed most political discourse. On the evangelical scene national churches were feeling the pressures of two sections slowly drifting apart. The Presbyterians would not split until 1857; the Methodists, however, could not remain together past 1844.[70] Scott, Lee, and Smith were in the galleries as reporters for the Wesleyans. The ideologies of the northern and southern camps had firmed since they had met four years previously. The northern wing was tired of being pushed around by the southerners; the pro-slavery clergy had an aggressiveness that did not bode well for a harmonious convention. The passage of the Few Amendment in 1840 still rankled in the breasts of antislavery ministers. Besides, they had watched as one congregation after another had seceded with many going over to the Wesleyans. They could be pushed no further. When the issue of Bishop James O. Andrew's slaves surfaced in the middle of May, the breach opened. By the time they adjourned, the Few Amendment had been rescinded and the southern delegates had seceded from the church. The main thing that bothered the Wesleyans in the galleries was the fact that the delegates had not acted out of moral courage but for purposes of expediency. Such charges appear justified. As soon as the new seceder church threatened to impact Methodist membership by drawing from it, the delegates suddenly saw slavery for the evil monster that it was. Had it really changed its behavior in the last year? It was about as satisfying to an abolitionist as a forced confession on the evils of slavery. That, of itself, probably ended any hope of reuniting on the part of the Wesleyan Methodists.[71]

Soon it was time to plan for the New York conference session, and Lee ran announcements on a regular basis to alert men within his boundary to prepare for the opening on June 19. Lee was elected president (he had been appointed to that office at Utica) and corresponding secretary of the Board of Missions. He was not stationed as pastor at Syracuse, a move that placed him in a position to be selected for work in the general conference.[72] Not surprisingly, he was also elected as a delegate to that conference scheduled to meet in Cleveland that autumn. The Methodist periodicals, still referring to the new church as "Scottites," reported on Lee's recently adjourned New York conference. Calling him "The 'Logical' Lee," they interpreted his assignment to be that of traveling the area in an effort to get more Methodists to secede, as well as to raise funds for his own salary, scoffing "Such a Missionary Work!!"[73] Undaunted, Lee continued his travels, stopping in Fulton, the place he had served as pastor six years previous. This time, however, he dedicated the new Wesleyan meeting house. His labors of writing and traveling consumed his energies until the first week in October, when he journeyed with his wife to Cleveland.

In the previous year, the Lees had agreed to permit their second son, then fourteen, to live with Mary's parents, who had moved into the Western Reserve area of Ohio. Now they were anxious to see the lad and their relatives. Working their way westward, lecturing along the way, the Lees were stunned when a letter reached them near the Pennsylvania line that their son in Ohio had died. After spending time with sympathizing friends in Jamestown, they moved on to Cleveland.

Lee was appointed president *pro tem* by a nominating committee. During the elections, Scott was elected president, but declined to serve for a variety of reasons. On the second ballot, Lee was elected president. Again, as at Utica, the secret society issue surfaced; this time in the form of a request to appoint a committee on secret societies. A disturbance accompanied the discussion, but the requested committee was appointed. In time the group recommended a rule that all members of secret societies be excluded from membership. Scott and Horton, remaining cool, argued against such a rule; Smith and J. Walker vigorously supported it. Smith managed to work himself into an ugly frame of mind, denouncing Scott and his arguments. Lee later observed that a debate on admitting the devil into membership could not have stirred more animation. Lee demanded that Smith come to order; Smith defied him. Lee tried again, "You will come to order if there's power enough in this house to bring you to order." The delegates rose to their feet affirming, "The chair shall be sustained."[74] Smith complied. The issue of secret societies took on geographical dimensions. Generally it was the West versus the East. Cyrus Prindle submitted a resolution that the connection be divided into two general conferences that would reflect the east-west opinions. Scott, Horton, and Prindle were particularly concerned about the negative effects of a strong stand against secret societies. To insist on rules against such societies could only impede future growth of their infant church. For the West, however, purity could not be subsumed to expediency, and Prindle's resolution mustered only three votes. Eventually the delegates passed the following rule, after a bitter struggle:

Question. Have we any directions to give concerning oath-bound societies?

Answer.   We will on no account tolerate our ministers and members in joining secret oath-bound societies, or holding fellowship with them, as in the judgment of the Wesleyan Methodist Connection it is inconsistent with our duties to God and Christianity to hold such connections.

The stage was thus set for future problems, since the founders, most of them Masons, argued that only the organizing convention in Utica had power to pass such restrictive rules.[75]

In other matters, the General Conference adopted the *True Wesleyan* as its official organ, and after substantial debate, especially by Scott and Horton who favored leaving it in Boston, ordered its removal to New York City. It also established a Book Concern, and selected Scott as Book Agent. Lee was elected editor of the publication and also of the *Juvenile Wesleyan.* Not everyone, however, was enamored with Lee's appointment; a hostile reporter wrote in another church paper that "they have jumped over O. Scott's head, and made Luther Lee editor, whose caustic and bitter pen will involve the Connection in quarrels with their neighbors."[76] Statistics from the six conferences are instructive:

Allegheny:	45 preachers, 2500 members;
Miami:	42 preachers, 2400 members;
Michigan:	22 preachers, 1300 members;
New England:	36 preachers, 2400 members;
Champlain:	not reported, 2500 members;
New York:	60 preachers, 3500 members.

In each of the annual conferences, significant growth had been reported, most of it coming in the recent months. President Lee admonished the delegates to remain solid in their purpose reminding them: "The eyes of the slave and the slave's friends are upon us. Our union is their only hope."[77] On October 10, the session adjourned, and wearily the Lees set out for Syracuse, where they must pack their household and then move to New York.[78]

Lee went in search of a ship bound for Buffalo. A search at several harbors along Lake Erie proved fruitless. The weary travelers were forced to resort to the stagecoach whose route paralleled the lake shore. Did the Lord not care about his weary servants and their need to make Buffalo? That night witnessed the most violent storm that local residents could recall. Bouncing along throughout the interminably long night in an unheated stagecoach, the Lees could see lights of ships out on the tempest-tossed lake, unable to enter a harbor due to the violence of the storm. The wind lashed and buffeted the coach in what Lee termed a "night of terror." God, however, Lee wrote later, had spared their lives by keeping them off the lake vessels. As they neared Erie, the effects of the storm became visible by the first light of dawn. As part of the 1844 presidential campaign, Whig supporters had erected ash poles for Clay; Democratic supporters of Polk matched their opponents utilizing hickory poles. Many of these had been snapped off at the ground as stark evidence of the viciousness of the storm.

Later, Lee viewed the devastating effects upon ships that had been out on the lake through the night. Along the shoreline, near the city of Buffalo, wrecked vessels lined the water's edge. Portions of the city had been flooded, houses had been broken in pieces by the waves, and ships had been driven by the storm far into the business section of the city. No vessel had escaped undamaged; many lives had been lost. The Lees continued on their way, thankful that Providence had kept them from obtaining passage on Lake Erie.[79] In November, the Lees moved to the largest city in the nation, locating near the Wesleyan Book Room at 6 Spruce Street.[80]

The next four years passed quickly for Lee. His work on the *True Wesleyan* consumed most of his time as well as reflecting that reform issues remained popular with him and his colleagues. He regularly reported the progress of such social issues as temperance (including support of the Washingtonians), female moral reform, female working conditions, educational reforms, and in the realm of politics, the Liberty Party candidates and letters from its candidates, especially Birney.[81] In national issues, the annexation of Texas filled several columns. Of course, Lee took a strong stand in opposition to those pro-slavery policies.[82]

Lee frequently was called upon by seceders from the old church to render assistance, especially if district presiding elders challenged the action. In March of 1845, Lee was summoned to Leicester, Massachusetts, for such an occasion. There he discovered that Methodist ministers had been going from house to house, informing the former members that they had been deceived. Lee preached three times on the weekend, and lectured on church government on Sunday evening. He was challenged to a debate by one of the other preachers. He accepted only to discover that the other had withdrawn his offer. Thus another congregation joined the Wesleyans.[83] Lee also organized a Wesleyan Church in Hackensack, New Jersey, in May of 1845.[84] On May 28, Lee presided over the New York Conference. For the coming year, however, Lee was not elected president; it is unknown whether he had declined to serve. He did receive the kindest thanks from his New York brethren for the services he had rendered since the Utica Convention.[85] On October 5, 1845, Lee assisted in the dedication of the new Wesleyan Chapel at 78 Allen Street in New York. On the larger religious scene in the nation, there were interesting developments. Lee found himself interested in the Millerite Controversy.[86]

During Lee's first year in New York, William Miller, a Baptist preacher, had predicted the second coming of Christ. That never materialized, much to Miller's chagrin and embarrassment. From that error, he espoused the concept that after death the soul ceases to exist—presumably, at least for the wicked. After writing some columns to refute the notion, Lee began to think in terms of writing another book, one that would discuss fully the implications of Miller's teachings.

In 1850 Lee finished the manuscript of *The Immortality of the Soul.*[87] In that same year he wrote a treatise that provided a philosophical rationale for the church polity adopted at the Utica Convention in 1843. He also wrote *The Revival Manual,* a how-to book for aspiring evangelists.[88] Despite Lee's commitment to all aspects of social and moral reform, the antislavery issues took precedence. Whenever a slave case, legislative enactment on the South, or some event based on abolitionism transpired, Lee did not fail to include articles about it.

One such case involved the arrest, trial, and subsequent imprisonment of C. T. Torrey, an old friend of Lee and Scott on the New England scene. Torrey had gone to Annapolis, Maryland, in January, 1842, ostensibly for the purpose of reporting on a convention called by slave holders to defend themselves against abolitionist's tactics. Licensed to preach by the Congregational Church in 1836, Torrey was happier as an antislavery editor than a pastor. In 1839 he joined

Garrison's opponents, ultimately editing the *Massachusetts Abolitionist,* the organ of the same state organization that had hired Lee as General Agent in 1839. In that year, Lee and Torrey had joined in debate against the Garrisonians on the issue of nonresistance. By the 1840s Torrey formulated plans to evangelize slave holders, and educate slaves—a potent formula for disaster.

Once in Annapolis, Torrey first fell afoul of the slavery men while posing as a reporter. After several days in and out of jail, he managed to extricate himself and return to Albany, where he edited an anti-Garrison paper. Later he returned to Baltimore, planning on going into the starch manufacturing business. He managed to get himself arrested again for allegedly plotting to assist the slaves against their masters. On June 24, 1844 he was ordered to stand trial. By August, he had written a letter to the Baltimore newspapers explaining his slave running activities, denying any moral wrongdoing. All over the North, sympathetic editors took up his cause, as did Lee. With each new item he received, he printed articles in the *True Wesleyan,* hoping to stir up support for Torrey. On December 1, 1844, Torrey was found guilty of enticing, persuading, and assisting slaves to escape from their masters. Sentenced to six years of hard labor, he died in prison on May 9, 1846, another martyr for the cause of antislavery.[89] Lee preached and later published a sermon on the occasion of Torrey's death: "The Supremacy of the Divine Law."[90]

The title of Lee's sermon reflected an ethical view that later antislavery politicians, especially William Seward, came to advocate: a "higher law" supercedes and transcends human laws. His Scripture text was from Acts 23:29, "Whom I perceived to be accused of questions of their law, but to name nothing laid to his charge worthy of death or of bonds." St. Paul had been accused according to civil laws. Lee also cited other cases of Biblical characters that had to resist civil law to obey God: Daniel, the three Hebrew men, Peter, and John. Lee cited the response of disciples: "We ought to obey God rather than men." When such Scriptural models are applied to civil laws that defend slavery, the latter must yield to the Bible. Lee declared that the acts of Torrey were at worst acts of "mistaken philanthropy," and that his sentence had already been "repealed in that higher and impartial court, where human actions are rightly weighed." Lee included a lengthy review of nineteenth century oratory:

> . . . and we say peace to his ashes, and let every one that shall
> visit his tomb and read his epitaph; whisper peace; and when slavery
> shall be no more, when the chain shall be stricken from the limbs of
> the last slave, when the light of the nation's jubilee shall break upon
> the land, then amid the joy and songs of that glorious morn, let his
> epitaph be written anew. Until then peace to his ashes, peace to his
> memory, peace to his martyr's spirit.[91]

This is vastly different from Lee's earlier position on civil law,
which he had advocated in the sermon on the death of Lovejoy in 1837.
At that time, Lee had appealed to the laws of the state to protect the
rights of reformers to speak their mind on issues. By 1846, however,
Lee was making reference to a higher law, one that permited "civil
disobedience" in pressing the cause of reform.

In May, Lee attended the American Anti-Slavery Society convention which held its anniversary in the Tabernacle in New York. Due to
ill health, Lee was unable to take many notes. While there he did
manage to secure a list of all American publications that Garrison
noted as supportive of the Liberty Party. Of course, the *True Wesleyan*
appears in the listing.[92] Near the end of the convention, Alvin Stewart
gave a moving eulogy on the life and death of Torrey. Curiously,
Luther Lee appears as a member of the executive committee of the
American Anti-Slavery Society for the 1846-47 year. Apparently, Lee
had mended some fences with Garrison, from whose organization he
had departed six years earlier.[93]

Events on the national scene appeared ominous that summer. War
with Mexico seemed more likely with each passing day. At the same
time the situation with Great Britain over ownership of the Oregon
territory had deteriorated. The two nations had endured joint administration for decades. American expansionists, shouting "54-40 or
Fight!" argued for annexation of the entire territory as far north as that
latitude. Neither side appeared willing to give ground. Pacifists and
antislavery people argued against war on both fronts. Lee and his
colleagues resorted to newspaper articles that denounced any attempt
to engage the nation in a war with Mexico, a conflict that clearly led to

the expansion of slavery into new territories. Thus the nation focused on diplomatic issues. Closer to home, Lee and his denomination, however, had not lost sight of their call to evangelize sinners even as they sought to change the social fabric of the nation.

The Wesleyans, ever resourceful when it came to spreading the gospel, attempted an innovative way of reaching the lost for Christ. In New York harbor they managed to secure an old sailing vessel as a means of ministering to lonely sailors. Naming the vessel the *John Wesley,* they formed the New York Wesleyan Methodist Bethel Association, complete with constitution and bylaws. The old hulk was moored at the foot of Rector Street on the North River, and it served to rescue worldly sailors from lives of loneliness and sin. Several of the ministers in New York preached on the decks of the floating church. Lee ran a sketch of the old ship, complete with a large message emblazoned on its bulkhead, "Supported By Voluntary Contributions."[94]

The same issue sounded the victory trumpet, "Friends of Freedom Rejoice! The Gag is Repealed," in which Lee exalted over "old man eloquence," John Quincy Adams, and his untiring efforts to end the gag rule in the U.S. House of Representatives. He ended his article by urging readers to "pour in the petitions on slavery, and especially against the annexation of Texas. *Wait not a day.*"[95]

During his tenure as editor, Lee and his colleagues never forgot the useful purpose that camp meetings served, not only in evangelism but also in the cause of antislavery, temperance, and other reforms of the era. A June, 1846 issue of the paper advertised such a camp. The purpose was to serve as the "annual feast of tabernacles" for the New York Conference. "All who believe the Gospel is opposed to slavery and intemperance, as well as to other sins, come and hear it preached in that beautiful grove," at Verplank's Point, fifty miles up the Hudson. Lee, one of the camp sponsors, ran an announcement that spoke of special travel arrangements with the boat lines for camp meeting goers.[96] Other matters , however, were not so pleasant.

Orange Scott had fallen victim to pulmonary tuberculosis. He had traveled since 1844 as the Book Agent of the connection. In the summer of 1847, his friends sensed that he could not live long. His years in the fight against slavery, as is frequently the case with humanity, had mellowed him. He had warned his colleagues against stubbornness, uncharitable condemnation, "heated and intemperate controversy," and curiously, "the worship of sect."[97] As he lay dying at his small farm in Newark, New Jersey, Lee was requested to go to Scott's home to take dictation from him for a narrative of his earlier life. Lee rode over to Newark to see his old friend. Scott, in his reverie, posed the question to Lee whether Lee had any doubt about one being conscious between death and the resurrection. Lee assured him that he had none.[98]

On July 31, Scott passed away. Lee had been designated to preach the funeral at the Scott home. The *New York Tribune* stated that Scott, "The Wesley of America," was to have his funeral preached by Lee at the Wesleyan Methodist Church on King Street (near Hudson).[99] Other funerals were preached in several cities throughout the connection. Scott was buried in Springfield, Massachusetts. Interestingly, he was buried the same day as Amos Phelps, a co-member of the American and Foreign Anti-Slavery Society with whom Scott had shared many hours and views. The entire connection mourned the one who had early on moved to the fore of the Methodist clergy in the cause of the slave. Numerous articles of eulogy were sent for publication in the paper.[100] Lee wrote concerning Scott's death, "I felt it as one of the most severe calamities of my life."[101] Another antislavery supporter died some months later. The paper of March 4, 1848 carried accounts of the death of John Q. Adams, a favorite politician of all the antislavery people.

The second General Conference convened on October 4 of the same year in King Street Chapel in New York City. Lee was not reelected as president. He was elected as editor, not, however, before some enemies tried to derail him. Immediately prior to the voting for editor, a resolution of censure against Lee was introduced. His opponent decried Lee's course in politics. As Lee later observed, "I never had any politics which were not part of my religion, and I had urged men to vote the Liberty ticket as a religious duty." Lee refused to defend himself, to the concern of his friends and enemies. Finally a gentleman from Wisconsin, formerly of northern New York and an obvious friend of Lee, "took the floor in defense of the editor, and the way he laid out those non-political Christians was workman-like."[102] The defense worked like magic; the resolution lost, and Lee was reelected editor. He vowed, however, it would be the last time he would serve. During the session, the *Discipline* was revised concerning methods of conducting church trials, and also to reflect the contractual relationship of pastors to their parish without outside interference. The conference ended without further controversy. The reporter for the conference submitted descriptions of several of the delegates and officers. His is the best description available of Lee:

> His is of about medium stature, full round chest, with head rather inclining forward. He had dark hair, very large dark eyes, and exceedingly prominent front teeth. These throw a shade over every other feature at first view, and alone arrest the attention of the stranger. He is not eloquent as a speaker, but is distinct in his articulation, clear in his ideas, and always speaks to the point, and is always heard when he does speak.[103]

Lee returned to New York City where that winter he managed to get involved in the antislavery cause as never before.[104]

The Joseph Belt case is not well known to students of antislavery.[105] In the years subsequent to the passage of the infamous Fugitive Slave Law late in 1850, the North took a decided step against slavery in general and slaveholders in particular. Among other things, the hated enactment required northern folk to assist in catching runaway slaves. Luther Lee, in December of 1848 had other ideas about slave catchers.

Joseph Belt, a young black, was traveling through New York City. On December 20 he was walking with a friend, Thomas Peck, on Duane Street at half past eight in the morning. Suddenly he was knocked to the sidewalk, handcuffed, and thrown into a carriage and carried away. As he was struggling, his assailants claimed that he had stolen a coat at a fire on the previous night. His companion was let go. Peck eventually went to Lee, a known humanitarian and abolitionist, to see if he might render any assistence. Lee enjoyed a friendship with Judge John Jay of the New York Supreme Court, who lived in the city. Lee went to him seeking advice, which Jay had given him in the past. Jay, not surprisingly, said nothing could be done until the man was found. Lee then secured the services of a well-known detective. Before taking the case, Lee had to visit some wealthy antislavery friends and secure the necessary financial backing. The detective agreed to seek the man.[106]

The detective established to his satisfaction that the man had not left the city travelling northward. After a closer search, he learned that the men had crossed on the Brooklyn ferry, either to Brooklyn or Long Island. He also discovered that a Baltimore clipper, anchored in the bay, was awaiting cargo to carry back to Maryland. He theorized that the ship was hired to transport runaway slaves. Miraculously, the detective discovered Joseph Belt, chained in an empty log house on the island ten miles from Brooklyn. He was brought before a judge. Young John Jay was secured and two other lawyers agreed to volunteer their services, no doubt at the urging of Lee, in defending the young man. In addition, the state law mandated that the district attorney must defend citizens whose liberty is threatened. In late 1848, John McKeon, later elected as a Democrat to the U.S. House of Representatives, was the district attorney for New York County.[107] Thus four lawyers were managing the case for the defendant.[108] Judge John Edmonds issued a writ of *habeas corpus* for ten o'clock the next morning.

At that hearing, John Lee of Frederick County, Maryland, appeared, demanding that his runaway slave be returned to him. He presented a lengthy affidavit in which he described Joseph Belt and told of Belt's flight to Lynn, Massachusetts, and then back to New York, acknowledging that he had hired the two men to pick him up on Wednesday morning. Belt, however, had his answer ready when the hearing reconvened on December 26.

In his sworn statement, he claimed never to have been *legally* [emphasis mine] held by his alleged master, John Lee, but claimed to be a free citizen of the United States. Belt did confirm that Peck had been seized along with him. When the assailants decided to free Peck, the released man agreed to tell Belt's landlord, Mrs. Jackson, of Belt's arrest.[109]

Soon John Lee was joined by a nephew who also corroborated his account of Belt as a runaway. The entire case came down to the legality of slavery in Maryland, and whether or not such laws actually existed. Judge Edmonds permitted McKeon to cross-examine Lee. McKeon denied that Maryland was a slaveholding state. He admitted that the evidence tended to indicate that Belt had been held as a slave, but had it been legal? The law must be produced. After a search was made, a volume of Maryland state law was brought into the court. McKeon denied that the book was legal; it lacked the certificate of the Secretary of State in the front. The judge demanded the book. On the title page he observed that New York law books contain the inscription, "Published by the authority of the State," but this alleged Maryland law book "reads, 'Published by authority,' but it does not say what authority. I decide that it is insufficient; the man must be discharged."[110] On a somewhat less judicial note, he turned to the young black man and announced, "You are free, and your legs are the only security that you will remain free." Luther Lee wrote that the youth shot from the room with the speed of an arrow. The slave owner in the court room feared that he was about to be lynched. He requested the court to grant him protection until he could leave town. That was granted. Lee had the pleasure of beating a slave catcher at his own game. He subsequently kept up a steady flow of articles in the *True Wesleyan* concerning his hatred of the Fugitive Slave Law passed in the autumn of 1850; he was especially effective in his discourse, since he, by that time, had firsthand experience with slave owners.

Lee wrote of other alleged runaway slave incidents, but none quite so dramatic. He continued to edit the paper and made regular forays into the region in the cause of enlarging the denomination, and, of course, to speak on behalf of reforms. One such outing found him in Penn Yan, New York, where he delivered a Fourth of July anti-slavery address. The trip from New York was made traveling by boat, an overnight express train, and a lake steamboat across Seneca Lake. On that same trip he spoke twice on temperance in the county courthouse and once in the Baptist church on the same topic. In July, Lee officiated at the wedding of his daughter Mary to John Benson.[111]

Lee finally made a return visit to New England, an area from which he had been absent for years. In October of 1850, he accepted an invitation to deliver antislavery lectures in Dover, New Hampshire, the home of Senator John P. Hale, a Free Soiler and one whom Lee had supported. Lee spoke at several churches in the area, commenting in the paper that the Wesleyan church there was small but growing.[112] In January Lee exalted in the passage of the famous Maine Law, a state enactment that shut down grog shops, led to pouring spiritous liquors on the ground, and in general, caused the state of Maine to go dry. He hoped that other states would soon follow suit.[113] In February Lee preached the dedicatory sermon for the new Second Wesleyan Methodist Church in Rochester, New York.[114] Early in the spring of 1852, Lee wearied of journalism and the editorship of the *True Wesleyan*. It was time for him to move on to other challenges. He resigned the editorship and accepted the pastorate at his old church in Syracuse. The issues throughout April were replete with accolades that various conferences and individuals sent in, recognizing the superior manner in which Lee had acquitted himself in that capacity. He chose to make the break prior to the New York Conference. Matlack finished out the last of Lee's five months on the paper.[115]

The previous nine years had provided Lee with a chance to prove the sincerity of his commitment to social reform and to the concept of a new antislavery church. When he saw the uselessness of remaining in the old Methodist Episcopal church, he boldly made the move of secession. We can never argue for certain that Lee would have made the break alone; however, once he decided, he never hesitated. His shaping influence of the Wesleyan Methodist Connection cannot be overstressed. His powers of persuasion were considerable, given the wide range of views that were being advocated by strong men at the Utica convention.

In the Joseph Belt affair Lee had his first experience with slave catchers and masters. Like Harriet Beecher Stowe, he had done his speaking and writing against slavery strictly on hearsay and written descriptions. By the end of his tenure as editor he laid aside that role as one with vast experience in his chosen field. Satisfied that he had done his best, he turned to the settled ministry to rest and catch his breath from the whirlwind activity of New York City.

NOTES

1. Sydney E. Ahlstrom, *A Religious History of the American People* (New Haven, Conn.: Yale University Press, 1972), 648-64; cf., John R. McKivigan, "Vote as You Pray and Pray as You Vote: Church-Oriented Abolitionism and Antislavery Politics," Alan M. Kraut, ed., *Crusaders and Compromisers: Essays on the Relationship of the Antislavery Struggle to the Antebellum Party System* (Westport, Conn.: Greenwood Press, 1983): 181, agrees that the secession of the Wesleyan Methodists forced the Methodist Episcopal church to open up to antislavery discussion.

2. See "Second Advent," *True Wesleyan,* April 12, 1845, for article on Storrs's involvement with the Millerites.

3. Donald G. Mathews, *Slavery and Methodism: A Chapter in American Morality 1780-1845* (Princeton, N.J.: Princeton University Press, 1965), 230; Whitney R. Cross, *The Burned-over District: The Social and Intellectual History of Enthusiastic Religion in Western New York, 1800-1850* (Ithaca, N.Y.: Cornell University Press), 296, 310.

4. Unfortunately, Nathan Hatch has identified this new paper as the *True Methodist,* and has erroneously attributed it to "the crusading abolitionists Orange Scott and La Roy Sunderland," when in fact Scott and Horton, living in Lowell, actually started the paper and Lee soon became the editor; Nathan O. Hatch, *The Democratization of American Christianity* (New Haven, Conn.: Yale University Press, 1989), 207.

5. Luther Lee, *Autobiography of the Rev. Luther Lee, D.D.* (New York: Phillips & Hunt; Cincinnati: Walden & Stowe, 1882), 238.

6. *Autobiography*, 238.

7. *True Wesleyan,* January 7, 1843.

8. *True Wesleyan,* January 14, 1843. Lee's article was dated December 12, 1842.

9. Matlack later would serve as a General Conference president, editor, educator, and in other positions of significance.

10. *True Wesleyan,* January 21, 1843.

11. *True Wesleyan,* February 10, 1844.

12. Smith is a significant figure in the early days of Wesleyan Methodism, especially on the issue of secret societies. He served as president of Allegheny Conference, one of the six original conferences. His formal withdrawal took place on April 10, 1843; L. C. Matlack, *The Anti-Slavery Struggle and Triumph in the Methodist Episcopal Church* (New York: Phillips & Hunt, 1881; repr., New York: Negro University Press, 1969), 318-19.

13. See *True Wesleyan,* May 13, 1843, for Lee's comments on the church at Andover. He stated that the congregation hardly qualified as Methodist Episcopal since the entire membership had seceded. He further stated that Methodism "has never been very flourishing in this place; as it is the seat of Congregationalism."

14. Actually, "superintendent" is the Latin translation of the Greek term *episcopius,* or "bishop" or "overseer."

15. *True Wesleyan,* February 11, 1843; Lucius C. Matlack, *The History of American Slavery and Methodism from 1780 to 1849, and History of the Wesleyan Methodist Connection of America in Two Parts* (New York: C. Prindle and L. C. Matlack, 1849; reprint, Freeport, N.Y.: Books for Libraries Press, 1971), 322-25; Lucius C. Matlack, *The Life of the Reverend Orange Scott: Compiled from His Personal Narrative, Correspondence, and Other Authentic Sources of Information, In Two Parts* (New York: C. Prindle and L. C. Matlack, 1847; reprint, Freeport, N.Y.: Books for Libraries Press, 1971), 210-11.

16. *True Wesleyan,* March 4, 1843.

17. *True Wesleyan.*

18. Pegler had come to Utica in 1842, to a church that he wrote had withdrawn from the Methodist Episcopal Church in 1840, following the General Conference; George Pegler, *Autobiography of the Life and Times of the Rev. George Pegler* (Syracuse, N.Y.: Wesleyan Methodist Publishing House, 1879), 391.

19. *True Wesleyan,* April 29, 1843.

20. *True Wesleyan,* April 22, 1843. Interestingly, that issue included a letter from a Mr. J. T. Sturtevant of Chagrin Falls, Ohio, located eighteen miles south west of Cleveland who reports his pleasure at reading the *True Wesleyan,* comments upon the strong influence of abolitionism in the area, and predicts success for the Wesleyans; Lee would pastor in that town in 1858; cf., Thomas Dublin, *Women at Work: The Transformation of Work and Community in Lowell, Massachusetts, 1826-1860* (New York: Columbia University Press, 1979), for an excellent analysis of the women's situation at Lowell.

21. Pegler wrote that the Wesleyan Chapel could not accommodate the crowd, and the Blecker Street Church had seating for close to three thousand, and that it was often filled.

22. Letter of William M. Sullivan, June, 1843, a delegate from Michigan in a letter written to his wife; in Joel L. Martin, *Wesleyan Manual, or History of Wesleyan Methodism* (Syracuse, N.Y.: Wesleyan Methodist Publishing House, 1889), 20-24.

23. Martin, *Wesleyan Manual,* 20-24.

24. Martin, *Wesleyan Manual,* 9-17; Matlack, *American Slavery and Methodism,* 333-45.

25. The *Christian Advocate and Journal,* the official organ of the Methodist Episcopal Church, began in August, 1843, to run a series of counterattacks against the "Scottites" and their *Discipline.* The editors charged that the Utica delegates had grievously erred by deleting items from their Articles of Religion that referred to "Romish" practices. They argued that the Scottites were "not a whit more Protestant than they are Methodists"; Luther Lee, *Wesleyan Manual: A Defense of the Organization of the Wesleyan Methodist Connection, With an Introduction by Cyrus Prindle* (Syracuse,

N.Y.: Samuel Lee, Publisher, 1862), 155-57; *Autobiography,* 247-48; William Goodell had been attempting to organize "come-outer" sects under one umbrella of churches in what came to be known as Unionism or the Union Movement (not to be confused with later merger attempts in 1865-66). He ridiculed Lee's "connexional principle" which he feared would permit sectarian control over individual congregations; cf., Douglas Mark Strong, "Organized Liberty: Evangelical Perfectionism, Political Abolitionism, and Ecclesiastical Reform in the Burned-Over District," unpublished Ph.D. dissertation, Princeton Theological Seminary, 1990, 240; see also the *True Wesleyan,* August 8, 1846, where Lee takes issue with Goodell for attempting to induce secessions from the Presbyterian and other churches in the area. See also "Why did we call ourselves Wesleyan Methodists?" in the *True Wesleyan,* December 13, 1845, for a further discussion concerning the choice of the name; Lee, *Manual,* 155.

26. Luther P. Gerlach and Virginia H. Hine, *People, Power, Change: Movements of Social Transformation* (Indianapolis, Ind.: Bobbs-Merrill, 1970), xvi, have defined a social movement as "a group of people who are organized for, ideologically motivated by, and committed to a purpose which implements some form of personal or social change; who are actively engaged in the recruitment of others; and whose influence is spreading in opposition to the established order with which it originated." They argue, further, that religious movements can actually develop strength when organizations split, realign, and combine with other groups—as long as recruiting new members to the long-term goal is the constant view.

27. See Nathan O. Hatch, "Demand for a Theology of the People," *Journal of American History* 67 (December 1980): 545-67, for a fuller discussion of social influence on church formation in this period, i.e., the impact of the Revolution on the concept of the sovereignty of the people in the realm of religion and society.

28. Jackson Turner Main, "Government by the People: The American Revolution and the Democratization of the Legislatures," *William and Mary Quarterly* 23 (July 1966): 391-407; Rhys Isaac, *The Transformation of Virginia, 1740-1790* (New York: W.W. Norton & Co., 1988); Rhys Isaac, "Evangelical Revolt: The Nature of the Baptists' Challenge to the Traditional Order in Virginia, 1765-1775," *William and Mary Quarterly* 31 (July 1974): 345-68.

29. One exception permitted a local church to be brought to trial for accepting improper members. If a church were to be found guilty of such a violation, it was dropped as a church from the connection.

30. Lee, *Manual,* 157-58; see Curtis D. Johnson, *Islands of Holiness: Rural Religion in Upstate New York, 1790-1860* (Ithaca, N.Y., and London: Cornell University Press, 1989), 175, where he states concerning Methodist Episcopal congregations, "their episcopal structure limited the ability of church members to reorient local church policy and doctrine to fit societal opinions." The delegates to the Utica Convention do not indicate that John-

son's argument is without exceptions. His observation, however, that "the Second Great Awakening was central in shifting evangelical congregations from a corporate to a 'modern' orientation," p. 173, conforms well with the attitude of those delegates to Utica.

31. Lee, *Manual,* 158-59.

32. The qualification that none of the General Rules be contravened became the basis for later protest by those who argued against enacting new tests of membership other than those established at Utica.

33. *True Wesleyan,* July 29, 1843.

34. Letter of William M. Sullivan to his wife, June 1843.

35. In September, Scott and Matlack also began publishing in Boston *The Juvenile Wesleyan,* a Sabbath school paper with stories and entertaining matter aimed at children. It was to be nonsectarian, "designed for use in all denominations." Several other denominational papers advertised it in their pages as well, *True Wesleyan,* September 30, 1843.

36. *The Discipline of the Wesleyan Methodist Connection of America* (Boston: Published by O. Scott, 1843), 72ff.

37. *The Discipline,* 22.

38. *The Discipline,* 22; *True Wesleyan,* June 10, 1843; see *True Wesleyan,* July 27, 1844, in which Scott responded to Smith's later letter on Masons. Scott played down the issue, recognizing it for its potential to divide dividing the Wesleyans just as slavery was dividing the Methodists. In August 10, 1844, letters to the editor began to appear, warning of the divisive potential that the secret society issue carried.

39. William J. Whalen, *Christianity and American Freemasonry* (Milwaukee, Wisc.: The Bruce Publishing Company, 1958), 1-13.

40. C. G. Finney, *The Character, Claims, and Practical Workings of Freemasonry* (n.p.: Western Tract and Book Society, 1869; repr., Chicago: Ezra A. Cook & Co, 1879).

41. Dorothy Ann Lipson, *Freemasonry in Federalist Connecticut* (Princeton, N.J.: Princeton University Press, 1977), 312-40; cf., *True Wesleyan,* June 21, 1845 wherein Lee observed that the charter of the Connecticut Grand Lodge of Odd Fellows had passed the state legislature. In that same issue Lee cites the celebration planned in Massachusetts for the revival of the Odd Fellows of the state which claimed seventy-five lodges and twenty thousand members.

42. Cross, *Burned-over District,* 113-25.

43. See the *True Wesleyan,* April 26, 1845, wherein Scott wrote, "I never joined but one secret society, and that was 22 years ago; and with that I have had no connection for nearly twenty years." In that same issue, Lee responding to an accusation in the *Olive Branch* asserted, ". . . We do not know, and cannot know that there are no Masons among the Wesleyans; but we have no knowledge of *one* Wesleyan who is an adhering Mason."

44. See Pegler, *Autobiography,* 310-15, for an account of parishioners who refused to support Masonic clergy sent them. Pegler suggests that the

Congregationalists and Presbyterians moved first to rid themselves of members of the lodge, due to the fact that they had more control over retaining their pastors; the Methodists, however, were usually at the mercy of the appointing bishop, and generally had to take whomever he sent them. If that be the case, we may account for Finney and his colleagues leaving the lodge as early as he did following the Morgan affair in Batavia. That might also partly account for why Antimasonic candidates got into politics when they did. Methodists, more often than not, supported Democratic candidates, especially in extreme rural areas.

45. *Autobiography*, 248-49.

46. *Discipline of the Wesleyan Methodist Connection, 1843*, 93: cf., William H. Brackney, "The Fruits of a Crusade: Wesleyan Opposition to Secret Societies," *Methodist History* 17 (July 1979): 239-52, for an overview of the process that antimasonry took in the new denomination. Lee Benson, *The Concept of Jacksonian Democracy: New York as a Test Case* (Princeton, N.J.: Princeton University Press, 1961), 19, delineates a bifurcation in society: the ranks of Masonry included wealthier upper classes, respresented in the ranks of wealthier landowners, bankers, and commercial elitists. Political antimasonry did better in rural areas, especially in western New York where its center was Rochester. Scott, Horton, and Sunderland were Boston and New York residents; Lee had been living in Utica and Syracuse. All of those cities were centers for banking and commercial interests.

47. The issue of secret society membership plagued the Wesleyans for decades after the Utica Convention; cf., *True Wesleyan*, November 16, 1844, in which Sunderland, a Mason, wrote concerning the proscriptive rule passed at Cleveland, that "if that rule, I cannot be admitted a member again. I am an Odd-Fellow, and have been a Mason for nearly twenty years: though I am not now a member of any lodge, and do not know that I ever should have become a member of any lodge again. But I deny the right of any church or conference, civil or ecclesiastical, to *forbid* my belonging to a lodge." That seemed to be the opinion of many who had been Masons before the secession began.

48. The boundaries of the original six conferences included:

New England: All of New England States, except for the portion west of the Green Mountains in Vermont,

Champlain: Vermont west of the Green Mountains, and north and east of the Black River, following a line from Carthage to the southeast corner of Vermont,

New York: All of New York excluding the area in Champlain, Eastern Pennsylvania, and New Jersey,

Allegheny: Pennsylvania west of the Allegheny Mountains, all of Ohio east of the Scioto River, and Western Virginia,

Miami: Ohio west of the Scioto River, Indiana, Illinois, and the Territories of Wisconsin and Iowa,

Michigan: All of Michigan.

49. See the *True Wesleyan*, June 17, 1843, for the complete text of the

Pastoral Address.

50. *True Wesleyan*, November 25, and December 2, 9, 1843, February 22, 1845, for a clear statement on Lee's doctrine of Christian Perfection; John L. Peters, *Christian Perfection & American Methodism* (Nashville, Tenn.: Pierce & Washabaugh, 1956; repr., Grand Rapids, Mich.: Zondervan Publishing House, 1985), for classical analysis of the subject from the entrance of Methodism into America to the present; cf., F. W. Conable, *History of the Genesee Annual Conference of the Methodist Episcopal Church,* (New York: Nelson & Phillips, 1876), 508-09, for evidence that the doctrine of Christian perfection did not have the unanimous support of all Methodist Episcopal clergy. The Genesee Conference of 1843, meeting in Lyndonville, Orleans County, discussed the matter, with the majority taking "the strictly Wesleyan view," as far as they were able to understand it. However a few dissented from that view as absurd, and favored the notion of the perfect purification of the new believer at the moment of his regeneration. That issue is precisely what the delegates at Utica meant to make clear: they were "strictly Wesleyan." The articles which Lee ran in the official paper reveal a proclivity on his part for the writings of Fletcher; cf., "Entire Sanctification," *True Wesleyan,* March 29, 1845. Lee chose *Watson's Institutes* as required reading for those in the New York Conference course of study, *True Wesleyan,* June 21, 1845; cf., "Sanctification, What It Is—and How It Differs from Justification and Regeneration"; *True Wesleyan,* April 17, 1852, "Christian Perfection," *True Wesleyan,* September 8, 1853; cf., Charles E. Jones, *A Guide to the Study of the Holiness Movement* (Metuchen, N.J.: Scarecrow Press, 1974), for a bibliography of the holiness literature; also Charles E. Jones, *Perfectionist Persuasion: The Holiness Movement and American Methodism, 1867-1936* (Metuchen, N.J.: Scarecrow Press, 1974) for an overview of perfectionism within the Methodist Church.

51. It is difficult to ascertain the time of Lee's movements; we do have a letter from him dated Saturday, July 8, 1843, written from Syracuse, so we can establish the very latest that he arrived there. On the next day, he wrote later, he visited the new Clay Wesleyan Methodist Church.

52. *True Wesleyan,* May 17, 1845, reported the Syracuse church as having fifty-six members; *Autobiography,* 252-53.

53. *True Wesleyan,* July 29, 1843.

54. *True Wesleyan,* July 29, 1843.

55. *True Wesleyan,* August 5, 1843.

56. *True Wesleyan,* October 7, 1843, in which Lee wrote that the pastor, a "Mr. Ball," whose brother was mobbed in Cincinnati for teaching a "colored Sabbath School, of which a young woolly-headed daughter of Harry of the West was a member."

57. *True Wesleyan,* October 7, 1843.

58. *True Wesleyan.*

59. Appearing under the title, "Our Poor Self," *True Wesleyan,* October 7, 1843, these two paragraphs give a sampling of Lee's whirlwind activities

during his church building days. It will not be necessary to further trouble the reader with such details to illustrate his industrious life.

60. *Autobiography*, 256-58; *True Wesleyan*, October 14, December 2, 1843, where Lee writes that the Jamestown membership had increased from forty-seven to sixty.

61. While viewing the falls, Lee composed a sonnet he entitled "Our Talk to the Falls," a soliloquy in which he muses upon his activities, *True Wesleyan*, October 28, 1843.

62. *Woman's Rights Conventions: Seneca Falls & Rochester, 1848* (New York: Arno & The New York Times, 1969), 3; *True Wesleyan*, October 28, 1843; cf., Lucille Sider Dayton and Donald W. Dayton, "Your Daughters Shall Prophesy: Feminism in the Holiness Movement," *Methodist History* 14 (October 1975): 67-92, who observe that the women went to the Wesleyan Methodist church, "knowing those who had opened their doors to blacks would also open their doors to women."

63. See *True Wesleyan*, February 17, 24, and March 2, 9, 16, April 13, 20, 1844, in which Lee published his arguments against the episcopal polity of his opponents; *Autobiography*, 256-64.

64. *True Wesleyan*, February 24, 1844; see Johnson, *Islands of Holiness*, 156-57, in which he observes that Methodists did not imitate the highly organized revival efforts of the Presbyterians and Congregationalists. In many Methodist revivals the pastor did not call an evangelist but served in that capacity himself.

65. *True Wesleyan*, April 20, 1844.

66. *True Wesleyan*, April 27, 1844, wherein he writes that Smith possessed excellent debating skills, and had the ability to keep "perfectly good-natured in all circumstances"; however, in debate at the first General Conference, it will be seen that Lee has differing views about Smith.

67. *Autobiography*, 266.

68. See Calvin Kingsley, *Round the World: A Series of Letters by Calvin Kingsley, D.D., Late Bishop of the Methodist Episcopal Church* (Cincinnati, Ohio: Hitchcock and Walden, 1870), 18-20, in which he argues that he bested Lee in the debate. Kingsley, an antislavery man, had graduated from Alleghany College in 1841. He was a traveling preacher, and an agent for the endowment fund for the college, in the year in which he debated Lee. He exemplifies those antislavery men who chose to remain with the old church, and when the 1844 split came, he raised his voice for the slave. Later Methodist historians, perhaps somewhat biased, wrote that Lee had been "over-matched by the logical Kingsley," Theodore L. Flood and John W. Hamilton, *Lives of Methodist Bishops* (New York: n.p., 1882), 956; cf., Matlack, *Antislavery Struggle and Triumph*, 214-18, for Kingsley's battle against slavery after the debates and the split in 1844.

69. *True Wesleyan*, January 27, 1844; cf., *True Wesleyan*, August 15, 1846, for a glowing report of the growth of the church in Jamestown. On one occasion, sixteen joined the church and fourteen received baptism, eight by

immersion and six by sprinkling; *True Wesleyan*, April 17, 1845, cites a membership in the Jamestown church of 172.

70. See Victor B. Howard, "The Anti-Slavery Movement in the Presbyterian Church, 1835-1861," unpublished Ph.D. diss., Ohio State University, 1961, for an insightful discussion of abolitionism in that church.

71. Luther Lee and E. Smith, *The Debates of the General Conference of the M.E. Church, May, 1844, To Which Is Added, a Review of the Proceedings of Said Conference,* (New York: Orange Scott for the Wesleyan Methodist Connection of America, 1845); Mathews, *Methodism and Slavery,* 246-70.

72. *True Wesleyan,* July 6, 1844.

73. *True Wesleyan,* July 13, 1844.

74. *True Wesleyan,* October 12, 1844; *Autobiography,* 272.

75. See George Pegler, *Autobiography,* 420-22, for a description of Smith. Pegler argues that Smith was chiefly responsible for the Wesleyans outlawing secret societies; cf., *True Wesleyan,* November 30, 1844.

76. From the *Olive Branch,* in the *True Wesleyan,* November 2, 1844. This official organ of the Wesleyans underwent several changes in its name in subsequent years: 1843-52, *True Wesleyan;* 1853-60, *The Wesleyan;* and in 1861 it was changed again to *American Wesleyan.*

77. *True Wesleyan,* October 19, 1844.

78. *True Wesleyan,* October 12, 1844; *Autobiography,* 273.

79. *True Wesleyan,* November 2, 1844; *Autobiography,* 273.

80. Matlack, *Life of Orange Scott,* 223.

81. Conspicuously absent in Lee's articles are discussions of the defeat of James G. Birney in the 1844 presidential election in which the Liberty Party captured the balance of power between the Whig Henry Clay and the Democrat James K. Polk. The result, however, proved to be a Pyrrhic victory that cost Clay the state of New York and ultimately the election; cf., Alan M. Kraut, "The Forgotten Reformers: A Profile of Third Party Abolitionists in Antebellum New York," Lewis Perry and Michael Fellman, eds., *Antislavery Reconsidered: New Perspectives on the Abolitionists* (Baton Rouge: Louisiana State University Press, 1979): 119-20.

82. See *True Wesleyan,* "Who Is Birney?" July 6, 1844; "Horton Will Vote for Birney," July 20, 1844; "Debate on Texas," March 16, 1844; "Oregon and War," May 2, 1846; and the "New England Conference Purchased the Dracut Academy," August 3, 1844, located one third mile from Lowell, with plans to open it in the fall, reveals the beginning of a commitment of Wesleyan Methodists to education; and "A Few Reasons Why Christians Should Not Smoke," October 11, 1845, for a sampling of Lee's attitude on general reform.

83. *True Wesleyan,* March 22, 1845; some of the seceders were convinced to return to the old church, ibid., April 5, 1845; and, "Episcopal Slanders," *True Wesleyan,* March 29, 1845.

84. "Visit to Hackensack, New Jersey," *True Wesleyan,* May 24, 1845.

85. *True Wesleyan,* June 7, 1845.

86. See Cross, *Burned-over District*, 288-321, for an overview of the rise of Millerism or Second Adventism.

87. Luther Lee, *The Immortality of the Soul* (New York: Wesleyan Methodist Book Room, 1850; rev. ed., 1859); *True Wesleyan*, November 16, 23, 1844.

88. Luther Lee, *Ecclesiastical Manual, or Scriptural Church Government Stated and Defended* (New York: Wesleyan Methodist Book Room, 1850); Luther Lee, *The Revival Manual* (New York: Wesleyan Methodist Book Room, 1850), a book of 108 pages, "divided into ten sections, and treats of revivals, of their nature, scriptural and philosophical character, their importance, and the best means of promoting and rendering them useful," *True Wesleyan*, June 12, 1850.

89. Hazel Catherine Wolf, *On Freedom's Altar: The Martyr Complex in the Abolition Movement* (Madison: University of Wisconsin Press, 1952), 80-99; *True Wesleyan*, December 7, 1844, March 28, May 16, 30, 1846.

90. Dayton, *Five Sermons and a Tract by Luther Lee*, 13.

91. Luther Lee, *The Supremacy of the Divine Law. A Sermon, preached on the occasion of the death of Rev. Charles Turner Torrey*, in Dayton, *Five Sermons and a Tract by Luther Lee*, 43-57.

92. The listing indicated that the *True Wesleyan* was the official organ of the Wesleyan connection that boasted four or five hundred clergy and twenty thousand members.

93. *True Wesleyan*, May 23, 1846.

94. *True Wesleyan*, December 7, 1844.

95. *True Wesleyan.*

96. *True Wesleyan*, August 1, 1846; Under "Editorial Ramblings," Lee frequently wrote of leaving the "city of dust, smoke, and noise, to travel to a camp meeting, where he frequently was an evangelist," August 25, 1849.

97. Matlack, *American Slavery and Methodism*, 245-53, 262-65, 283.

98. Matlack, *Life of Orange Scott*, 278-91.

99. *New York Tribune*, August 14, 1847.

100. Matlack, *Life of Orange Scott*, 278-91; *True Wesleyan*, November 6, 1847.

101. *Autobiography*, 278-79.

102. *Autobiography*, 281.

103. *True Wesleyan*, October 21, 1848.

104. Matlack, *American Slavery and Methodism*, 364-65.

105. Lee did not supply dates, or names, with the exception of the prosecutor's name, for this episode. John W. Edmonds, *Reports of Select Cases Decided in the Courts of New York, Not Heretofore Reported, or Reported Only Partially*, 2 vols. (New York: S. S. Peloubet & Co., 1883), from which salient facts can be corroborated.

106. See "Fugitive Slaves," *True Wesleyan*, January 26, 1850.

107. *Biographical Directory of the United States Congress, 1774-1989*, Bicentennial Edition (Washington, D.C.: GPO, 1989), 1472.

108. See "A Case of Kidnapping," *Liberator,* December 21, 1848, for the speed at which Garrison learned of the case and placed it in his paper, so soon after the episode began, which gives some indication of the interest that abolitionists had in this case. In December 23, Garrison wrote that Belt's location had been found due to "the indefatigable exertions of some gentlemen of this City," meaning Lee and his helpers.

109. Edmonds, *Select Cases,* 93-107.

110. Edmonds, *Select Cases,* 93-107; *Autobiography,* 330-31; *New York Tribune,* December 25, 26, 27, 28, 1848.

111. *True Wesleyan,* July 13, 20, 1850.

112. *True Wesleyan,* October 21, 1850.

113. "The Maine Law," *True Wesleyan,* January 10, 1852. Lee saw it as a propitious time to run a notice of the published address, *A Sermon for the Times—Prohibitory Law,* which he preached to the town of Lowell in 1841, announcing its availability through the Book Room.

114. *True Wesleyan,* January 31, 1852.

115. "The Editor's Farewell," *True Wesleyan,* April 24, 1852.

Chapter Seven

1852-1860: Pastor and Professor

In 1852 Harriet Beecher Stowe published *Uncle Tom's Cabin,* one of the most powerful pieces of abolitionist propaganda ever written. An immediate best seller, the book rocked the nation, selling in excess of 300,000 copies within the year. An enormous audience read the fictionalized account of how the vicious Simon Legree had brutalized his innocent slaves. The nation could not help reading accounts of slave catchers pursuing alleged runaway slaves under the protection of the dreaded Fugitive Slave Law. A combination of newspapers and novels kept the brutal system before the eyes of the North in the year that Lee departed New York City and returned to Syracuse, his former place of residence.

When Lee gave up the editorship of the *True Wesleyan* and accepted the settled ministry of a pastor, he had reached an epochal time in his life. In the next eight years Lee manifested new interests. While he continued to fight slavery, as evidenced by his famous oration at John Brown's grave in 1860, his focus was more on his parishioners, especially the problems that confronted women of that era. He took an active interest in female rights, education, and if challenged, he would not run from a good debate on theological matters. All of that activity prepared him more fully to write the *magnum opus* of his life, *Elements of Theology*, a systematic theology that became the standard text in holiness circles for years. His reputation became evident on a national basis; it earned for him a call to enter higher education.

In the years following his editorship, Lee at age fifty-two began to evidence a maturity and a mellowing that come only with years. The church in Syracuse had grown, and he would not need to pursue such a whirlwind schedule as he had nine years previously, when he attempted to dig out churches where none existed. Syracuse also had grown and developed in the intervening period. It had reached the size where large conventions frequently used facilities in the city for reform activities and functions. National and state political conventions had met in the city, as well as feminist, temperance, educational, and other reform groups.[1]

The Syracuse *Standard* did its part to welcome Lee back to the city, announcing his introductory sermon to be preached in the Wesleyan Methodist Church on the corner of Onondaga and Jefferson Streets.[2] Lee was frequently called from the city to deliver speeches on various occasions. He had barely gotten situated in his house when the call came to dedicate the new church in Watertown, where he had pastored in 1835.[3]

In June the New York Temperance Society, an all-male society, met in Syracuse. In its call for delegates no designation had limited the sex of those invited. The newly formed Woman's State Temperance Society sent Susan B. Anthony and Amelia Bloomer. When the convention met, it refused to seat the women. In fact it denied them entrance to the hall. Lee made a speech on their behalf, but it fell on unheeding, chauvinistic ears. He then invited them to assemble in the Wesleyan Methodist Church for a night session. The grateful women accepted. They requested Lee to speak; he happily complied.[4]

Lee's interest in politics had not diminished. In September, the Congregational Church and his Wesleyan Methodist church co-hosted the Free Democrat and the Liberty Party Conventions, respectively. On September 30, 1852, abolitionists, including Frederick Douglass, Gerrit Smith, Garrison, Lucretia Mott, Lucy Stone, and Luther Lee, spoke from the Wesleyan pulpit in the afternoon and the Congregational in the evening.[5]

On October 6-14, 1852, the third quadrennial conference of the Wesleyan Methodists met, by coincidence, in Syracuse. Cyrus Prindle was elected president. The delegates then tackled the issue of an episcopal form of polity again. Edward Smith, the president of Allegheny Conference, had never reconciled himself to a non-episcopal form of church government. He particularly sought to have the laity excluded from any appointive powers. To that end, he introduced a series of pro-episcopal articles to the church periodical, apparently timing the mailing of his materials so that they would be published in the final days before the Conference met. By so doing, no one on the other side of the issue could write rebuttals and get them printed in time to influence voting. Lee's friends in New York alerted him to the stratagem, and supplied Lee with the galley slips so that he could refute in print the points that Smith wanted passed. Smith led a debate on the issue on the floor, but when the votes were counted, Lee had success-fully ended the controversy. The matter never surfaced after that.

Only one other item negatively impacted the session: Horton had returned to the ME church in the previous year. He published his reason for doing so in an article entitled, "Reverend Jotham Horton's Reasons."[6] In it he stated that his ideas on the episcopacy had changed, the church was now amenable to antislavery men, and he viewed the old church as one best suited to "spreading scriptural holiness" in America. Once the session ended, life returned to a modicum of normalcy. In December, Lee's thoughtful parishioners, ever mindful that their pastor was a man who lived a meager life, honored him with a donation visit (a shower of food and monetary gifts), which took place in the afternoon and evening of the 22nd. Probably the spirit of Christmas motivated their kindness.[7] In the following year, Lee showed himself capable of acts of kindness. His charitable deed to a young woman in the area, however, proved to be an act that catapulted him into national prominence.

Antoinette Brown (1825-1921) of Henrietta, New York, which is near Rochester, had attended Oberlin College in the 1830s. Oberlin, an evangelical school that welcomed blacks and women as students, was a hotbed of social activism. With Lucy Stone and other future leaders in the cause of woman's rights, Brown had studied under the approving eye of Charles G. Finney, Professor of Theology. Not content to merely complete an undergraduate degree, she prevailed upon the faculty and administration to approve her taking the ministerial course, but she really was an unofficial student, and could not receive the same degree as the men in the seminary. As a student she was exemplary. Her Greek professor, Asa Mahan, so approved of her exegetical work, he thought it suitable for publication in the *Oberlin Quarterly Review*.

Ironically, it appeared in the same issue with a published speech by Professor Fairchild: "Women's Rights and Duties." Brown left Oberlin in 1850 at the age of twenty-five; her name, however, did not appear on an official list of theological students until 1908![8]

Brown entered the lecture circuit along with Anthony, Elizabeth Cady Stanton, Bloomer, the Grimké sisters, and other females who created an uproar wherever they went, at least among the male listeners. She traveled from city to city speaking in behalf of temperance, female moral reform, educational reforms, and, of course, women's rights. She enjoyed a unique advantage in that she had theological training.[9] By the summer of 1853, she was willing to assume the pastorate of a small Congregational Church in South Butler, located between Rochester and Syracuse. The congregation, impressed with her speaking abilities, had invited her to be their pastor for three hundred dollars per year. The church had previously hired a black minister. Such unconventional practices proved rather bold, even for an abolitionist church, but that probably was the result of the man's willingness to preach for such a paltry sum, rather than from any strong desire on its part for a black minister. In early summer, she rented rooms in the village, and began to preach. She enjoyed the strong support of Gerrit Smith, a man whose support counted for much since he was the wealthiest man in New York. By mid-summer, the membership wanted her to be ordained.[10]

As was common in Congregational churches, the ordination took place at the local level. The church in South Butler had no qualms about her ordination. They recognized, however, that such a public step would somehow proceed better if someone such as Gerrit Smith were present to give public support to the event. He agreed to attend and speak. All that was needed was some minister who would preach an ordination sermon. The local governing board took care of planning the rest of the occasion. At an ordination, it was customary to seek out a clerical member of one's own denomination to deliver the sermon. Brown discovered, however, that the nearby Congregational preachers were less than enthusiastic about having their name attached to such a novel event. When she turned to her Unitarian preacher colleagues, they feared that her strong orthodoxy might cast them in a negative light if they participated. Their hesitancy did not appear to be over the fact that she was female despite the fact that no member of that sex ever had been ordained in a mainline church in America. One man in the area came to mind. The Wesleyan Methodist minister in Syracuse had a reputation for advocating women's rights. In her hour of extremity she turned to Lee for help.

Brown had known Luther Lee for some time, having made common cause with him in the interests of social reform. Earlier in that same year she had spoken along with Gerrit Smith and Frederick Douglass in the Wesleyan Church in Syracuse at the Liberty Party Convention.[11] Lee had met her again at a state temperance rally. In the fall of 1853 she turned to Lee to preach her ordination sermon. Wesleyan Methodists had not sanctioned the ordination of women by that juncture. That would have to wait until the 1860s. In fact, four years previous, Lee was aware of a division of thought within his denomination on the use of women in a leadership role. In November of 1849, Lee had published an article submitted to him that had raised the issue of women serving as class leaders.[12] Lee, never one to shirk from something merely on the basis of public opinion, consented to preach the sermon.

On September 15, 1853, a substantial crowd gathered for the epochal event. Many social reformers graced the village church. Lee took his place at the podium and began the oration, using as his text Galations 3:28, "There is neither male nor female; for ye are one in Christ." Lee began by acknowledging that his text was a typical for routine ordination sermons, but this was a "novel transaction," since a woman was the candidate for ordination. Applying his logical approach, Lee reasoned to the assembly that should he decline to approve of her ordination, "what reason can I give for so doing?" To his knowledge, she possessed mental and educational preparation and manifested no moral defects. His conclusion was reached by this route:

> I acknowledge the candidate to be in Christ; if I deny her the right to exercise her gifts as a Christian minister, I virtually affirm that there is male and female, and that we are not all one in Christ Jesus, by which I contradict St. Paul, and though he is not among us to reply to me, to know myself at variance with him, would give me more uneasiness that to differ from the modern doctors of divinity,

and divinity schools. I am then brought to this conclusion, which I will state in the form of a proposition . . . . Females have a God-given right to preach the Gospel.[13]

Lee cited examples of prophetesses in the Old Testament, and to Joel 2:28 in which he stated, "I will pour out my Spirit upon all flesh; and your sons and your daughters shall prophesy." He included most of the references to female workers of any rank in the New Testament, arguing that qualification for the deaconate implied women were permitted to function in any capacity as men. He closed his oration by invoking a Triune blessing upon both the preacher and the people. It must be stressed that Lee did not ordain Miss Brown, he only preached a sermon for the occasion. That fact is noteworthy, because in the following year, she wrote to him, requesting that he provide her with a certificate of ordination, a request that he refused to grant without providing a reason. As he reminded her in his letter, "All I did was to preach a sermon . . . [and] I thought at the time there was a want of formality, and raised the question how you was to obtain your certificate . . . [to which you replied] . . . that a certifcate would be of no use."[14]

Lee was happy to preach the sermon but distanced himself from anything that smacked of legal complications by refusing to perform the act of ordination or a certificate to that effect. He did, however, involve himself with other issues confronting women of the era. Ever since Lee had voted against Scott and other antifeminists in the split with Garrisonians in 1839, he revealed an increasing interest in the plight of women.[15]

Samuel J. May, the Harvard-trained Unitarian pastor in the city, had also advocated female rights. Within months the two men joined together in the woman's rights battle. Before that happened, however, they must bury the theological hatchet that lay between them. That could only be done through a series of debates. The city of Syracuse had never witnessed such a spectacle. The whole community focused on the event that took place in its city hall.

The most important debate of Lee's career transpired in the Syracuse city hall, an event that spanned an entire month.[16] The contest came about almost by accident after Lee out of curiosity attended a convention that lambasted religious denominationalism and creedalism. May was present and engaged a friend of Lee's about creeds. Lee came to his friend's aid. In his autobiography Lee reports that this "led to a slight pass between Mr. May and myself, and I thought nothing more of it."[17] A week or so later Lee received a challenge from May to debate the doctrine of the Trinity. Due to his attendance at the Women's Rights Convention in Albany, it would not suit May to begin until later in the month. In February of 1854, they initiated the debates that ran for eleven evenings; the two debated for two hours, each speaking twice for thirty minutes in the same sequence of Lee, May, Lee, May. They arranged the debates, sometimes in consecutive order and at other times with open evenings in between.

The sustained nature of the clash over a period of four weeks shows the seriousness with which these two men took their task. Lee claimed that the debate drew "the most learned and pious people in the city," who crowded the large hall every evening. May was better known in the city, but Lee attracted the principal pastors of the city to his house where they helped him prepare his replies. Lee said that he had carefully prepared his direct arguments in advance in support of the affirmative side, that "there is but one living and true God . . . [who consists of] three persons, of one substance, power, and eternity, the Father, the Son (the Word), and the Holy Ghost."[18]

The careful planning by Lee of his verbal strategies in the debate is revealed in his own account of how he proceeded:

> The course I pursued was to open each speech after the first with a brief rejoinder to his reply, and then prosecute the direct argument to the end of my half hour. By this course I kept my argument clear and distinct before the audience until it was finished, closing in, closer and closer, upon my opponent as I progressed. When I reached the end my summing up was brief, logical, and beyond the reach of an answer, as it was too late for my opponent to go back and attempt to refute my arguments upon which my conclusions rested. This he had failed to do as they were delivered, but had rather sought to amuse himself with his own objections to, and caricatures on, the doctrine of the Trinity, which I brush from my path as I proceeded; and now I wound my chain of argument around

him. . . . [19]

The purpose here is not to analyze Lee's theological arguments, as such, but to describe his argumentative structure and his concern for evidentiary proof in support of his arguments.

One of the strong pieces of evidence for characterizing Lee's approach as extremely argumentative is his opponent's own admissions throughout the speeches. May acknowledged Lee's reputation as a logical debater numerous times throughout his twenty-two speeches. For example, on the third evening, May argued that Lee in his first speech had gone too far in his proof of an argument which, if it proves too much, "proves nothing." Later, May said, "If, however, my brother on the other side does not and cannot see this as I do, I will put him upon the horns of a dilemma, though I know it will be an uncomfortable position for so good a logician as he is."[20]

In May's second speech of the same evening, he opened with a reference to Lee's preoccupation with proof texts to support his argument. May began,

> It is extremely unfortunate for my friend's argument that, notwithstanding his formidable array of texts from the Old Testament and the New,—numerous and explicit enough—which he thinks prove beyond a question, that Christ was not a created, but a self-existent, eternally existent being, possessed of all the attributes of the Deity; it is extremely unfortunate for him, I say, that we have the most express declarations of Christ and his apostles, on every point, exactly to the contrary.[21]

May proceeded to attack Lee for being willing to accept the language of creeds when the language of the Bible does not provide primary evidence in the words of Christ that he was God. May attempted to cast doubt on Lee's credibility as a debater for having produced "all the passages to which [they] have been listening" but yet not being able to show "some explicit statement of this doctrine of the Trinity, in the very words of the Great Teacher." May concluded that "the plain declarations of himself outweigh all [Lee's] texts and arguments."[22]

May was quite concerned about Lee's reputation as a debater

who could establish proof by means of logical argument. In the final debate May appealed to his listeners "to judge fairly between [him] and [his] opponent" and to be aware that "the larger, much the larger part" of the audience was probably sympathetic to the views of his opponent. Acknowledging Lee's ability to build a formidable wall of proof texts to tear down, May said that if he "had followed Mr. Lee step by step, taking up every text he had laid down," giving his interpretation and his reasons for his interpretation as being different from Lee's, he could not, "in the time allowed, have traveled over half the ground he did, and should have left [his] argument in a much more unfinished state" than it was.[23]

After explaining his inability to meet Lee on his own argumentative terms, May admitted: "I came not here to measure my skill with Mr. Lee's as a tactician in debate" but rather, to "establish a great truth" and to offer "the principles of biblical interpretation" that have been "obscured . . . by the theology of the Churches." May deprecated his opponent's flair for "arguments and proof texts," emphasizing instead his own possession of the facts that enable his listeners "to discover for themselves the truth on this great subject." Lee, May continued, "has repeatedly more than intimated that my logic was defective . . . [but logicians] have played, and do play, such queer pranks with the truth, that I distrust them." May reiterated his acknowledgment of Lee's use of logic when he concluded, "My opponent may be a logician, sir, but what has his logic proved? What can it prove against the simple statement of the contradiction and absurdity in the proposition he has undertaken to defend?"[24]

The second body of evidence for characterizing Lee's approach as being extremely argumentative is his own admission of the kind of language and structure that he used. Lee's language consistently and repeatedly disclosed his motives and abilities in argumentative discourse. He knew the rules of debate and used them against his opponent. After the first three debates on consecutive evenings, four days elapsed before Lee and May resumed. When the debate began, Lee reminded his audience that, as he had the affirmative, he had the obligation "to spread [the] arguments before those who choose to hear, whether they are immediately replied to or not."[25]

Because May did not take up Lee's arguments in consecutive

order as Lee wanted him to do, Lee told his audience that he would leave his replies to May until the conclusion of the "direct arguments." He wanted to avoid "breaking up the chain of my argument," he said, "so that I cannot defend them in the order in which I have advanced them. . . . [But] I shall only correct some errors in matter of fact, make some brief explanations, or announce what will be the ground of my reply on a given point, and then press on with my direct argument to its close."[26] In careful debate style, Lee wanted to keep clear at all times where he was in the discussion as he developed his "chain of argument."

In good refutation style, Lee attempted to expose his opponent when he moved off the subject. He accused May at one point early in the series of having "a misapprehension of the question in discussion. The question was not, is it right to make creeds; but is the doctrine of the Trinity true." In addition, Lee attacked him for engaging in "a false principle of reasoning" by placing "one class of texts against another" without making any attempt to examine the arguments or the texts quoted to show that their meanings were not what Lee had said they were. Opposing one text with another text gains nothing, argued Lee, for "it is a false method of arguing."[27]

In rebuttal the Wesleyan minister also pointed out that he would use his opponent's evidence for his own case. Lee stated,

> The texts which he has quoted in reply to me on the attributes of Christ, are absolutely essential to my theory; they are the very texts which I shall quote to prove the humanity of Christ. He is thus urging against me, that upon which I rely for support. I affirm that Christ is both God and man, and he replies that he is not God, because he is man. Is this fair argumentation? This matter we will settle hereafter.[28]

The above argument was typical of Lee who preferred to appeal to the rules of debate and to whether the debate was being conducted properly, or whether his opponent was being fair. Another excellent example is in Lee's closing speech of the debate on the last evening. He referred to the fact that he had a great amount of ground to cover and may run out of time in answering everything. He reminded his listeners that he would have no opportunity to reply to May's closing speech. "It is always understood, however," he continued, "that no new matter is to be introduced in the closing address, and I have no doubt that my friend will abide this universally recognized rule."[29]

There were a few occasions throughout the eleven evenings when the debaters interrupted each other. During one of May's speeches, May referred to Lee's statement about the well-known theologian of the day, Theodore Parker. The interchange that follows is an example of the cross-examination they both engaged in:

> Mr. Lee—My friend is mistaken. I did not hold Mr. Parker up
> as a model Unitarian, much less as a great theologian. I
> could not so belie my idea of a theologian. You mis-
> represent me.
> Mr. May—What did you say, then?
> Mr. Lee—I said distinguished Unitarian.
> Mr. May—You said distinguished theologian.
> Mr. Lee—Oh, no! You misunderstood me.
> Mr. May—I am sure you did.
> Mr. Lee—If I said so I will take it all back, for I will not stultify
> my own common sense by saying or persisting in
> saying anything like that.[30]

Lee's efforts to adhere to the rules of debate included providing a manuscript of his speech so that his opponent could have adequate opportunity to reply. On another occasion Lee handed May a tract during the debate that he had written on keeping the Sabbath, so that May could read his views regarding the inspiration of the Scriptures.[31] Both men made reference in the debate to the fact that their proceedings would be published and then readers could judge for themselves what had been said.

Reference has already been made to Lee's use of the analogy that his argument was a chain with iron links. He also used the analogy of a river. Lee self-confidently stated,

> At this point it may be observed that [my] argument gains strength at
> every step. Like the progress of a river, the argument deepens and

widens as it flows, by receiving at every step the tributary strength of small streams. So the previous arguments I have offered hold their own strength and are increased by each successive proposition that I establish.[32]

Such comments disclose his argumentative motives and strategies as a debater. His opponent seemed far less preoccupied with the language of argumentative style and structure, and was more concerned about substance.

Every one of Lee's twenty-two speeches in the debate on the Trinity follows a similar pattern of keeping clear what the main proposition was, what the arguments were, what his supporting texts were, what the rejoinders to his opponent were, where his opponent failed to meet his arguments, where he strayed from the proposition, where he engaged in false arguing, and where he came short of his responsibilities on the negative side. The 160 pages of fine print with double columns is a text worthy of careful analysis by theologians for the detailed use of scriptures and doctrines and by both ministers or rhetorical scholars for the extensive use of argument, reasoning, evidence, and persuasive attempts to influence the audience toward a particular view of religious reality.

Lee's own perception of what happened in the debate is explained in his autobiography. He felt very satisfied with his efforts and in 1883 described the result in the following passage:

[May] had every appearance of honesty and candor in the opening of the discussion, and I believe he thought he had the right side of the question, and expected to be able to triumphantly defend his views and overthrow what he regarded as the absurdities of Trinitarianism. It appeared to me that he had been educated a Unitarian, and taught from his youth to believe that Trinitarianism was a concatenation of impossibilities, absurdities, and contradictions, which he had only to touch with his wand of reason to see the whole system fall to pieces. He appeared not to understand Trinitarianism, and to have no conception of the chain of iron-linked logic by which it could be defended. When he came to face an opponent quite as experienced in debate as himself, and who had thoroughly studied both sides of the question, he found the discussion anything but the pleasant recreation he had anticipated, and was driven to positions he little thought of when he commenced the debate.[33]

Such a description illustrates how Lee believed that he had won the debate. The phrase, "the chain of iron-linked logic," was one that Lee liked to use to characterize his style of debating. In Lee's obituary many years later, the writer used the phrase, "under the weight of Dr. Lee's sledge-hammer strokes," to describe why "Mr. May became terribly perplexed" in the course of the debate.[34] Just as Lee's sermon on the death of Lovejoy had brought him national attention as an abolitionist, so his debate with May served as the epitome of his public disputations on religious and social issues.

A most pleasant sequel to the debating episode is the fact that Lee and May joined together in organizing the Syracuse Female Seamstress Association. This organization addressed the manner in which working women of the city were being exploited on a regular basis. Such social activism suited Lee perfectly. After his willingness to argue with Garrison in favor of female roles in antislavery organizations, and his willingness to preach at the ordination of Antoinette Brown, to shrink from lending his influence to female workers would have been out of character for Lee.

Logic dictated to Lee and to May that if slaves could be happy in their lot in life, they were degraded humans; if women could be happy locked away in a "cult of domesticity," they too, shared an element of degradation. Ever since the women had insinuated themselves into the fight against slavery in the early 1830s, reflective abolitionists like Lee and May were forced to reevaluate the role of women. Beyond that, the men were humanitarians. How could any reformer worth his salt stand on the sidelines as female workers were exploited without raising a voice against it? Lee throughout his tenure as editor of the *True Wesleyan* had printed numerous articles against such inconsistencies in an age of social reform.[35] Although the salt works had long been the chief industry of the city, textile manufacturing was rapidly developing as one of the largest sources of employment, especially for women. Captains of industry discovered that it was easy to exploit female workers, the first significant wave of factory workers in the North.

The Syracuse daily newspapers regularly printed anonymous articles in defense of women such as: "Wages of Females," "The Wages Paid to Females," "The Female Advocates of Woman's Rights," and "Women's Wages," all of which ran during 1853 in the Syracuse *Tribune* and *Daily Standard.* The articles provide no clue to the writer, but it is likely that Lee or May was responsible.[36] Once the theological debates had ended in the spring of 1854, the two men set about to do something tangible for the laboring women of Syracuse.

May had urged the seamstresses outside the city to end their production in the hope that the stoppage would drive up the wages in the city. That accomplished nothing.[37] He and Lee together called for an organizational meeting of the needlewomen to meet on April 27. Lee opened with an overview of events that had led to the organizational meeting. May followed by reading Thomas Hood's "Song of the Shirt," a poem that described the plight of seamstress workers. Its final lines poignantly portray the dismal life of a seamstress:

> With fingers weary and worn,
>   With eyelids heavy and red,
> A woman sat, in unwomanly rags,
>   Plying her needle and thread;
> Stitch—stitch—stitch!
>   In poverty, hunger and dirt;
> And still with a voice of dolorous pitch—
> Would that its tone could reach the rich!
>   She sung this "Song of the Shirt"!

May concluded his reading by stating that many women in Syracuse paralleled the poet's representations. Next the meeting agreed upon a constitution for the "Sewing Female Protection Society," after which Matlack read the report of a committee that earlier had investigated working conditions in the city among women who were engaged in "Slop Work," in which numerous cases of unbearable conditions came to light. In a stroke of humor Lee exhibited a pair of pantaloons that had been made for fifteen cents, declaring that "he did not know whether they were made for Jews or Gentiles." In the discussion a general feeling of helplessness predominated but Lee and his colleagues urged the women to attempt to remedy the evil.[38]

First they appealed to the local ministers to initiate reform. Then they canvassed the city to secure lists of destitute women. A partial list was read, citing the names, marital situation, dependents, hours worked, and wages received for a dozen or more actual cases current in Syracuse. Lee advocated such reforms and continued to lend his time and voice for the women in his city. While the organization should not be construed as a union, its charter contained language that sought "to obtain just compensation" for its members, demanded fairness in wages, would aid striking workers through a support fund, and would assist "fallen women" to find respectable lives and incomes. The *Daily Standard* published the proceedings along with the constitution. The two men continued to make common cause in social reform until Lee left Syracuse.[39]

The Syracuse Wesleyan Methodist Church members loved their pastor and were not bashful about demonstrating their appreciation. On January 11, 1854, they ran the following announcement in the *Daily Standard*: "The Reverend Luther Lee's friends are invited to make him a pastoral visit . . . Wednesday . . . afternoon and evening at the Wesleyan Chapel. . . . Refreshments will be provided freely for all who call."[40] On July 4, 1854, Lee delivered a rousing oration, "The Nation's Peril—Liberty or Slavery," in the city hall at Syracuse.[41] His reputation as an orator had steadily increased; he had improved immeasurably from the first faltering sermon that he had delivered in the home of Jacob Dubois thirty-three years earlier. His oratorical skills were frequently employed by committee chairmen in the city.

A Syracuse annual occasion since October 1, 1851, was a Jerry Rescue Celebration. On that date Jerry, a resident of the city, accused of being a runaway slave, had been rescued from slave catchers by local citizens. The gathering drew people from all over the North.[42] The keynote speaker on September 30, 1854, was none other than Luther Lee.[43] Gerrit Smith presided; Frederick Douglass and other significant antislavery people were in attendance. Charles Sumner had been invited but could not attend. He sent his regards in a published letter. Douglass spoke in the afternoon, followed by Garrison. The gala event never ceased to inspire the city's residents to press ahead in the cause of the slaves. According to Lee, Syracuse was one of the most active points on the underground railroad in the nation.

Lee declared that during the three years that he lived in that place he "did the largest work of my life on the Under-ground Railroad," assisting as many as thirty slaves in a month. He argued that until the passage of the Fugitive Slave Law, most slaves felt safe in the area. After the bill received passage, slaves did not rest until they reached Canada. During those years Lee wrote innumerable passes to friendly train conductors who permitted runaways to ride for free. Escorting them from his residence at 39 Onondaga Street to the cars, Lee instructed his charges to "keep their seats until they crossed the suspension bridge, and then they would be in Canada." Lee claimed, "My name, the name of my street, and the number of my residence, came to be known as far south as Baltimore, and I did a large business." To safeguard against surprise by "slave catching officers," a particular ring of the bell in the Congregational church announced for a distance of four or five miles that help was wanted for a fugitive slave.[44]

One of the last speeches that Lee gave in Syracuse developed out of a fugitive slave case in Wisconsin. The nation ultimately learned about the efforts of two people who defied the Fugitive Slave Law. In the case of *Ableman v. Booth* the Wisconsin Supreme Court declared the law to be void and ignored the U.S. Supreme Court when it overruled the state court. Sympathetic abolitionists in Syracuse organized a meeting in honor of their daring colleagues of Milwaukee. Popular antislavery people gave speeches and passed resolutions as the mayor of the city presided. Lee gave the concluding oration of the evening. In it he declared that the federal law that assisted slave catchers to be immoral, "a war upon God, upon his law, and upon the rights of humanity; that to obey it, or to aid in its enforcement, is treason against God and humanity, and involves a guilt equal to the guilt of violating every one of the ten commandments. . . . I never had obeyed it—I never would obey it."[45] He concluded the speech by stating his home address and declaring that if any federal authorities should want to pick him up and "lock me up in the Penitentiary on the hill; but if they did such a foolish thing as that I had friends enough in Onondaga County to level it with the ground before the next morning."[46] The immense crowd leaped to their feet and shouted "We will do it! we will do it!" In that frame of mind, it is reasonable to assume that they would have made good on their boast should the need present itself. On that note, Lee concluded his abolitionist activities in the city.

By the spring of 1855, Lee concluded that his labors in Syracuse had come to an end. With regret he submitted his resignation. Even his old debating opponent, Samuel J. May, submitted a kind article for the paper, entitled, "Farewell to Mr. Lee."[47] Lee kindly responded to May, the Unitarian, in the next paper:

> Here I grieve the friends I love,
> And they in turn, grieve me?
> But, O, My Father, grant me grace,
> That I may not grieve Thee.

> Luther Lee

> Fulton, May 22, 1855.[48]

While the church was barely able to settle its accounts with Lee, due to the poor income of the church, Lee wrote that he was able to leave Syracuse "without owing a dollar."[49] He subsequently accepted the Wesleyan Methodist Church at Fulton, the same town at which he was pastor when he converted to abolitionism in 1837.

Many of the members of Lee's old ME church had seceded; most of those who did had joined the Wesleyans. Once the old church had split and the gag rule had been implicitly repealed, the lure of Wesleyanism diminished. By the time that Lee arrived there in 1855, he found a substantial Wesleyan congregation with which to labor. While at the village of Fulton, Lee concluded three of his literary works, *Elements of Theology,*[50] *Slavery Examined in the Light of the Bible,*[51] and the second volume of his *The Evangelical Pulpit,*[52] a series of bound sermons that he had been editing for several years. Evidence of his poor financial condition was substantiated by the fact that he could not publish his theology without a loan from a parishioner. Perhaps the fact that his work at Fulton located him some distance from larger cities and since he had no editorial responsibilities, Lee's literary reform efforts received less attention. The only evidence that he had remained interested in the antislavery cause can be seen in the town of Mexico, sixteen miles to the northeast of his home. There on September 11, he attended a speech given by Frederick Douglass, the famous former slave, and editor of the *North Star*, the antislavery paper published in Rochester. Lee gave the invocation on that occasion in which abolitionists had gathered to dedicate a monument in the memory of Asa S. Wing, one of their own who had died prematurely of tuberculosis. Douglass's oration focused on the slavery problems in "bleeding Kansas." Through the winter Lee attended to his duties as pastor. Early in the following spring, Lee received an unexpected visitor who changed the course of his life.[53]

Lee's caller turned out to be Seymour A. Baker, the agent for Leoni College, a fledgling school begun by the Michigan Conference in a small hamlet to the east of Jackson, Michigan, where the local citizens had donated ten acres for the construction of a college. In 1847 a brick kiln was constructed on the property, and a building program began to develop. By the following year, a tiny institute of higher education began training youths from all over the Connection. Between fifty and sixty students attended the school in its first year. In 1848, the State Legislature issued a charter for Leoni Literary and Theological Institute. Early in the next decade, the name was changed to Michigan Union College. The college was blessed with a number of men on the faculty who were not only excellent educators, they also were solid Wesleyans. Most of these had been colleagues of Lee for years. In 1852 Prindle accepted a professorship at the college.[54] By 1855 John McEldowney was appointed Professor of Systematic Theology, Seymour Baker, Professor of Sacred Rhetoric and Pastoral Theology, Professor William Crane, Ecclesiastical History, and an opening existed for a professor of Hebrew and Literature. With men of such high caliber, the future of the college appeared promising, indeed.[55]

The purpose of Baker's visit soon became manifest; he wanted the pastor of Fulton to consider heading up a theological department at the college. Lee's volume of systematic theology, along with his other considerable literary accomplishments, had not escaped the notice of reflective men. Now he must make a decision. The agent promised a new house on an acre of land, to sweeten the offer. Lee had planned to remain in Fulton for a lengthy pastorate. He insisted that his church must give him its blessing before he would entertain the notion of leaving them so soon after his arrival. Lee's church members agreed to permit their pastor to move on to the new post of duty, and by early May the Lees had moved to Michigan.[56]

Lee appeared to be jubilant at what he found when he arrived at Leoni. The white frame house that had been provided for his family was of two stories with a "good cellar." It had cost nine hundred dollars to build.[57] The town, located about seventy miles west of Detroit, boasted a clean atmosphere, free of profanity, street noises, and "papists"—for Protestants such as Lee, the epitome of everything evil. He cannot be accused of racism, but he certainly had been well infected with a certain class bigotry. One is tempted to conjecture that since Lee had associated with Masonry, he could be reflecting their nativism.

Lee arrived late in the semester, and the academic year ended June 18. Part of the closing activities called for students to present orations. He noted that the men and women gave exemplary speeches—mostly on aspects of social reform. The students were dealing not with the world as it was, but as it should be. Lee presented an address entitled, "The Culture of the Mind," as part of the activities. The student body numbered 323, with hopes of an even higher enrollment in the fall semester.[58]

During the summer a concerted drive attempted to raise $10,000 to endow a professorship for Lee. At that time Lee held the post of president of the Institute as well as his professorship. As an inducement for possible donors, the paper carried a series of very positive reviews of all of Lee's published works. It was a sales pitch to justify a man of Lee's abilities.[59] Another section of the paper depicted Lee as personable and in touch with youth and that he desired to meet with each of the new students on registration day. Late in June, Lee was in the Syracuse church where he preached both services with Prindle, the editor of *The Wesleyan,* in the audience. In the following issue, the editor rhapsodized the sermon. Referring to Lee as a distinguished theologian, and commenting on Lee's accolades from the venerable Bishop Hedding, Prindle asserted that Lee "was undoubtedly one of the ablest divines now living."[60]

If things appeared too good to be true to the Lees, that is because they were. Professor Lee enjoyed his teaching and position as college pastor. Several of his theological students later entered the ministry and acquitted themselves well. Lee attended the fourth General Conference at Cleveland, where he was elected its president for a second time. The nation, however, had positioned itself for another economic downturn. Back at Leoni the impact of the Panic of 1857 devastated fundraising and the students' ability to pay tuition. The college was unable to open for the fall semester. Other towns, however were anxious to have such a college and offers of assistance in the amount of $50,000 had been tendered. The trustees continued to explore the options. By August, Lee, a man who always seemed to live at the edge of poverty, was far behind in his salary. Viewing the Leoni situation as hopeless, he resigned. He must return to pastoring. The *Miami Conference Journal* reported that the Committee on Pastoral Relations had assigned Lee to the church at Felicity, Clermont County, Ohio. Selling his furniture to pay his bills, and then the house to cover his share of the investment, he managed to leave Michigan on September 16 to accept a Wesleyan Methodist Church across the Ohio River from slave-holding Kentucky. He would, however, live to return to Michigan, and as an educator.[61]

Traveling by rail to Detroit, then by boat across Lake Erie to Sandusky, the Lees then rode the night train to Cincinnati. The train was forced to lay over in Dayton around seven o'clock in the morning. Lee spent most of the layover time attempting to locate breakfast in a place other than a bar. Back on the train, the Lees managed to make Cincinnati by late morning. They then proceeded to find an Ohio River boat which carried them to a landing fifty miles upstream from the Queen City, where a member of the Felicity congregation was to meet them with a hack. The member greeted them, but as they left the landing they discovered that the hired hack for some unknown reason had left. Lee, his family, and the welcoming committee of one were forced to find lodging for the night, "feeling a little vexed that the hack-man had left us." The next day they discovered that the hack had overturned on the dark rainy road and been destroyed. By noon, they reached the hamlet where the new pastor was to preach both morning and evening the following day. The congregation did its best to give the Lees a warm welcome. As for Lee, he hoped the church and the village would live up to the name of Felicity.[62]

Located four miles from the river, most of the westward expansion of the nation had passed Felicity by. Until recent days, the town had been a busy station on the underground railroad. For unexplained reasons, Lee wrote that nothing was being done in that business when he arrived. In 1847, a Wesleyan Methodist congregation was organized, consisting of ex-Cambellites, Methodists, and Free Presbyterians. The Miami Conference had met there a few years earlier, an indication that the church had a modicum of stability.[63] A small meeting house had been constructed in September of 1850 for the 112 members. The congregation had outgrown that building. In 1857 the church, primarily made up of seceders from the ME church and a few converts from the area, was in the process of finishing a new house of worship just as the Lees arrived. The brick structure of 45 by 65 feet was not small. One member had gone to the city to find a bell; others were completing the painting. The dedication was first set for November 1; then it was delayed to November 22. In the meanwhile, Lee submitted articles to the connection paper, which appear throughout the next several years.[64]

The day of dedication arrived on the heels of several days of hard rain followed by plummeting temperature. Lee lamented that no "foreign help" could assist in the ceremony, due to the weather. Ever optimistic, Lee wrote of the full house for all of the Sunday services. Even the bell, a first place winner at the Ohio State Fair, added to the joyous occasion. The building was located near enough to the center of the business district that the town fathers had purchased a large clock for the place. Lee asserted that the house of worship was as fine as any in all of Wesleyan Methodism.

In February, Matlack visited the church to conduct a revival that ran on the seventeenth to the twenty-fifth of the month. He reported that the church was growing, and based upon results of the protracted meeting, the prospects appeared bright.[65] While he labored for the Lord, Lee never forgot the plight of the slave. Even though his interests were in education, and even though he was a professor in between jobs at the moment, whenever opportunity opened, he spoke for the blacks in bondage. Such an occasion began with what he entitled as "The Glorious 4th in Felicity."[66]

Each year the town managed to work itself into a fever pitch on the anniversary of the nation's liberty. The Wesleyan church bell pealed out freedom's songs to hearers six miles away. Kentucky residents, both masters and slaves, who lived two miles inland from the southern shore of the Ohio River, could hear the bells. Somehow, however, the good citizens of Felicity managed to overlook the bondmen across the Ohio River in Kentucky. A venerable Methodist preacher delivered a magnificent invocation at the huge celebration, but, as Lee sarcastically observed, "he forgot to pray for the slave, and not a word was uttered in his prayer, from which anyone would know that there is any slavery or oppression in the world. . . . But he remembered to pray for their [Methodist] Quarterly Meeting, which he told the Lord in the hearing of all the people, would commence that afternoon."[67] The next speaker, a local lawyer, obviously soft on slavery, fell short in the same manner.

Mr. Swing, Esq., had the honor of being the speaker of the day. Lee pointed out with a pun that Swing, like the ME preacher, "managed to 'swing' entirely clear of the subject of slavery," and his hearers would never suspect "that he had ever heard of the existence of slavery in this nation." Finally Lee got his chance at the podium. What to do? Should he tell the crowd what it apparently wanted to hear— nothing of slavery? Not Luther Lee! As he later affirmed, "We long since made up our mind that when we let fly the arrow of truth, if men get hit by getting between us and the devil, the fault is theirs not ours." He then proceeded to vilify the institution of slavery in general, and slaveholders and defenders of slavery in particular, using language that no person in his audience could possibly misunderstand. As he progressed in his oration, he observed one man who had fled from the speakers' stand, and others from the audience were leaving. "Seeing the state of things, and wishing not to further expose any of the small boilers to the danger of explosion, or a collapse," he ended his comments, thanking God that he at least had freedom in his own pulpit, and that on the morrow, he would speak freely on the subject of slavery—which he did to a full house.[68]

The Miami Conference was scheduled to meet in Felicity on the first day of September. Lee set about to prepare himself for the entertainment of the delegates. During the session it was reported that no new ministers had been added during the year, and additions in the membership had been slight. Since many of the churches were small, a number of the pastors were forced to provide their own living. Everyone departed, however, on an optimistic note, expecting the new year to produce solid gains.[69] Things were also looking up in the realm of the Wesleyan's college at Leoni.

In April, the trustees at Leoni decided to move the college to Adrian, Michigan.[70] By June a full complement of faculty had been found. Reverend Asa Mahan, a close friend of Finney and co-laborer with him at Oberlin College, had been voted president of Adrian College. The names of Prindle and McEldowney graced the new catalogue as professors. Lee, in a somewhat different fashion, could appear better equipped, if the occasion should open to him again. It came as a total surprise, in the form of an official letter from Vermont.

Middlebury College came to birth as one of nineteen new colleges chartered in America between 1782 and 1802. While it did not begin as a religious institution, Middlebury's faculty and students were significantly impacted by the Second Great Awakening, shaping it into a religious bastion. Many of its students moved to the forefront of social reform in the Jacksonian era. It was entirely appropriate that such an institution recognize the arduous labors of Luther Lee. Always poor, Lee certainly never funded any endowments for the school; he did not graduate from there, had not visited Middlebury College, in fact, Lee had never even heard of the place! The trustees, however, in response to the recommendation of the Committee on Honorary Degrees, voted in their session of August 10, 1859, to honor Lee with the title Doctor of Divinity. He received official notice later that month in Felicity.[71] By September, for reasons unknown, Lee had concluded that it was time for him to move on. At the Miami Annual Conference, Lee was stationed at Chagrin Falls, Ohio.[72] Interestingly, a minister of the Methodist Protestant Church, a group with whom the Wesleyans had been considering a merger, went to Felicity. On September 11, Lee preached his last sermon there, and headed for Cuyahoga County, to a village "about eighteen miles east of Cleveland," a decidedly more "comfortable" territory for abolitionists.[73]

Chagrin Falls could be reached by means of a stage that ran morning and evening between Cleveland "on an excellent plank road all the way"— at least that was true in 1846.[74] The town nestled "in the midst of Yankeedom of Ohio, where Democratic slave hunting is unprofitable."[75] The Chagrin River divided the village into two parts. The clear water cascading over a large and a small falls within the town's border provided the townspeople with power to operate saw, flour, woolen, and paper mills. A foundry did a bustling business. In time the farmers from the surrounding territory made it their place of business. The Congregationalists in 1835 were the first to organize in the village. The Methodists followed in 1844, and soon thereafter came Wesleyan Methodists and the Free Will Baptists. Abby Kelley and Stephen S. Foster had delivered antislavery speeches in the Methodist meeting house, shortly after the defeat of Henry Clay and the election of James K. Polk in 1844.[76]

Lee's new assignment called for the minister to travel one hundred miles and preach at eleven different places within two weeks to cover the circuit. When Lee arrived in the village, the Wesleyans and an Independent Congregational group were worshipping together and jointly provided for the salary of the minister. The latter owned a large commodious building but had failed for several years to secure a pastor. At best they could only get "supply men" who never stayed for more than one year. The former owned only one half of a house for their meetings. The two congregations then made common cause for a period of time. Cyrus Prindle, editor of the church paper, visited them that fall, commenting favorably about Dr. Lee and the large congregation he had rallied for a weeknight meeting. Prindle sensed that good days were ahead for the church and the community. Just before the visit from the editor, however, an event of enormous consequences transpired far from Chagrin Falls, on the banks of two rivers, at the confluence of the Potomac and the Shenandoah Rivers. A former resident of the area just to the west of Lee's circuit struck a blow for freedom of the slaves.[77]

On October 16, 1859, John Brown conducted his infamous raid upon the federal arsenal at Harper's Ferry. Gathering a group of devoted followers in the previous winter, he had made plans without considering how to proceed after the initial seizure of the armory. Assuming that the slaves would dash to the Blue Ridge Mountains where he could arm them against their masters, old Brown never got out of Harper's Ferry. He and his twenty-two followers never stood a chance. Wounded in the charge against his men bottled up in the engine house by the United States Marines, he had no hope of escape.

Placed on trial for murder, inciting insurrection, and treason, Brown managed to use his defense speeches as a platform from which to position himself as a victim of slavocracy. Republican politicians such as Abraham Lincoln and William H. Seward attempted to distance themselves from Brown. Opponents of slavery, however, used the event to extol Brown. Henry Thoreau compared Brown to Christ, calling him an angel of light. Emerson claimed that Brown made the gallows as glorious as the Cross. Garrison, although a pacifist, wished success to every slave insurrection in the South. Douglass, who had consulted with Brown prior to the raid, supported such violence since a system of brute force had to be met with its own tactics. The act generally was interpreted by most antislavery people as heroic; something needed to galvanize the North and its politicians into action.

The shock waves rolled over the Western Reserve of Ohio. By the time Brown mounted the "glorious" gallows in Charlestown, having been found guilty of treason against Virginia, Lee had prepared to preach a funeral sermon in Brown's honor, just as he had done upon the deaths of Lovejoy and Torrey. Although Brown had once lived just beyond the horizon from Chagrin Falls in the village of Hudson and also in Franklin Mills (the modern town of Kent), Lee was not sermonizing about him as a local citizen, but as a national hero of the abolitionists. Nor was he merely following the prescribed course of action recommended by the American Anti-Slavery Society on November first that "impartial friends of freedom throughout the Free States . . . observe that tragical event."[78]

The time of the oration on Brown is not known. The location and its title are known because, as Lee frequently did after delivering what he considered to be a major address, he published it. He entitled it, "Dying to the Glory of God," delivered "in the Congregational Church at Chagrin Falls."[79] Lee took for his text John 21:18 and 19,

> Verily, verily, I say unto thee, when thou wast young, thou girdest thyself, and walkest whither thou wouldst: but when thou art old, thou shalt stretch forth thy hands, and another shall gird thee, and

carry thee whither thou wouldst not. This spake he, signifying by
what death he should glorify God.

The outline for his oration proved to be quite simple: (1) Peter
would die a violent death, and (2) Peter should honor God by the death
he should die. Employing his tools of logic, Lee deducted that "a man
may glorify God in death . . . [based upon] the life he has lived, the
cause and circumstances of his death, and the manner in which he
meets his fate."[80] He then flatly stated that Peter had so glorified God,
and so had John Brown. Conversely, the authorities of Virginia, men
who seemed to have such a penchant for honor, had dishonored
themselves.

Lee concluded a transition that began after Lovejoy's death at the
hands of the mob. At that time, Lee argued that the laws of the land
must be employed to deter those who would deny humans the right to
speak out against evil. On the occasion of Torrey's death, Lee demonstrated that civil laws that were morally wrong must necessarily be
broken in the cause of moral duty. Upon the death of Brown, he
advocated the use of force to accomplish moral duty. Even Garrison,
the peace advocate, would some day come to look upon violence with
less jaundiced views. Lee relied heavily upon the model of the American Revolution. When the patriots had no alternative, they resorted to
arms against tyranny. Lee made no attempt to extricate Brown from
being a felon against the laws of Virginia. He had lifted up the sword
against that Commonwealth, but all revolutionaries must so do. In a
moralistic tone, Lee asserted that Brown was a Christian, citing to his
satisfaction those aspects of Brown's life that qualified him as such. He
also, however, took words from a letter that Brown had written to his
wife, and one to a "Judge Tilden" of Cleveland, to further establish
what he claimed by "commending them to Christ."[81] He concluded his
peroration by declaring Brown a martyr, and in so being, his manner of
death "has condemned slavery and sealed its doom."[82] The sermon not
only demonstrates Lee's unwavering commitment to the destruction of
slavery, but it caught the attention of Brown supporters all over the
North. It would later earn for Lee a request from the widow of John
Brown that he deliver an oration in the following year at North Elba,
New York. That materialized in the following summer. Lee, after the

flush of excitement over the Brown affair, busied himself with his work in Chagrin Falls.

The circuit had once comprised eleven preaching points. By the time Lee arrived, however, the work at Russell had closed and several of the others had organized as separate groups or drifted off to other denominations. Lee alternated between two places on Sunday, Chagrin Falls and Solon. On occasion he exchanged pulpits with ministers in Cleveland. By February, the hopes that he initially had entertained for the town had dimmed. Commenting that "Chagrin Falls has more infidelity in it than any other place of its size we ever knew," he requested the prayers of *The Wesleyan*'s readership. One gets the distinct impression that Lee would soon be looking for other pastures—greener or not.[83] He also responded to calls to deliver antislavery speeches.

He received such a call from Reverend D. S. Kinney, a minister near South Windsor, twenty-five miles east of Chagrin Falls. Kinney asked Lee to preside at his quarterly conference and then to deliver antislavery speeches there, at Mesopotamia, and at Windsor. Lee had some misgivings due to the extremely muddy conditions; but he decided to proceed. The country between Chagrin Falls and his destination was "one unbroken wilderness of mud . . . the only variety there was in the prospect, the mud was deeper in some places than it was in others."[84] It was agreed that Kinney would bring his wife to visit Mary Lee, while Lee and he returned to the scheduled meetings, battling the mud together. The Kinneys set out for Chagrin Falls, but twelve miles from home, one of the horses gave out. They put up for the night with sympathetic strangers. The next day they secured another horse and arrived by that night. The travel back to South Windsor defies description. After the meeting there, Lee, driving the buggy with Kinney's sister riding also, had the hitch break loose from the buggy. The horses went on, the buggy rested solidly in mud up to the axles and Kinney "on the shore" helped the stranded riders to safety. They finished the tour with Lee lecturing at Green, Farmington, and Gustavus. The effort proved to be successful; Lee sighed in relief when he arrived safely home. By the time that the April showers had brought the May flowers, Lee had turned his attention to two orations that he was to give far from his home. The first would take him to Adrian, Michigan, where he was to speak at the laying of the cornerstone of the college chapel on June 12.

Lee must have had conflicting emotions as he rode across the southeastern portion of Michigan. He had departed the state three years previously as an ex-professor of Leoni Institute. In 1860 he was returning to celebrate the end of the first year of Adrian College, the successor of the former. The activities climaxing the academic year would run from June 7 to 12. He listened to President Asa Mahan speak of the aims of the college. Lee listened intently to the student orations. On the next to the last day, he went to the site where he was to speak. The foundation walls of the chapel had been laid to a height of three feet above the ground. In the selected corner rested the rectangle of Cleveland sandstone, inscribed with the year, 1860. Under it was a recess in which was to be placed a box containing a directory of the city of Adrian, three different daily newspapers, all bearing the date of June 11, 1860, a listing of all administrators and faculty, a plate of the college buildings, a copy of a scholarship certificate, a copy of the *New York Weekly Tribune* and *The Wesleyan,* a list of the officers of the State of Michigan, various papers of the college, and a "Likeness of Reverend Dr. Lee, the orator."[85] A stand had been prepared in a grove and the crowd moved to that location as Lee spoke. His oration clearly had his academic audience in mind. He urged the college to include a healthy balanced curriculum of secular as well as sacred studies. He spent a large portion of his time projecting the influence of graduates from such a college upon the nation. He closed by declaring the value of an education as "a fortune of which one cannot be robbed or deprived by any misfortune. . . . Abroad it is an introduction to the wise; an adornment to youth and manhood; 'and to age it is a crown of glory on the brow. O may it be ours.'"[86] That evening the guests crowded the local Odd Fellows Hall for the climax of the activities. To Lee the future appeared bright for Adrian College. His mind, however, was already on his next oration on Independence Day at North Elba, Essex County, New York. The focus of that speech had nothing to do with academia. The focus of that occasion would be upon the martyr of Harper's Ferry, the hero of every slave in the country.

John Brown was born in Torrington, Connecticut, in the same year as Luther Lee and Orange Scott. The family later moved to the

Western Reserve, finding a home in Hudson, Ohio. Brown tried a variety of vocations, and never succeeded at any of them. He had raised sheep in Hudson, had operated a wool cooperative in Springfield, Massachusetts (one in which not only the sheep, but the investors were shorn!), and even taught a small rural school for blacks near Meadville, Pennsylvania. In the late 1840s, he learned of Gerrit Smith's plan to assist blacks and freedmen. Being the largest landowner in New York, that reformer and Liberty Party man donated 100,000 acres for a new start in life for them. By 1846 Smith had made out two thousand deeds to forty-acre tracts of land for the lots. Most of the new residents had no knowledge of farming. Brown visited the area in 1848, and after consultation with Smith, he agreed to purchase 244 acres of land on which he would model for the others the best methods of farming.[87]

When guerrilla war broke out in Kansas, old Brown took his sons and headed out to strike a blow for the freedom of slaves, ultimately butchering six proslavery men in the middle of the night by way of avenging the sacking of Lawrence, Kansas. He hatched the plan to attack Harper's Ferry in conjunction with the "secret six" abolitionists who financed him. After the trial and hanging, Brown's body was taken to New York City where it was kept on ice, the rope removed, and a new walnut coffin selected. Then the cortege moved out toward his home at North Elba. Wendell Phillips delivered an oration at the burial. The next year the family sought to honor him on the day on which the nation proclaimed anew its freedom.[88]

A huge celebration was being planned by prominent abolitionists all over the North for the Fourth of July. It was to take place at the John Brown farm in the highlands of the Adirondack Mountains. Mary Brown, John's widow, had requested that Lee (who went by the name "Dr. Lee" after he received the honorary degree) give the oration of the day. The editor of *The Wesleyan* had placed an announcement concerning the affair, which was to include a dinner. He ended the piece by stating "that Luther Lee, D.D., has accepted the invitation of the committee, and is to be present to deliver an oration." Late in June, Lee departed for North Elba (the name of the town; Lake Placid is the village at the edge of the Brown farm), and traveled by railroad to the head of Lake Champlain. From there, he took a boat to Port Kent and completed the rest of his journey by stage. On the weekend before the gala event, he preached in the Wilmington Wesleyan Methodist church. On July 4, he arrived at the Brown farm where he was greeted by a throng of twelve hundred citizens who had come from far and wide. The farmhouse rests in the center of a large meadow; the graves of Brown and some of his sons are approximately one hundred feet beyond the residence. A huge boulder, standing five or six feet high and perhaps fifteen feet in diameter, overshadows the graves.[89]

The service began at ten o'clock. After an appropriate hymn by a selected choir, Lee was introduced as orator of the day. Reverend N. Wardner, a fellow Wesleyan who pastored at nearby Wilmington, presided. He declared the speaker to be "a man who believes in the Bible, and the Declaration of Independence; in Bunker Hill, and Harper's Ferry; in George Washington, and John Brown; the Reverend Luther Lee, DD., of Ohio."[90]

With that rousing introduction, Lee mounted the rock, and launched into a two-hour production that he later claimed was "the oration of my life, the most radical and, probably, the most able I ever delivered."[91] The speech was a logical *tour de force* in which the speaker restated the principles of the Declaration of Independence as a premise, and developed a logical deduction of those principles in relation to the crime of slavery. Points that he made include: all governments that suppress liberty have no moral force and thus no claim upon the people being tyrannized; slaves have the right to take their liberty "any way in which they can get it"; everything that impedes the slave from securing liberty is sinful, and anything that enables him to find freedom was morally right.

> . . . If money, a horse, or a boat, will enable a slave to secure his liberty, and he cannot secure it without, he has a right to take them, because his right to liberty is inalienable, and greater than another man's right to property, which is not inalienable, and the smaller right is lost in the greater, as rights cannot conflict. . . . I place on the ground of necessity, and the law of necessity knows no higher law; it is the law of nature, of which God is the author. . . . As liberty is before life in importance, and as our right to liberty is inalienable, we have a right to strike through and strike down whatever rises

between us and our liberty.[92]

Lee did not stop with granting to slaves the right to seize anything needed to flee slavery; he called for *vi et armies* and argued that "if it be right for a slave to escape from his bondage, it must be right, and a duty, to help him in his flight, as his necessity may demand."[93]

When Lee uttered such seemingly rash statements, he was treading the ground of many abolitionists. Lewis Perry argues that since abolitionists regarded slavery "as a violation of divine government. . . . As their radicalism increased, they tended to denounce human government."[94] Lee, as we know, did not denounce human government, but rather sought to harness government in the cause of social reform. Thus, he does not fit Perry's profile. Certainly the Garrison school of abolitionism conforms well to his anarchy theory *vis-à-vis* his burning the Constitution. What can be said about Lee's position at North Elba? He merely established a hierarchy of laws (and of governments) and indicated that some laws (and governments) have greater or lesser weight depending upon a given context. Here we speak of the nineteenth-century concept of the "moral government of God," a phenomenon that Lee chose to label the "higher law."[95]

He then moved prophetically to assert that "When the time shall come that the oppressed shall feel prepared to strike for freedom, it will be the right and duty of freeman to strike with and for them. If this is not true, why did our fathers invoke and receive the aid of France?"[96]

Lee spoke of an "irrepressible conflict" between liberty and slavery, arguing that the slaves must be made free, or free laboring men and women must be made slaves. In making such striking statements, he was reflecting the fears of the North that if the slave power were not stopped, slavery would be exported, not only into the territories, but ultimately into the North. Invoking the language of Patrick Henry, he likened the present situation of slavery to the plight of the patriots in 1776. Lee managed to remove any stigma that may have accrued to Brown in Kansas. Defending the butchery of the pro-slavery men, Lee affirmed that: "I have no doubt a development of all the facts would not only fully justify him, but place him on the roll of the most brave and noble of heroes."[97]

His summation is freighted with the language of rhetoric and logic: "Deny the *conclusions* I have *deduced.* . . . Deny these *conclusions.* . . . One blind dash of proslavery *logic.* . . . One other *conclusion* from the *premises* [emphasis mine]. . . . John Brown is dead, and his dust has found its place of calm and last repose beneath the shadow of this rock; but his work is not done." The final paragraph is classic nineteenth-century oratory:

> When that day shall come—when the Declaration of Independence shall become a practical reality in the nation;—yes, I must insist upon the Declaration, to maintain which my own father watched the campfires of the Revolution for seven years, and fought through many a battle where brave companions around him licked the dust;—when the Declaration of Independence shall be carried out in the land—when the bondman's chains shall be broken, and liberty shall be proclaimed through all the land, to all the inhabitants thereof,—then, if this mortal that stands before you shall still be above the sod, and this heart still beat and this head still think, then send for me again, and I will come and once more stand upon this rock; and then let freemen rally, and let the freed slave come and wave his unmanacled hands here, and we will raise one long loud hallelujah over the grave of Freedom's first martyr, and the nation shall respond in a loud Amen.[98]

After two hours of oratory, Lee descended from his stone rostrum. He later wrote that as he came down from the rock, he shook hands with each member of the Brown family. The second son exclaimed to Lee as Lee took his hand, "It electrifies my arm clear up to my shoulder and makes my heart jump to take hold of your hand."[99] John Brown, Jr., introduced as "the noble son of a noble sire," gave a speech followed by Owen Brown, and then several of the survivors of Harper's Ferry were introduced.[100] By three o'clock in the afternoon, the guest walked to a grove where a "20 rod-rod table" had been prepared for them. Lee received the thanks of Mary Brown and her brood, and wearily turned his steps toward Chagrin Falls.[101] His pastoral duties must be cared for since he had spent considerable time on the road that summer. Besides, the General Conference would take place in less than three months and Lee had been elected as a ministerial delegate from Allegheny Conference, in which Chagrin Falls was located.

The fifth quadrennial conference met in Fulton, New York, a place not unfamiliar to Lee, since he had pastored there for the Methodists and the Wesleyans. He found himself appointed as president *pro tem,* as he had on many other occasions. Matlack was soon elected president and Lee busied himself with committee work for the next seven days of business. Lee writes that it was "a quiet Conference, and but little transpired which can properly fill space in my personal history."[102] That, however, masks the severity of the debate that raged over the secret society question.

For hours the delegates fulminated against the Rule as it had been passed at Utica, in which the matter had been left to local churches and annual conferences. The 1844 rule, passed at Cleveland, had not satisfied everyone, especially the founders of the Wesleyan Methodists. So they tried again to find a satisfactory resolution. Reverend G. W. Bainum moved the adoption of a change which would read accordingly:

> Question. Have we any directions to give concerning Secret Societies?
>
> Answer. We will on no account tolerate our ministers in joining or holding fellowship with Secret Societies, such as Free Masonry or Odd Fellowship; as in the judgment of the Wesleyan Methodist Connection, it is inconsistent with our duties to God to hold such connection.[103]

The resolution was finally adopted by a vote of thirty-three to fifteen. The minority immediately sought to enter their solemn protest to the rule, claiming the new section to be unconstitutional since the Utica Convention did not empower subsequent General Conferences to change the General Rules without submitting such rules to the annual conferences for ratification. They argued that the Utica Convention had only given "advice" on the matter, thus it should not subsequently be made a test of membership. In 1852, the General Conference had footnoted the rule: "*This Section the General Conference ordains as law." That too had been officially protested as unconstitutional. In so doing, the minority argued, the Conference had admitted that no rule really existed. Interestingly, Lee did not sign the protest, nor, of course, had he voted for it.[104]

On that occasion Lee responded to a would-be dress reformer, an extremist on the subject of dress who had sought him out for an opinion on proper attire for Wesleyan Methodists. Lee had always held that specific rules on dress should not be incorporated in the *Discipline*. To write rules as to what a person ought to and ought not to wear would only invite problems. Lee argued, as had John Wesley, the founder of Methodism, that the best results within the membership of the church would be effected by simply insisting on plainness of dress, based upon Scriptural authority. To legislate "concerning the cut of coats and the number of buttons to be put upon them, or the size and shape of bonnets, and the length and breadth of ribbon with which they should be trimmed, could do no good." He continued, "I said it must be allowable to wear gold in some cases." After all, he reasoned, "The Church required a minister to put gold on the finger of a bride, and I could not see how it could be right for me to put gold on a lady's finger which it would be wrong for her to wear."[105] He stated that he did not wear gold-bowed glasses only because of his financial limitations. To his utter amazement, a group of friends had a small social affair, made a speech, and presented him with a pair of gold-bowed spectacles, which he gladly wore until they were no longer serviceable.

At that Conference, Lee received a unique appointment; he was elected "general missionary," in which capacity he would travel the entire connection as a lecturer, evangelist, church organizer, or whatever duty demanded. Thus, at the close of the session, he resigned from the church in Chagrin Falls, and relocated his family to Syracuse. At the age of sixty, he threw himself into the work with a vengeance; and also threw himself into a physical breakdown that forced his resignation from the post in April of 1861. He accepted the pastorate of a Wesleyan Methodist Church at Sprague's Corners on the border of the St. Lawrence and Jefferson Counties, not far from his old stomping grounds of thirty-five years earlier. The church only boasted thirty members, and only four of them were landowners. With the rise of the new year, the editor changed the name of the organization's paper to

The American Wesleyan, giving it a more cosmopolitan ethos. Lee responded by writing a lengthy poem to mark the occasion.[106]

As Lee took up his work at Sprague's Corners the nation was taking up arms to settle the slave issue once and for all. The abolitionists had done their work well, at least from their perspective. For Lee and his fellow abolitionists, the North had finally seen the slave power for what it was as the Confederate States seceded one by one. He demonstrates a remarkable understanding of political theory, and resorting to his customary logic, exposed the error of the Southerners:

> No State has or can have a legal right to secede or withdraw from the Union. The United States Government is not a Government of States, or by States, but a Government of the people; not the people of separate and individual States, as such, but of the whole people, of all the States. The constitution commences, "We the people". . . . The people are above States. This shows that no power can annul any part of the compact, less than the direct action of a majority of the whole people. . . . [concerning the war soon to be in progress] Government has no constitutional power to compromise the matter; no power to make peace with rebellious States, only on condition of their entire submission . . . this they must do, or it must be decided by the sword. . . . When the Government, sustained by the North, is conquered by the South; or the South is subdued, then and not till then can the war cease.[107]

His understanding of the national government, of course, reflects that of the organic concept of the Constitution as opposed to that of the compact theory of states rights as set forth by its chief proponent, John C. Calhoun. When it came to a grasp of constitutional issues and war aims, Lee evidenced more perception than many bellicose abolitionists.[108]

Lee continued to regain his strength while at the small pastorate. In January the congregation surprised him with a donation visit. "The gathering was in the church, and refreshments were provided as usual on such occasions." The members contributed $180.96 and a new buggy valued at $115. After the "repast" had been cleared away, the secretary called upon Lee for a speech. His heart welled up with joy at the kindness of the members and the community.[109] At the next Syracuse Conference, he was honored by his colleagues by being elected as Conference President.

During the war years Lee kept a series of articles running in *The American Wesleyan* entitled "Slavery and War." His incisive insights into the goals of the Union and the treatment of the freedmen reveal the thoughts of a man who does not equivocate. The war was a moral issue, and as such must be fought to a moral conclusion. Compromise with the South could not be considered. As he wrote his columns, he kept an eye on developments at Adrian College.

Significant advances had been made at Adrian. The local citizens stood solidly behind the enterprise, financing many of the capital improvements on the campus with trust funds and stocks. The college had reached a point at which it could offer the degree of Bachelor of Arts and Bachelor of Science, and felt significant enough to confer an honorary doctorate on Asa Mahan in the graduation exercise of 1862. The school had eight full-time professors, and 250 students, of which eighty-two were women.[110]

The college was placing a strong emphasis upon holiness. President Asa Mahan submitted articles pertaining to entire sanctification on a regular basis to the editor. He, of course, had linked up with Finney in espousing "Oberlin Perfectionism."[111] Finney, the "New School" Presbyterian, had been led into the experience by reading John Wesley's *Plain Account of Christian Perfection.* Finney preferred to call it "entire sanctification," and Mahan adopted the term "Christian perfection."[112] That theology of Wesley, minus the teaching of original sin, plus a major emphasis upon the will, constitutes the foundation of Finney's perfectionism. The Methodist-oriented professors at Adrian would be pure Wesleyan in their approach, not founding perfection in natural ability as Finney argued, but in the atonement of Christ. At any rate, holiness was the watchword at the college.[113]

In that same year Lee published his *Wesleyan Manual,* in which he discussed the causes of the secession in 1842 and focused on the church polity of the Wesleyan Methodists. He also continued to write upon war issues, as well as to turn his attention to what should be done with the slaves. Upon the issuance of the Emancipation Proclamation by Abraham Lincoln, Lee wrote an article, "Liberty Proclaimed," in which he stressed that the president had done more than Jehovah had done for Jews when he had "deliver[ed] the spoiled out of the hand of the oppressor."[114] Just as Lee was exalting in the freedom of slaves, at least those behind enemy lines, he began to see himself as free from the labors of public life. At the age of sixty-two it was time for him to build a home for his retirement years; he too sought freedom. But it was not to be. Late in the winter of 1864, Lee received letters from Prindle and others advising him not to accept another year in Sprague's Corners. A plan was afoot to endow a professorship for Lee at Adrian College. Thus, in the summer of that year, Lee found himself returning to Michigan. This time he would not be leaving.

NOTES

1. Carol M. Hunter, *To Set the Captives Free: Reverend Jermain Wesley Loguen and the Struggle for Freedom in Central New York, 1835-1872* (New York: Garland Publishing, Inc., 1993), 234, notes that there were twenty-four churches in Syracuse in 1851. Of those, only Luther Lee's Wesleyan church and Samuel J. May's Unitarian church did not practice racial segregation. She states that "Rev. Luther Lee, one of the original founders of the new denomination, was located in Syracuse during the formative years of 1843-1846," but fails to note that he returned to the city during 1852-55. Hunter erroneously states that "Rev. Hiram Mattison . . . the minister of the First Methodist Church in Syracuse from 1856-57, . . . carried on an acrimonious debate with the Wesleyan leader, Rev. Luther Lee on the divinity of Christ," 219. The debate to which she alludes was between Luther Lee and the Unitarian Samuel J. May. No Methodist preacher ever would question the divinity of Christ! She also fails to note that Lee had left the city one year prior to the "debate"; the New York State Temperance Convention was held in Syracuse on June 17, 1852. That occasion is noteworthy since Miss Antoinette Brown attempted to deliver an address but was shouted down. The rebuffed women were invited to use the facilities of Lee's church, which they did, with great appreciation to Lee, *True Wesleyan,* July 3, 1852.

2. Syracuse *Standard,* May 8, 1852.

3. *True Wesleyan,* June 12, 1852.

4. *Lily,* July, 1852; Nancy A. Hardesty, *Women Called to Witness: Evangelical Feminism in the 19th Century* (Nashville, Tenn: Abingdon Press, 1984). 142-43.

5. "The City of Conventions," *True Wesleyan,* October 9, 1852.

6. "Rev. Jotham Horton's Reasons," *True Wesleyan,* July 5, 1851. As an

editor's comment, Lee faulted Horton for assuming that the bishops were any less arbitrary than they had been.

7. Syracuse *Standard,* December 22, 1852.

8. Elizabeth Cazden, *Antoinette Brown Blackwell: A Biography* (Old Westbury, N.Y.: The Feminist Press, 1983), 41-42, 52.

9. Many editors did not approve of her, and were not hesitant to say as much, e.g., the Syracuse *Standard,* April 4, 1853, wherein is asked, "We would like to know what . . . Brown would make of the Apostolic injunctions, that women should not be suffered to teach, and that they should keep silence in the Church!! . . . If some Samaritans took the trouble to give the loquacious Antoinette a jolly good ducking . . . it might improve both her manners and her morals," and, ". . . Brown says that if Providence had given her an 'invalid husband and half a dozen children, her salary as a clergyman is amply sufficient to pass them comfortably through life.'" See Nancy A. Hewitt, "Feminist Friends: Agrarian Quakers and the Emergence of Woman's Rights in America," *Feminist Studies* 12 (Spring 1986): 27-49, for a balanced overview of the roots of feminism; Hardesty, *Women Called to Witness,* 16-19, 97-103, 122-163; cf., Blanche Glassman Hersh, "'Am I Not a Woman and a Sister?': Abolitionist Beginnings of Nineteenth-Century Feminism," in Lewis Perry and Michael Fellman, eds., *Antislavery Reconsidered: New Perspectives on the Abolitionists* (Baton Rouge: Louisiana State University Press, 1979), 252-83, for an overview of how women, in an age of Jacksonian optimism and social change, were challenged by their attempts to free themselves, as well as the slaves, from the slavery of womanhood. The arguments that they propounded to justify their entry into abolitionism became the basis of feminist ideology; Blanche Glassman Hersh, *The Slavery of Sex: Feminists-Abolitionists in America* (Urbana: University of Illinois Press, 1978).

10. Cazden, *Antoinette Brown Blackwell,* 74-78.

11. "The Liberty Party," *Wesleyan,* February 24, 1853; "The Women and Temperance," *Wesleyan,* April 28, 1853, in which is the account of Brown and Susan B. Anthony addressing a temperance rally in the Syracuse City Hall. Brown erroneously stated that there was no organization of churches that made total abstinence a test of membership. She betrays her ignorance concerning the Wesleyan Methodists who had done that very thing. In her speech she argued for state legislation, modeled on the Maine Law. In June, the State Senate passed such a bill by a vote of seventeen to thirteen, *Wesleyan,* June 23, 1853. Lee added an article "The Maine Law Right," to lend his support to the legislation that he had suggested as early as May 1841 in his Lowell speech; *Wesleyan,* July 14, 1853; cf., "Temperance Triumph in Leoni," *Wesleyan,* December 8, 1853, for the account of Michigan's passage of a Maine Law.

12. See "A Grave Question," *Wesleyan,* November 30, 1849, in which the writer argues that the *Discipline* states, "Let each leader carefully inquire how every soul in *his* [emphasis mine] class prosper. . . . All the leaders should be . . . *men* [emphasis mine] truly devoted to God." The writer failed to see

room for woman class leaders in such language; cf., Curtis D. Johnson, *Islands of Holiness: Rural Religion in Upstate New York, 1790-1860* (Ithaca, N.Y., and London: Cornell University Press, 1989), 168-69, in which he argues that women took the lead in revivals and formed the strength of the congregation in many churches in central New York. As women were displaced by men in the 1850s, evangelistic success declined drastically.

13. Luther Lee, *Woman's Right to Preach the Gospel, A Sermon Preached at the Ordination of the Rev. Miss Antoinette L. Brown, at South Butler, Wayne County, N.Y., Sept. 15, 1853* (Syracuse, N.Y.: By the Author, 1853; repr., Donald W. Dayton, *Five Sermons and a Tract by Luther Lee*. Chicago: Holrad House, 1975), 79-100.

14. Letter of Luther Lee to Antoinette Brown Blackwell, April 30, 1855, Blackwell Family Papers (used by permission of John Blackwell); cf., David W. Odell-Scott, *A Post-Patriarchal Christology* (Atlanta, Ga.: Scholars Press, 1991), and David W. Odell-Scott, "Women Speaking in Corinth," *Biblical Literacy Today,* (Spring 1989): 14-15, for a novel approach to the issue in which he understands that Paul is not forbidding women to speak, but is merely reflecting back to the Corinthians, an earlier question. He is not agreeing with the idea of barring women from speaking in public; newspapers for miles around carried articles on the affair; cf., Syracuse *Standard,* September 22, 1853; *New York Daily Tribune,* September 19, 1853; cf., Lucile Sider Dayton and Donald W. Dayton, "Your Daughters Shall Prophesy: Feminism in the Holiness Movement," *Methodist History* 14 (October 1975): 67-93, for an excellent overview of the development of the use of women within the holiness churches; Rosemary Radford Ruether and Rosemary Skinner Keller, *Women and Religion in America,* Vol. 1: The Nineteenth Century (San Francisco: Harper & Row, 1981), 194-99, 214-17. Their work, in addition to presenting the nineteenth-century arguments for women preachers, describes the *Woman's Bible,* a work accomplished in 1898 under the leadership of Elizabeth Cady Stanton, in which a committee revised all biblical texts that refer to women or exclude them; Hardesty, *Women Called to Witness,* 97-98, has written an excellent overview of the ordination of Brown, however, on page 16, she has made a serious error in stating that "in 1844 . . . resulted in Orange Scott's formation of the Free Methodist Church, and then the holiness controversy in 1860 which spawned B. T. Roberts, and Luther Lee's Wesleyan Methodist Connection. . . ." The Free Methodist church did have its beginning in 1860; however, Luther Lee had nothing to do with it! Furthermore, Orange Scott certainly did not form a Free Methodist church in 1860, since he had died in 1847!

15. The one exception, of course, that is found in the literary sources is the citation above at the Boston Convention May 28, 1840.

16. L. C. Matlack, ed. *Discussion of the Doctrine of the Trinity, between Luther Lee, Wesleyan Minister, and Samuel J. May, Unitarian Minister.* (Syracuse, N.Y.: Wesleyan Book Room, 1854.)

17. Luther Lee, *Autobiography of the Rev. Luther Lee, D.D.* (New York:

Phillips & Hunt; Cincinnati: Walden & Stowe, 1882), 285.

18. *Autobiography*; cf., D. Ray Heisey and Paul L. Kaufman, "Luther Lee: 19th Century Evangelical Debater and Reformer," an unpublished essay presented to the Religious Speech Communication Association Convention, November 1994, in New Orleans.

19. *Autobiography*, 287.

20. Matlack, *Discussion of the Doctrine of the Trinity*, 34.

21. Matlack, *Discussion of the Doctrine*, 40.

22. Matlack, *Discussion of the Doctrine*, 41.

23. Matlack, *Discussion of the Doctrine*, 149.

24. Matlack, *Discussion of the Doctrine*, 150.

25. Matlack, *Discussion of the Doctrine*, 43.

26. Matlack, *Discussion of the Doctrine*, 44.

27. Matlack, *Discussion of the Doctrine*, 45.

28. Matlack, *Discussion of the Doctrine*, 45.

29. Matlack, *Discussion of the Doctrine*, 153.

30. Matlack, *Discussion of the Doctrine*, 47.

31. Matlack, *Discussion of the Doctrine*, 59.

32. Matlack, *Discussion of the Doctrine*, 66.

33. *Autobiography*, 288-89.

34. *Christian Advocate*, December 19, 1889.

35. E.g., "Song of the Shirt," March 4, 1844; the formation of the Women's Sewing Association by thirty widows in Rochester to "protect themselves from the rapacity of employers," April 6, 1844; the Needle Women of London, mostly "females of tender years who were exploited in the labors in sweat shops," August 10, 1844; statistics on female operatives in Lowell, reporting 6,320 of them, 2,714 connected with Sunday schools, either as teachers or scholars, 2,272 church members, their earnings range from 75 cents to $4.85 per week, and they have on deposit $1,000,000 in the Savings Bank at Lowell; "Capmakers Wanted on Trial," in which girls make dozens of caps to secure a job, only to have fault found with each item—more exploitation, April 11, 1846; "Wrongs of American Women," April 11, 1846; "Female Labor," November 11, 1848; "Doctor arrested in Boston for murder of a young woman for producing abortion, a midwife to be tried on three similar charges (also Boston)," January 4, 1845; "Divorce," September 6, 1845.

36. Lee and May conjoined their efforts to organize female laborers in Syracuse in 1854.

37. Syracuse *Daily Standard*, April 8, 1854.

38. Syracuse *Daily Standard*, April 8, 1854.

39. Syracuse *Daily Standard*, April 27, 1854.

40. Syracuse *Daily Standard*, January 11, 1854.

41. *Wesleyan*, July 20, 1854, carries the full text of the speech.

42. See *Autobiography*, 332-33, for Lee's account of the Jerry Rescue.

43. See *Wesleyan*, October 12, 1854, for the complete text of Lee's oration.

44. *Autobiography*, 333-35.

45. *Autobiography*, 335-36.

46. *Autobiography*.

47. "Farewell to Mr. Lee," *Wesleyan,* May 23, 1855.

48. "Farewell to Mr. May," *Wesleyan*, May 30, 1855.

49. *Wesleyan*, April 25, 1855.

50. Luther Lee, *Elements of Theology or An Exposition of the Divine Origin, Doctrine, Morals and Institutions of Christianity* (Syracuse, N.Y.: S. Lee, 1856; 12th ed, Syracuse, N.Y.: A. W. Hall, 1899); the Syracuse *Standard* of February 1, 1856, cited the work, stating that "Reverend Luther Lee, formerly of this city. . . [has completed an] elaborate work on theology. . . [that] embraces the field of morals, doctrines and ordinances, and is in the hands of printers," cf., *Wesleyan,* January 30, 1855.

51. Luther Lee, *Slavery Examined in the Light of the Bible,* (Syracuse, N.Y.: Wesleyan Methodist Book Room, 1855); cf., *Wesleyan,* August 15, 1855, for the preface and a review of the work. The volume contains Lee's most definitive analysis of slavery. Motivated by the doctine of the moral government of God, and rooted squarely in Scripture, Lee presents an exposition of virtually every biblical reference to human bondage, man stealing, and trafficking in humans. The Bible opposed every form of oppression. This *tour de force* insisted that since Deuteronomy 33: 15-16 commanded, "Thou shalt not deliver unto his master the servant which is escaped from his master unto thee: He shall dwell with thee, even among you, in that place which he shall choose . . . thou shalt not oppress him." That called for every Christian to get involved in the business of assisting the slave to freedom, from aiding in the underground railroad to military and political action. See William C. Kostlevy, "Luther Lee and Methodist Abolitionism," *Methodist History* 20 (January 1982): 90-103, for an excellent overview of Lee's use of the moral government of God in attacking slavery.

52. Luther Lee, ed., *The Evangelical Pulpit,* 3 vols. (Syracuse, N.Y.: Lee & Masters, 1854, 1856, 1864).

53. John W. Blassingame, *The Frederick Douglass Papers, Series One: Speeches, Debates, and Interviews,* Vol. 3: 1855-63, (New Haven, Conn.: Yale University Press, 1985), 107. The text of Douglass's speech appears in the New York *Daily Tribune,* September 14, 1855; *Autobiography,* 290-91; *True Wesleyan,* January 1, 1845, cites a book, Luther Lee, *Wesleyan Review,* no copies of which are known to exist.

54. See "Leoni Institute," *True Wesleyan,* January 12, 1850; Margaret Burnham Macmillan, *The Methodist Church in Michigan: The Nineteenth Century* (Grand Rapids, Mich.: Michigan Area Methodist Historical Society and William B. Eerdmans Publishing Company, 1967), 156-57; cf., *True Wesleyan,* September 21, 1850, wherein the editor had projected 100 students for that fall enrollment; "Michigan Wesleyan University," *True Wesleyan,* October 4, 1851; *True Wesleyan,* March 20, 1852.

55. "Leoni Theological Institute and Michigan Union College," *Wes-*

leyan, August 22, 1855; ibid., April 30, 1856, lists Lee's mailing address as Leoni, Jackson County, Michigan.

56. L. C. Matlack, *The Anti-Slavery Struggle and Triumph in the Methodist Episcopal Church* (New York: Phillips & Hunt, 1881; repr., New York: Negro University Press, 1969), 355; *Autobiography,* 290-92.

57. "Our Home in Michigan," *Wesleyan,* January 28, 1857.

58. "The Schools at Leoni, Michigan," *Wesleyan,* July 2, 1856.

59. *Wesleyan,* July 30, 1856.

60. "President Lee," *Wesleyan,* June 24, 1857.

61. *Autobiography,* 292-94; cf., *Wesleyan,* September 16, and October 21, 1857 for the financial situation at Leoni. Leoni did continue to operate; the 1857-58 academic year had 163 students enrolled. Interestingly, the college catalogue issued in the spring of 1858 still listed Lee as professor of Natural Theology and Moral Philosophy. The April 15, 1859 issue reports the purchase of acreage in Adrian for a new college.

62. "At Home in Felicity," *Wesleyan,* September 30, 1857.

63. *Wesleyan,* September 22, 1853.

64. See the *True Wesleyan,* June 14, 1845 for the account of the formation of the Wesleyan Methodist congregation in Williamsburg, twenty-three miles north of Felicity; *True Wesleyan,* January 26, 1850 indicates that the Felicity congregation began under like circumstances; cf., *True Wesleyan,* January 26, 1850, and April 12, 1851. Lee wrote, "The Worship of God," *Wesleyan,* November 11, 1857; "Felicity and Its Surroundings," *Wesleyan,* July 7, 1858.

65. "Dedication in Felicity," *Wesleyan,* December 9, 1857; "Meeting at Felicity," *Wesleyan,* March 10, 1858; "Withdrawal from the Wesleyan Church," *Wesleyan,* June 23, 1858.

66. "The Glorious 4th in Felicity," *Wesleyan,* July 21, 1858.

67. *Wesleyan.*

68. *Wesleyan.*

69. "The Miami Conference," *Wesleyan,* September 22, 1858.

70. In December of 1859, the first term of the college began with approximately fifty students, *Wesleyan,* February 1, 1860. The spring of 1860, enrollment reached eighty-two, *Wesleyan,* April 25, 1860.

71. "Minutes of the meetings of the President and Fellows of Middlebury College, August 10, 1859"; "Fifty-Ninth Anniversary of Middlebury College, Commencement August 9, 10 and 11, 1859"; Dune L. Robinson, compiler, *General Catalogue of Middlebury College* (Middlebury, Vt.: Publications Department, 1950), 1035; David M. Stameshkin, *The Town's College: Middlebury College, 1800-1915* (Middlebury, Vt.: Middlebury College Press, n.d.), 1-5; *Autobiography,* 294; *Wesleyan,* September 7, 1859; cf., "D.D.'s," *True Wesleyan,* September 27, 1845, for Lee's opinion on the distribution of cheap honorary doctorates; cf., "Doctorate of Divinity," *True Wesleyan,* March 16, 1850, where Lee claims that honorary doctorates commenced being used in the mid-twelfth century with Peter Lombard being the first recipient.

72. *Wesleyan,* October 12, 1859. His successor at Felicity wrote to the editor in February reporting a glorious revival in which thirty had joined the church. They had been holding meetings day and night for over a month, *Wesleyan,* February 22, 1860.

73. "At Home Once More," *Wesleyan,* November 2, 1859.

74. *True Wesleyan,* March 14, 1846.; cf., *Wesleyan,* August 18, 1853, for the notice that Allegheny Annual Conference was to meet in Chagrin Falls.

75. *Wesleyan,* August 18, 1853.

76. C. T. Blakeslee, *History of Chagrin Falls and Vicinity* (Chagrin Falls, Ohio: By the author, 1874; repr. Friends of Chagrin Falls Library, 1969), 36-43; "A History of the Federated Church United Church of Christ, 1835-1985," unpublished manuscript by the church.

77. *Wesleyan,* November 23, 1859; February 15, 1860.

78. *Wesleyan,* November 9, 1859.

79. Luther Lee, D.D., *Dying to the Glory of God. A Sermon Preached on the Occasion of the Execution of Capt. John Brown, In the Congregational Church, Chagrin Falls, Ohio* (Syracuse: Samuel Lee, 1860; repr., Donald W. Dayton, *Five Sermons and a Tract by Luther Lee* (Chicago: Holrad House, 1975), 103; cf., *Wesleyan,* January 18, 1860, for the announcement that Lee's sermon on Brown had been published and was then available to the public for nine cents each or one dollar per dozen.

80. Lee, *Dying to the Glory of God,* 103.

81. Lee, *Dying to the Glory of God,* 112-15.

82. Lee, *Dying to the Glory of God,* 118.

83. "Chagrin Falls," *Wesleyan,* February 15, 1860.

84. "A Short Excursion," *Wesleyan,* March 21, 1860.

85. "First Annual Commencement of Adrian College," *Wesleyan,* June 27, 1860.

86. *Wesleyan.*

87. Edwin N. Cotter Jr., "John Brown in the Adirondacks," 9 (Summer 1972): 9-12; *Autobiography,* 295; Letter of Boyd B. Suttler to Edwin N. Cotter Jr., November 20, 1967; Edwin N. Cotter Jr., "John Brown at North Elba," unpublished essay by the Superintendent of the John Brown Farm and Grave, n.d.; Lee made the same incorrect assumption as many others have—that Smith donated land to Brown. The fact is that Brown paid $244 for the land, or one dollar per acre.

88. See Paul Wallace Gates, *Fifty Million Acres: Conflicts over Kansas Land Policy, 1854-1890* (Ithaca, N.Y.: Cornell University Press, 1954), 72-76, for a revisionist view of Brown's activities in Kansas. Since the federal government had permitted squatters to settle as pre-emptors on *unsurveyed* land, many fights broke out when surveyors later adjusted the pre-emption claims to the new boundaries. Old Brown might just as likely been killing men over disputed land claims as much as for them being pro-slavery settlers.

89. "North Elba Fourth of July," *Wesleyan,* June 27, 1860.

90. "North Elba Fourth of July," *Wesleyan,* June 27, 1860.

91. *Autobiography,* 295.

92. "Fourth of July Oration, Delivered from the Rock above the Grave of Capt. John Brown, at North Elba, N.Y., by the Rev. Luther Lee, of Chagrin Falls, Cuyahoga Co., Ohio," *Liberator,* August 3, 1860. The writer is greatly indebted to Mr. Edwin N. Cotter Jr., Superintendent of the John Brown Farm and Grave, for assisting me in locating the oration. Professor Donald W. Dayton, of North Park Theological Seminary in Chicago has collected all of the important speeches and sermons of Lee. In his volume *Five Sermons and a Tract by Luther Lee,* concerning the oration at Brown's grave, Dayton states, "Unfortunately this speech has not survived. Lee loaned the manuscript to a reporter and never saw it again," p. 19. Lee also states that in the *Autobiography,* 295. After exhaustive searches of my own, I found Ed Cotter to be of assistance. He recalled in his files a piece of correspondence from Boyd B. Stutler of Charlestown, W.V., to himself, dated November 20, 1967. It was he who had found the oration in the *Liberator.* Garrison had heard of the celebration and had secured the services of a reporter from Vermont to be there as Garrison's reporter. Doubtless, it was that reporter who asked for the manuscript and forwarded it to Garrison. The fact that Lee in 1881 still had no knowledge of its whereabouts provides a clue as to how much of an avid reader of *Liberator* he actually was!

93. *Liberator,* August 3, 1860.

94. Lewis Perry, *Radical Abolitionism: Anarchy and the Government of God in Antislavery Thought* (Ithaca, N.Y.: Cornell University Press, 1973), 33.

95. See William C. Kostlevy, "Luther Lee and Methodist Abolitionism," *Methodist History,* 20 (April 1982): 90-103, for an extended discussion of the "moral government of God" theology of the period.

96. *Liberator,* August 3, 1860.

97. *Liberator,* August 3, 1860.

98. *Liberator,* August 3, 1860.

99. *Autobiography,* 295.

100. Bartly Coppic, a Quaker lad from Salem, Ohio, had remained on the north bank of the Potomac on the night of the raid. His brother Edwin, was less fortunate, having been captured and eventually hanged, despite intervention by his Uncle John Butler, a pious Quaker from Damascus, Ohio, who made a trip to Richmond to intercede with the state legislature and Governor Wise, on behalf of his nephew. Bartly had only recently returned from Canada, where he had fled from Virginians seeking him. He arrived at North Elba ill, and did not speak.

101. "North Elba Fourth of July," *Wesleyan,* June 27, 1860; "North Elba," *Wesleyan,* July 25, 1860; "Fourth of July Celebration at John Brown's Tomb," *Wesleyan,* August 15, 1860.

102. *Autobiography,* 296.

103. *Wesleyan,* November 7, 1860.

104. *Wesleyan,* August 15, 1860; cf., "The Union Question," *American*

Wesleyan, April 4, 1866, for a full history of the issue by Lee.

105. *Autobiography,* 296.

106. "The American Wesleyan to Its Patrons," *American Wesleyan,* January 2, April 17, 1861; *Autobiography,* 296; an announcement appeared in the paper which stated that he would live in Sommerville only a mile away from the church in Sprague's Corners, as he was "recovering from his long and painful illness"; *American Wesleyan,* April 24, 1861.

107. "The Pro-Slavery War," *American Wesleyan,* June 5, 1861.

108. See William W. Freehling, *Prelude to Civil War: The Nullification Controversy in South Carolina, 1816-1836* (New York: Harper & Row, 1965), 159-73, and Charles S. Sydnor, *The Development of Southern Sectionalism, 1819-1848* (Baton Rouge: Louisiana State University Press, 1948), 197-201, 279, for a helpful discussion of Calhoun's concurrent majority and compact theory and how these contrast with the organic interpretations of antistates rights theorists.

109. *American Wesleyan,* January 5, 1862.

110. "Adrian College Commencement," *American Wesleyan,* July 2, 1862.

111. Mahan was a Presbyterian also, having served the Sixth Street Presbyterian Church in Cincinnati. He was also a member of the board of trustees during the Lane Revolt. By 1835 he was president of Oberlin College, a post he held until 1850. An aborted attempt to start Cleveland University at the present site of University Heights left him out of academia. He pastored a Congregational Church in Jackson, Michigan, near Leoni, and then at the Plymouth Church in Adrian.

112. See "The Holiness Revival at Oberlin," in Timothy L. Smith, *Revivalism and Social Reform in Mid-Nineteenth-Century America* (Nashville, Tenn.: Abingdon, 1957), 103-13, for a fuller account of holiness of the period.

113. "A Letter from Asa Mahan," *American Wesleyan,* September 24, 1862; "Have Ye Received the Holy Ghost Since Ye Believed?" *American Wesleyan,* November 26, and December 24, 1862.

114. "Liberty Proclaimed," *American Wesleyan,* December 24, 1862.

Chapter Eight

1860-1889: Return to the Methodist Episcopal Church

As the nation approached mid-century, a marked shift in the mainline denominations was discernible. Nathan Hatch also observes this new emphasis in a section of his *The Democratization of American Christianity,* which he labeled, "The Lure of Respectability." The quest for respectability among the Methodists, the Baptists, and the Disciples of Christ called for a more educated ministry and less emotional religious services than the first generation membership of these groups had known. Those who opposed such measures lamented the drift toward decorum and education, and identified the cause as "a Yankee triumph." The new emphasis produced over thirty colleges for the Methodists and twenty colleges for the Baptists in the three decades prior to the Civil War.[1] The same trend away from his frontier circuit riding days to a more settled ministry can be traced in the life of Dr. Luther Lee as he passed middle age. That shift in Lee manifested itself in the epochal step that he took when he abandoned the Wesleyan Methodists and returned to an even more modernizing Methodist Episcopal church.

At the age of sixty-four Lee took up his new assignment at the thriving Adrian College with a new spring in his aging heels. As professor of theology, he took charge of the department, organizing a sequence of course such as was typical for the day. He also taught homiletics and natural theology (philosophy), and on occasion offered courses in mental and moral science (psychology and ethics). The student enrollment continued to increase steadily. Some events on the national scene were shaping the destiny of the Wesleyan Methodists in general and Adrian College in particular. As the Methodist Episcopal church and other mainline denominations became abolitionized by the Civil War, the appeal of the Wesleyans and their antislavery church waned in a marked fashion. That had a major impact upon membership in the churches. Many smaller congregations began to dry up. One after another, churches went out of existence as members drifted away to larger churches.

The shift had enormous effects on Adrian College. But another process had been placed in motion by farseeing administrators of the college. The Wesleyan Methodists were not unaware that an earlier secession had taken place from the Methodist Episcopal church as early as 1830. Rejecting the arbitrary bishops, the new group called itself the Methodist Protestants. It had, however, retained the position of the old Methodist Episcopal church on the issue of slavery. By the mid-1860s some discussions transpired between men from both denominations to explore the possibility of merging. What made the concept particularly attractive to both parties was the college. The Methodist Protestants had none, but they had fifty thousand dollars toward one. The Wesleyans had a college and a mountainous debt to go with it. Thus the discussions took place.[2]

In February of 1865, Cyrus Prindle, then the Publishing Agent, met with George Brown and A. H. Bassett, two Methodist Protestant ministers in Springfield, Ohio. They agreed to initiate a process that would lead to a convention in Cleveland that would be open to all non-episcopal Methodists, hoping to lure any maverick followers of Wesley into a new denomination. The session would meet in June of 1865. At that point, the group of delegates in session was analogous to the ones who attended the Utica Convention in 1843. No one had elected them; they represented no official governing bodies from their respective denominations. Officers elected included: Reverend John Stott, a Methodist Protestant, president; and John McEldowney, a Wesleyan, secretary. Matlack presented a paper in which he spoke favorably for the formation of such a church. The delegates adjourned, agreeing to call for another convention in Cincinnati in May 1866, to determine how to effect the union.[3]

The problem with all of these decisions stemmed from the fact that there existed no official sanction by the denominations for them. Only the Michigan Conference had appointed delegates to attend. None of the other conferences had acted. It became clear that the majority of the Wesleyans would oppose such a move. Actually it was the faculty at Adrian that pressed the issue. The money and possible students were too appealing to be passed over.

The Non-Episcopal Methodist Convention met in Cincinnati on May 9-16, 1866, hopefully to climax the "Union Movement." Luther Lee attended along with Prindle and McEldowney and others for the Wesleyan camp. Reverend S. Baker, a Wesleyan from New York, was elected president. Lee was the second out of twenty-four placed on the Committee on Basis of Union. They chose the name "Methodist" over "United Methodist" by a vote of 107-24. But there were other problems in addition to a name for the new denomination.

The matter of Secret Societies refused to go away. G. W. Bainum, the one who had sponsored the resolution to prohibit Masons and Odd Fellows from joining the Wesleyan Methodists, was on the same committee with Lee.[4] The delegates declined to make that a test of membership in the new denomination. The constitution had passed the committees; it would take one more meeting, a General Conference in May 1867 (analogous to the one in 1844 at Cleveland by the Wesleyan Methodists), to officially organize. There was to be one delegate for every thousand church members being organized at that convention. Free Methodists, Primitive Methodists, and any others were invited to participate.

On June 6, 1866, Lee wrote to the *Western Methodist Protestant* a letter in which he spoke positively of the proposed merger. In the letter he added that "the sequel of the Wesleyan disaffection toward the Union shall be considered later."[5] In the next month, Lee met in Springfield, Ohio, with Dr. John Scott and others to effect a *Discipline*. As things were rapidly moving toward a culmination, Lee and several other of his erstwhile colleagues were getting cold feet. By the time the General Conference of the Methodist Church was to meet in Cleveland, Lee had changed his mind. Lee, then president of the board of trustees of Adrian College, could see that the finances had reached a crisis. Unless something was done, the college would default and be lost to its creditors. To that end, representatives met earlier at Egypt,

Michigan in February 1866. Thus, while negotiations were taking place to merge denominations, a meeting to discuss merging Adrian College took place.[6]

Lee, who had been at the Egypt Convention, wrote a strong article to protest the charges in print that the college had been given away or the Wesleyans betrayed. He asserted that financial help had not been forthcoming from the Wesleyans, therefore something must be done. He asserted (1) that he favored union, (2) he predicted that union would eventually take place, and (3) when it did, membership in secret societies would not be a test of membership.[7]

Eventually the trustees opted to merge the college with the Methodist Protestants, despite the outcome of the Cleveland Convention. The Wesleyans had received numerous entreaties for financial help—all to little avail. Just when it appeared that the merger would work and the college could be saved by joining efforts with the Methodist Protestants, a "plot was developed by a selfish Methodist Protestant connected with the college to secure control, and make himself president by slander and falsehood directed against my friends."[8]

Lee, then sixty-six, had wearied of turmoil. The fight had gone out of him. He announced to his friends that he was contemplating rejoining the Methodist Episcopal church. Early in 1867, Lee, Prindle, and Matlack invited all persons interested in returning to the Methodist Episcopal church to a meeting in Adrian, Michigan. By the middle of February, they had published a lengthy article under the title, "A Calm Appeal to the Ministry and Laity of the Wesleyan Methodist Connection of America." In it they reviewed the origins and the present state of the Connection. In summation they intoned: "We have now reached the conclusion of the whole matter . . . that our work as a separate body is finished . . . that our continued existence is neither practicable, nor desirable, nor justifiable."[9] With the advent of the Civil War and the subsequent emancipation of southern slaves, the Wesleyan founders saw no purpose in remaining a separate body. The fact that they continued to advocate the deletion of rules on Masonry could only have propelled them toward the old church. Lee soon made it official.

On April 10, 1867, Lee submitted a valedictory to his friends in an article, "Last Words." In it he recapped his career as a Wesleyan. He then reported on Adrian College by simply stating, "Adrian College is now in the possession of the Methodist Church, that is the late Methodist Protestant Church. . . . For it I am not responsible, nor are the other late Wesleyan members of the Board of Trustees." He then wrote for two columns on the mechanics of how the other group gained control of the college. After twenty-five years as editor or a contributing editor, Lee was writing his last column.[10] At least he thought he was. In the July 3rd issue, he wrote two columns in defense of former President McEldowney against false charges. He signed off by regretting the publication of matters of a personal nature; however, duty demanded that he correct an error with truth.[11] The Wesleyans continued to use Lee's books, and to advertise them, and new editions of them whenever available. Lee remained at Adrian College through the academic year. By late spring, having set his things in order, he resigned from the faculty and requested membership in the Detroit Conference of the old church from which he had seceded twenty-five years earlier.[12]

Lee did not proceed to full membership until the Detroit Conference convened in the fall. In the interim he supplied the Methodist Episcopal church at Port Huron throughout the summer. In September, he traveled to Saginaw City for the annual conference session. He was introduced to the body along with six others who were applying for readmission by the presiding elder of the Adrian District. Out of the six, Dr. Lee was noted by name. In a moving speech the presiding elder described Lee as a zealous man who did what he had to in order to live with his conscience. Of Lee he declared,

> He left honestly. He had fought the battle bravely, ever being found in the thickest of the fight. He has fought until he has heard the shout of victory, and now that the battle is over, he returns to seek a home in the Church of his early choice.
>
> To be sure, he returns not as he left, in the full vigor of early manhood, but he comes bearing the impress of years, and with whitened locks, which have been bleached upon the moral battlefields which he has so nobly contested; but he is yet strong and brave, and ready for service. . . .[13]

Lee then made appropriate remarks so freighted with emotion that most of the house wept as he spoke. He ended his words and then offered his hand to the bishop, asking, "Will you take my hand, in behalf of these my brethren."[14] At the conclusion of the session Lee was assigned to the Court Street Methodist Episcopal church in Flint, one of the largest in the conference.

After two productive years there, he went to the Ypsilanti Church in 1869-70, and then to Northville for the 1870-71 year. His labors in the latter two churches were singularly devoid of anything particularly outstanding. There is evidence, however, of Lee's activities at Northville outside the church.

A notice appeared in a Northville newspaper in November 1870, in which Lee appeared as one of eight members on the committee of examination for the Northville Union School. The next month contained an account of a surprise party for him. Under the title, "Reverend Luther Lee, D.D.," the reporter wrote of a celebration of Lee's seventieth birthday. Lee provided them with a brief sketch of his life which appeared in the paper in a subsequent issue. In the month of December, the Masonic fraternity held a public installation of officers in their hall over W. P. Hungerford's store. Over 160 people turned out for the festivities, most of them women. When the master of ceremonies called the group into session, Lee "invoked the Divine blessing."[15]

Upon the completion of his one year of service at Northville, Lee was superannuated at the annual conference of 1871. His health had been poor during recent months. The Lees continued to live in Northville. In July, Lee officiated at the wedding of his granddaughter.[16] When the *Northville Record* began publication, Lee wrote a poem of dedication, "A Sonnet to Northville Record," in which he personified the paper and urged it ever to be mindful of the poor, the weak, and the cause of temperance.[17]

Not completely unmindful of Lee, the bishop requested that he preach a semi-centennial sermon at the next session at East Saginaw in 1872. Lee responded with alacrity. During the sermon he spoke of his years of fighting for the slaves. He mentioned that he had been mobbed five times for his efforts and had one suit of clothes destroyed—for which he had never been repaid. No sooner did his sermon end, than one of the clergy leaped to his feet and moved that Dr. Lee be paid for the suit. An offering was speedily taken, and Lee left with fifty dollars more than he came with. At the close of the session the bishop urged pastors to use Lee for special services or pulpit supply. The editor of the *Michigan Christian Advocate* repeated the same, challenging the ministers to call Lee, seeing he had something worthwhile to say and could use the finances. He chided them gently:

> If the Doctor should come before your people and throw you a little into the shade by his superior ability, as you are comparatively young, you will have time to recover from it. As the brethren have been a little dilatory in regard to their resolution the forepart of last year [passed at the 1872 Conference], let the invitations now pour in upon the Doctor thick and fast.
>
> O. Whitmore[18]

Unfortunately, requests arrived neither thick nor fast.

Lee agreed to supply the Milford Church for the 1872-73 year. On November 30, his birthday, he took violently ill with typhoid fever. He indicated that he was at the point of death, "I listened for the sound of the coming boatman's oar, but it pleased God that I should recover."[19] With renewed health, he appeared at the annual conference seeking to help out. He received the Petersburgh Church for the 1874-75 year. On February 18, 1874, the church honored him with a party in which he received a donation from his friends amounting to over one hundred dollars. That summer Lee did not forget the ladies. On June 26, 1874, he appeared in Detroit at a convention of the friends of woman suffrage. The gathering took place at the Detroit Theater. Lee gave a characteristic "lengthy speech" in which he asserted the same sentiments concerning women's rights as he had decades earlier.[20]

On July 31, 1875, Luther and Mary Lee celebrated their golden wedding anniversary. Lee was not prone to complain about his lot in life, but he was forced to admit to his poor finances. He felt that by standing by his convictions, he had sacrificed financial security for a clear conscience: "I really believe I might have secured wealth had I devoted myself to it as ardently as I did to what I believed to be truth and righteousness." He continued, "This course which I believed it my duty to pursue would bring me neither popularity, wealth, nor many friends; and so I have lived and come down to old age without them." His battles with local preachers, stewards, class-leaders, and church members had not been without a price since "it sometimes made my loaf of bread smaller than it would otherwise have been. . . . This warfare, waged for conscience' sake, secured for me more poverty than money, and more enemies than friends." Lest he appeared to be whining, he asserted:

> I have preserved my integrity, and come out of life's struggle an honest man, having never sold myself for place or pelf. . . . I claim nothing for myself more than the honor of having lived an honest man. . . . It is better to die in a poor-house, true and honest, than to die surrounded by friends and luxuries purchased at the expense of integrity.[21]

Recognizing that he had been among his colleagues for only eight years, he had little reason to expect much help from them. On that occasion, however, an offering of $450 was received for the Lees. The paper stated that the indebtedness on Dr. Lee's property had been reported at about $350.[22] After Lee left the area, its citizens did not forget him. Five years later an announcement stated: "The venerable Dr. Luther Lee, residing at Flint, was tendered a donation by his friends in that city, receiving about $170." His many friends in Milford did not forget him on this occasion. Lee was returned to superannuated status in 1875. That move had nothing to do with his pastoral abilities; in that year he had missed preaching on only two Sundays when he visited his eldest son who lay dying in Syracuse.[23]

In 1878 Lee finished writing his autobiography.[24] In it he exhibited a memory that was remarkable. Consistently, in any item in the manuscript in which he cited a date, name, or event, when it can be validated by other sources, Lee proved to be accurate. In that year T. J. Joslin reported that "Rev. Dr. Lee, of this conference has a manuscript autobiography, and the conference requested that he publish the same." The enterprise did not advance beyond that point until the conference of 1881 when the minutes stated that a committee took "into considera- tion the expediency and feasibility of publishing the autobiography of

Dr. Luther Lee." Later in the session, "J. M. Arnold was allowed opportunity to secure promises from the Conference for the sale of the autobiography of Dr. Luther Lee." In that year the story of Lee's life finally reached the publisher and the public.[25]

By 1878 Lee and his wife moved back to Flint.[26] He did not officially hold any offices in the large Methodist Episcopal church that he had pastored ten years previously. In the winter his article on the influence people have on one another appeared in the *Northern Christian Advocate*. He assisted the pastor by preaching on occasion, and sometimes he conducted the funeral of older parishioners who had known him as their pastor. In June the conference organ printed Lee's article, "Excellencies and Defects of Modern Sunday-school Teachings and Methods." Lee manifested his continued interest in religious instruction for children and adults, alluding to his first efforts of 1826 in which he had to answer charges for his conduct before the presiding elder. In a December article, "Infidelity Poorly Disguised," he manifested a strong reaction to German higher criticism. A friend had given Lee a recent volume entitled *The Religion of Israel,* which alleged that the Old Testament was essentially the work of later redactors and editors. Lee refused to subscribe to any biblical interpretations that were not orthodox.[27]

The Court Street Church initiated an unofficial practice concerning Dr. Lee. Every year on the Sunday before his birthday, November 30, he preached the Sunday morning sermon. He usually managed to incorporate incidents from his many years as a social reformer. The church always took up a donation for him and his wife. The Detroit Conference did the same. Almost every annual conference journal during the years of his retirement contains the record of a love offering that was taken for him from among the delegates. He proved to be consistent in his attendance at annual conference. The record indicates that he missed roll call only two times in all his years in that conference—no small accomplishment for one who had retired from conference service. In the spring of 1880, Lee published an article against the practice of Catholic confession to earthly priests. He made his point in the form of a conversation between a Catholic woman and an evangelical Christian who showed the errors of auricular confessions.[28]

The pace he set for himself would challenge a man half his age. In

June of 1880, Lee missed the annual conference for one of the few times in his life. He did not absent himself out of dereliction of duty; he did have a satisfactory reason for being elsewhere. From early June until the end of July he traveled seven hundred miles from his home to Lake Superior where he "preached and lectured through the copper region for two months, speaking from four to six times a week, and all this without a traveling companion."[29] In 1883 Lee attended the annual conference that met in Flint. At that time he was given $200 from the conference aid fund.

The Court Street Methodist Episcopal Church published a weekly paper entitled *The Recorder*. This little periodical provides many details of the final years of Lee's life. The paper carried the announcement that the last Sunday of November had been designated Historical Day. On November 30, 1884, that very day fell on Lee's birthday. He had completed his eighty-fourth year of life. He preached the morning sermon to a full sanctuary. The presentation told his life story "in well composed verse."[30] Following that the pastor received an honorarium of forty-two dollars.

By the following March Lee's wife had become quite feeble. The Lees' daughter, Mary Lee Benson, cared for her in the house that the Lees and their daughter shared. In the meanwhile, the finances of the family continued to be a drain upon them. The two Methodist Episcopal churches, Court Street and Garland, regularly took offerings for them. In an April donation party an offering of $327 from local and distant friends helped considerably. Mary Lee, however, was losing her struggle for life, and on June 16 at the age of eighty-three she passed away. The Lees had braved the hardships of life together for sixty years. Her funeral was conducted at their home on West Court Street. Dr. Lee could not afford to pay for the funeral or purchase a burial lot for her. Neighbors and "friends" helped to cover the burial expenses and the Detroit Conference paid for a section of plots in Glenwood Cemetery that would accommodate the body of Mrs. Lee and twenty-five other indigent elderly preachers who were unable to purchase them. Curiously, the local Masons had no part in rendering assistance, but perhaps it was because Lee had not kept an active affiliation with them.[31]

Lee, sorrowing over his beloved Mary, probably could comfort others in bereavement with even more sympathy than before his recent loss. The very next month after burying her, in the absence of the pastor, he conducted the funeral of a member of the Court Street Church. In August the *Northern Christian Advocate* printed an article by Lee, "There is Salvation in no Other Way." The contents reveal that Lee had not deviated a bit from his understanding of the gospel message since his earliest days of preaching in the 1820s. At the annual conference that year, due to the full house, ". . . many of the venerable fathers, among whom were . . . Luther Lee . . . sat within the altar."[32]

Back home in the Court Street Church he continued to assist in dispensing the elements of communion at the church, as he had done since his retirement. The church paper listed him among the ill during the fall months, but by the end of November he was ready to preach his annual birthday sermon. By the following summer, Lee appeared to have preached a Sunday evening sermon, and assisting in the "love feast." In September of 1887, his indomitable courage and strength motivated him to visit his daughter Loretta in Elkhorn, Wisconsin. He had not seen her for sixteen years and knowing his life was winding down, he made the trip. By April the Court Street Church remembered his finances and honored him with a donation party that produced $415 to "the worthy veteran and that paid his current debts and promises to keep him in comfort for the year."[33]

In 1889, Lee's last year to live, the church paper reminded the congregation that Lee would be preaching his customary birthday sermon on November 30. It continued, "His mind is clear, his faculties strong, his voice vigorous and ringing, and while rather feeble in body he walks a mile or two almost every day and is regular in attendance at church." He preached that sermon as though he sensed it to be his last. His text, "The time of my departure is at hand," later appeared particularly appropriate, and somewhat prophetic, for the occasion. He closed the sermon by quoting the lines:

> My latest Sun is sinking fast,
> My race is nearly run;
> My strongest trials now are past,
> My triumph is begun.
> Oh come angel bands,

Come and bear me away on your snowy wings
To my immortal home.[34]

Lee walked home and then back to church that evening. He went to town and back each of the next three days, again on foot. Those were the last good days for him, however. On December 13, 1889, he passed away quietly in his home at the age of eighty-nine.[35]

Judging by the size of his funeral, Dr. Lee had many friends. Two newspapers competed in Flint at that time; both of them claimed that no occasion had ever surpassed Lee's funeral in the Court Street Methodist Episcopal Church. That event was the largest the city ever had witnessed until then. Nine hundred persons attended the services. Ministers from most of the Methodist Episcopal churches in the District and surrounding counties packed the platform. Bishop Bowman traveled by train from St. Louis to deliver the funeral sermon. One obituary stated that he had joined the Masonic lodge at the age of twenty-one. Accordingly, members of the Flint and Genesee Lodges, Free and Accepted Masons, numbering almost one hundred, assembled at the Masonic Temple. From there they proceeded to the Lee home from which they conveyed his remains to the church. The middle row of pews had been reserved for them. Following the funeral service, the Masons performed their rites, after which pallbearers from the local lodges conveyed the body to the cemetery. They also participated in the committal at the Glenwood Cemetery where Lee was buried beside his wife.[36]

NOTES

1. Nathan O. Hatch, *The Democratization of American Christianity* (New Haven, Conn.: Yale University Press, 1989), 201-205.

2. "Thoughts on the Proposed Union," *American Wesleyan,* March 11, 1866; "The Convention in Egypt," *American Wesleyan*, March 21, 1866; "Union Among Methodists," *American Wesleyan,* March 14, 1866.

3. Ira Ford McLeister, *History of the Wesleyan Methodist Church of America,* revised edition by Roy Stephen Nicholson (Marion, Ind.: Wesley Press, 1959), 80-83.

4. See "The Union Question," *American Wesleyan,* May 9, 1866,

wherein Lee states his most mature judgment on the Masonic issue. He writes that "I, and many with me, believe that a Mason or an Odd Fellow may be a Christian and, of course, I am conscience bound to receive them into the Church, as well as in the fellowship of my own spirit; so far as my influence can go towards bringing them into the Church. To obey my conscience, in such a case, is to violate the rule; to obey the rule, is to violate my conscience. . . . It never has been and never can be proved that to belong to a Secret Society is, *ipso facto* a transgression of any one command of the gospel."

5. Edward J. Drinkhouse, *History of Methodist Reform in the Methodist Protestant Church*, 2 vols. (Baltimore, Md.: Board of Publication of the Methodist Protestant Church, 1899), 2: 474-76.

6. "The Convention at Egypt," *American Wesleyan*, January 31, 1866; "The Convention at Egypt," *American Wesleyan*, March 28, 1866.

7. "The Union Question," *American Wesleyan*, March 21, 1866.

8. Luther Lee, *Autobiography of the Rev. Luther Lee, D.D.* (New York: Phillips & Hunt; Cincinnati: Walden & Stowe, 1882), 301.

9. *American Wesleyan*, February 13, 1867.

10. "Last Words," *American Wesleyan*, April 10, 1867; McLeister erroneously writes that Lee and the others returned "in the fall of 1866," *Wesleyan Methodist History*, 86. He correctly added that "Luther Lee by his writings, debates, and lectures did more than any other man the Church in its early life to set up the ideal of the independence of the local church," 88.

11. "The Assault on President McEldowney," *American Wesleyan*, July 3, 1867.

12. *Autobiography*, 301-304.

13. *Autobiography*, 305-306.

14. *Autobiography*.

15. *Northville Record*, November 12, December 3, 24, 1870.

16. *Northville Record*, July 20, 1872.

17. *Northville Record*, February 3, 1872.

18. *Michigan Christian Advocate*, n.d.; *Autobiography*, 311-12.

19. *Autobiography*, 312.

20. *Northville Record*, February 28, June 20, 1874.

21. *Autobiography*, 342.

22. *Northville Record*, July 31, 1875.

23. *Milford Times*, March 22, 1879.

24. *Autobiography*.

25. *Minutes of the Detroit Annual Conference of the Methodist Episcopal Church* (Detroit, Mich.: John F. Eby, 1881), 19, 22.

26. He lived in a modest home on the corner of Court Street and Stockton, about five blocks west of the town square; H. G. Osborne, *Flint City & Genesee County Directory, 1881-82* (Flint, Mich.: W. I. Beardsley's Steam and Job Printing, 1881), 64.

27. "The Influence We Exert," *Northern Christian Advocate*, February 22, 1878; *Michigan Christian Advocate*, June 28, 1879; "Infidelity Poorly

Disguised," *Michigan Christian Advocate,* December 14, 1878.

28. "Priest Fraud Defeated," *Michigan Christian Advocate,* March 20, 1880.

29. *Autobiography,* 342-43.

30. *Recorder,* December, 1884.

31. *Recorder,* July, 1885.

32. *Minutes of the Detroit Annual Conference of the Methodist Episcopal Church* (Detroit, Mich.: John F. Eby, 1885), 18; *Northern Christian Advocate,* August 20, 1885.

33. *Recorder,* August, 1885-April 1888.

34. *Recorder,* December, 1889.

35. One week prior to his death, *Michigan Christian Advocate,* December 7, 1889, printed an article by Lee entitled, "Our Wonderful Nation History," in which he outlined salient points of American history from the perspective of one who viewed God's hand in all the major events.

36. *Flint Daily News,* December 13, and 16, 1889; *Wolverine Citizen,* December 21, 1889; *Christian Advocate,* December 19, 1889; *Michigan Christian Advocate,* December 21, 1889; *Recorder,* December, January, 1889; a search of the courthouse indicated that Lee died without a will, probably due to the fact that he had nothing of value to leave. He shared the house on Court Street with his daughter, Mary Benson, but it appears to have been in her possession at the time of his death. No death certificate could be located.

Chapter Nine

Conclusion

Thus ended the closing scene of the venerable Lee's life. Unfortunately, it was in a paradoxical fashion. Great luminaries of the Church such as Luther, Calvin, Edwards, and Whitefield are frequently viewed as being controversial. Lee must share in that dubious distinction. He had been the president of the General Conference of the Wesleyan Methodist Connection for twelve years, an organization that early on had moved to outlaw membership in secret societies. Curiously, the death of Lee revealed a major aberration of his life: a lifelong affiliation with the Masonic lodge. It is appropriate to observe with another historian: "In a sense, this last unpleasantness was fitting: for one who had made controversy a foundation of his career, a little controversy at the end represented the perfect capstone."[1]

The greatest paradox of Luther Lee proved to be his ambivalence on the issue of the Masonic lodge. A diligent search of lodge records in many of the towns and cities where he lived produced no evidence that he continued an active affiliation with the Masons. In most cases, the earliest records have been discarded, lost, or destroyed. Research in many of the places in which he resided reveals no evidence that he attended one lodge meeting. The only evidence to the contrary occurred when he lived at Northville, Michigan. In his seventies he was invited to deliver an invocation at a public gathering of the local Masons. The event cannot be classified as a regular secret meeting of the lodge. Women made up the largest part of the crowd. It is reasonable to assume that Lee invested that public occasion with no more importance than if he had given an invocation at a Fourth of July celebration. Since he appeared to be quite civic-minded in his declining years, he probably received such invitations on a regular basis for

221

any and all types of civic functions. Some will argue that his action renders tacit approval to Masonry by so doing. Lee cannot defend himself, so that matter must rest in obscurity.

The question invariably surfaces: Why did he, along with Scott, Sunderland, and others, join the Masons? In light of the fact that antimasonry so thoroughly had swept the Northeast and the burned-over district, it seemed so out of character for these otherwise upright men. Finney had long since left the lodge along with thousands of others. The answer appears to lie in the social networking that such membership opened for them. In the East, away from the tenant-owner controversy of New York, the social class lines were less sharply drawn. It is clear that the farther into the frontier one went, the more the elites were marked men.

Finney and his Presbyterian colleagues were in a less structured ecclesiastical setting because their church polity lacked the hierarchy and power flow from the top down, as with the Methodists. They answered more directly to their congregations, whereas the Methodists answered to the bishops. Futhermore, Methodist preachers knew they would move every two years whether their congregation liked them or not. Because Presbyterian preachers did not move, they were more likely to respond to antimasonic impulses within their congregation than would the Methodists. While they constituted a large percent of Mason preachers, they were the first to leave, and did so in large numbers.

Dorothy Lipson's findings that lodges waived membership fees for clergy explains how poorly paid clerics could enter the fellowship of the lodges. That made it easier and more respectable for Methodist ministers to join. In 1821 when Lee joined the Masons, he was probably as poor as any man in all the state! An even stronger lure to the lodge, however, than these issues must be explored.

Masonic lodges offered temporal benefits beyond the social. Not only did the members enjoy social connections between towns and cities through the lodge membership, it provided them with a communications network that otherwise would be unavailable to them. Added to that were other more tangible benefits. Low income ministers such as Scott and Lee, if they joined, were eligible to receive weekly medical payments; their wives and children could expect widows and orphans assistance in the event the breadwinner passed away. The Oneida Lodge in Utica presents an example. Under the Section on "Contributions and Benefits" is outlined the following:

> Every *bonafide* member . . . shall, in case of sickness or disability, be entitled to and receive such weekly benefit as may be fixed by law, from the funds of the lodge.
>
> In the case of the death of a Brother . . . there shall be allowed from the Lodge, a sum not less than thirty dollars, to defray the expense of burial, which shall be paid over without delay, to the deceased Brother's nearest of kin.
>
> On the demise of the wife of a Brother, qualified as provided by Clause 2, he shall be entitled to a sum not less than fifteen dollars, for the purpose of assisting in the funeral expenses.[2]

To a relatively low salaried preacher, such benefits must have appeared significant.

At the Utica convention Lee and Scott were not ready for the strong attack of Smith and his western delegates. It was not that significant to them, but I suspect that Lee did not intend that they should push him and his eastern delegates out of something he viewed as harmless. Clearly the New Englanders did not agree with all the charges that Finney and others had made against Masons. Thus, whenever debate arose, he always argued from the General Rules formulated at Utica as the original test of membership. To tamper with those meant to ostracize the Wesleyans and hamper the recruitment of new members. To a church builder such as Lee, that was a critical issue. When the Union issue materialized, he could see that to insist on the rule in the face of a proposed merge with an organization that had no such rules would be fatal.

That brings us to the Masonic rights at his funeral. Here we have little information with which to proceed. One could assume that Lee maintained fellowship with the Masons and the Odd Fellows in Flint until his death. To do so requires us to call Lee a liar. He had affirmed as late as 1864 that he knew of no one who *affiliated* with secret societies. The funeral benefits described above were not paid to Lee. If they had been, the conference would not have paid for Mrs. Lee's burial and grave. It is reasonable to assume that he was not entitled to such payments. That could only result from his not being a member; otherwise the lodge made payments for members who were unable to pay dues. There is no solid reason to disbelieve him, based on the evidence examined. One cannot blame the lodges of Flint for wanting to link their organization as closely as possible to a man who could draw nine hundred citizens to his funeral. What organization would not? Were those elaborate plans made with Lee's consent? No doubt his daughter Mary, with whom he lived, agreed to the funeral service. Perhaps she held different views of the lodge than her father. Possibly her husband was a Mason and he influenced her to involve the lodges in the funeral. We will never know. The rabbis cautioned the living not to speak evil of the dead. Charity directs us to believe that Lee ended his days the way he had lived and believed, as a man that someday would give an accounting in a higher court to a "higher law." To level the charge of duplicity or deception against an otherwise devout minister is to speculate and indict without recourse to all the facts.

Historians seek to identify and explain continuity and change within the social, religious, economic, and political sphere of life. To be sure, these are intricately interwoven and are not easily identified or separated. The student of Jacksonian America can identify a number of strands in the *persona* of Lee. Each of these, taken by itself, would not yield a satisfying profile of someone unique. Any number of antebellum reformers can illustrate the typical abolitionist, temperance reformer, woman's rights advocate, or any other discrete movement. When, however, all the anomalies, apparent contradictions, and uniqueness of Lee are integrated, a gestalt figure emerges that is enormously more complex than the components.

Nathan Hatch and Richard Hofstadter have persuasively argued that society of the Jacksonian era was steeped in anti-intellectualism. It had grown weary of a deferential, hierarchical structure of society. No longer would the commoners defer to their "betters" in society, religion, and politics. The nonintellectual laity of the churches active in the Second Great Awakening refused to look to a highly educated ministry as earlier. Such leadership smacked of privilege and elitism, and in the day of the common man, the common man would have none of it. Nourished in the roots of the impoverished and insignificant classes, Luther Lee never strayed from his identity with them. From that foundation he developed an egalitarian mentality that defined the church polity he shaped. In his antipathy to arbitrary, domineering, gag-wielding bishops, he merely reflected the ethos of the commoners of the day. Class and elitism defined episcopalian polity. Lee and his class-hating parishioners could never abide such an organization. Thus Wesleyan Methodism incorporated a republican polity that never permitted the levers of government to be located far from the hands of the laity.

Lee's humble origins and total lack of formal training or a classical education placed him in the center of the hearts of his congregations. But therein lies an anomaly. Harnessing a solid intellect with a rigorous self-discipline, Lee, after barely passing his deacon's examination, mastered the mind of representative Wesleyan theologians, along with the methodology of classical rhetoric and logic, and combined them into a potent debating machine—a polemicist that routed his most experienced and Harvard-trained opponents. Beyond that he published a definitive systematic theology text that went through twelve editions. In grounding himself so thoroughly in Christian orthodoxy, he, unlike many of his peers and colleagues in reform, did not veer off into unorthodox sects. Theodore Dwight Weld, Elizur Wright, Antoinette Brown Blackwell, La Roy Sunderland, Angelina Grimké, George Storrs, James G. Birney, Elizabeth Cady Stanton, and Lucretia Mott are but a partial listing of those who ended their careers in Adventism, Mesmerism, Spiritualism, Unitarianism, and even atheism. Lee appears to have nurtured and guarded his pristine faith to his last sermon when in his ninetieth year.

While Lee does not inform us of his politics prior to the Liberty Party, it is reasonable to assume that he and his fellow reformers voted the Whig ticket. The vast majority of frontier Methodists were Democrats (e.g., Peter Cartwright versus Abraham Lincoln in the Illinois state house election of 1846), but that model did not hold true in the cities of New York and New England. When Lee set about to improve the country, he certainly practiced the Whig philosophy of social reform, one that mandated that the politicians get involved in social reform. Moral suasion did not suffice. Whereas Jacksonian Democrats feared government intermeddling in social issues (and played upon those fears in campaign rhetoric), Whig politicians sought to employ the engine of government to accomplish their reforms. In their vote-getting efforts, they appealed to the voters' hopes. That Whig concept was manifested in Lee's temperance speech to the citizens of Lowell. He strongly advocated the right and need for government to control the liquor traffic of the city, state, and nation. Any Democrats, if present, would have replied that government has no business in such matters.

Our examination of Lee yields a challenge to two models of abolitionists. The historiography manifests a wide range of interpretations of the people who participated. The Garrison school frequently gets juxtaposed with the Finney-Weld school. Lee in his earliest days of abolitionism in New York appears to fit the model of Gilbert Barnes who saw the antislavery impetus as a western phenomenon that originated with Theodore D. Weld. That posits a western model.

On the other side of the issue, James Ford Rhodes viewed the storm center of abolitionism in Garrison and his eastern followers. In that model the center is Boston, not the burned-over district and the West. The problem for us is that Lee fits that profile, also. Once he linked up with Orange Scott at the Albany Convention, he increasingly was drawn into the orbit of Garrison. That also can be said of James G. Birney. Won over from colonization and gradualism to immediatism by Weld, Birney ended up on the executive committee of Garrison's American Anti-Slavery Society with Lee. Barnes and Rhodes failed to identify the overlap between the two sections. Actually in the middle 1830s, a degree of unity developed—only to fall apart on issues of no-human government, the feminist issue, "come-outerism sects," and entering the arena of politics.

Lee's seeming indifference to the plight of the slave after 1860 parallels the career of many abolitionists. James M. McPherson traces the various responses of antislavery people after the war began. Most antislavery people did not heartily embrace the conservative stance of the Republican Party, but joined nevertheless, realizing that the party embodied the best hopes of the North for ending slavery. Some Liberty Party adherents refused to align themselves with either the Free Soil or Republican parties, declaring that the platform of both organizations had yielded too many abolitionist principles in an effort to appeal to a greater number of voters. In 1860 they organized as the Radical Abolitionist party under the leadership of Gerrit Smith, William Goodell, and Frederick Douglass. Many took the position that once the shooting actually commenced, the freedom of the slave was assured. It only remained for the military and the politicians to finalize matters. Luther Lee best fits the latter group. While he continued to write antislavery articles for the Wesleyans paper, for the most part his time was consumed by the events at Adrian College.[3]

As one interested in taking reformism into the political arena, Lee was quite consistent. Once committed to that course, he steadfastly adhered to it throughout the years that he edited the *True Wesleyan*. On occasion, his Wesleyan brethren faulted him for such doctrinaire doggedness, but his refusal to give up his insistence on harnessing government to fight slavery never wavered. It almost cost him his editorship in 1848, but wiser heads prevailed. Lee continued to push the Liberty Party and its ideals until the war.

Once war broke out, Lee revealed amazing insight into the theory of the formation of the federal government. He understood that the aims of the war could be achieved only with the destruction of one of the two governments. His understanding of the organic theory of the Constitution, that America was a government of the people, enabled him to see that compromising with the Confederacy, as McClelland and some Peace Democrats were urging in 1864, was theoretically impossible. The concurrent majority or compact theories of Calhoun found no place in the political philosophy of Lee.

In Lee's fundamental principles of antislavery and how best to end human bondage, one can identify three discernable steps that led to his mature position. He first awakened to the reality of human bondage with the death of Elijah Lovejoy. At that point he concerned himself with the right guaranteed in the Bill of Rights for citizens to speak out on any issue. In so arguing, he *affirmed* government. His next step was taken when he preached the sermon commemorating the death of Charles T. Torrey. At that time he moved to the position that there existed a "higher law" that transcended human law in such cases as Torrey's. In so doing he did not nullify human law per se. He merely affirmed that for some situations, God's moral law overruled in the affairs of men. Here the law was *transcended*. In his sermon at Chagrin

Falls, Lee reinforced that concept of civil disobedience. While no evidence indicates that Lee disobeyed civil law, he certainly approved when Torrey and Brown ignored civil statutes that protected the institution of slavery.

The final step in Lee's shift appears in his lengthy oration at North Elba. Then Lee did not stop at giving permission to break the law if an occasion so required; he insisted that in moral causes it *must* be broken. If a slave needed a horse to flee from bondage, he is free to steal one. (That would be the second step applied). If, however, it comes to one's knowledge that a bondman is attempting to flee, a citizen is bound to do anything to assist him—legally or illegally. Here the law is *shattered.* With Lee's metamorphosis from the affirmation of law, to permission to violate the law, and then to the necessity of breaking the law by resorting to force, he arrived at a revolutionary, radical stage in his abolitionist thought.

As an advocate of women's rights, Lee evidenced a solid commitment to reform. He did not simply stand on the sidelines and mouth pious platitudes, he entered the fray regardless of deleterious results to himself. When all the Presbyterians and Congregationalists refused to preach the ordination sermon for Antoinette Brown, Lee hurled aside reputation and charged to the rescue of the female cause. At the time of the ordination Lee discussed the need for proper certification. The following year Brown wrote Lee to secure proper credentials and Lee demurred stating that he had merely preached the sermon and not performed the ordination.[4] Lee never indicated why he deemed it improper to provide such a certificate. It is understandable that since Lee was not a Congregational minister, such official acts should properly come from a cleric of Brown's own church. The incident in no way detracts from the constancy of his lifetime of commitment to women's rights.

Lee had lived all his life in the North. His formative years took place in a society that never quite saw that "We the people" included blacks. While various states were passing antiblack laws and voting down referenda that aimed at extending the franchise to blacks, Lee steadfastly argued that they, along with women, were entitled, not only to their freedom, but to the right to vote. One cannot uncover a trace of racism in any of Lee's statements, written or spoken, public or private.

Where then does Lee fit in the context of his day? To place him at the highest echelon of the ranks of the abolitionists would only be suggested by a filiopietistic student of Lee. Without appearing overly ambitious, we can safely assign him status alongside of Amos Phelps, Charles Turner Torrey, Orange Scott, Charles B. Storrs, Alvin Stewart, and William Goodell. These were men who comprised a second layer or tier of individuals in the ranks of abolitionism. Lee clearly epitomizes a Methodist preacher with roots in the burned-over district of New York. In that Western context he mirrors the abolitionist profile of Barnes who argued for the importance of the homeland of Finney's earliest revivals as the seedbed of abolitionism. Lee's move into New England in 1839 brought him into the orbit of Methodists who had been enrolled abolitionists by Garrison's influence. That move placed Lee in a curious West-East blend that neither Rhodes nor Barnes attempted to separate in their writings. A premier debater who willingly confronted the unorthodox preachers, Lee built a reputation that none has bested. A consistent supporter of perfecting society through the use of evangelization and politics, he never wavered in his commitment to the reforms of the Jacksonian era. The Wesleyan Methodist Church that he molded and fashioned reflected the republicanism that characterized antebellum thinking. His theology remained true to that of Methodism's founder, John Wesley. His story, complete with all its anomalies, contradictions, and paradoxes, provides students of the Early National period of America's story with a fresh example of the "new man, the American."

NOTES

1. Cf., Harry S. Stout, *The Divine Dramatist: George Whitefield and the Rise of Modern Evangelicalism* (Grand Rapids, Mich.: William B. Eerdmans Publishing Co., 1991), 280, on the dispute concerning the burial of Whitefield.

2. *Constitution and By-Laws of Oneida Lodge, No. LXX, I.O.O.F.,* Chartered May 21, 1842 (Utica, N.Y.: Grosh & Walker, 1842), 10-11.

3. James M. McPherson, *The Struggle for Equality: Abolitionists and the Negro in the Civil War and Reconstruction* (Princeton, N.J.: Princeton Uni-

versity Press, 1964), 4-6, 295-301.

4. Luther Lee to Antoinette Brown, April 30, 1855.

Bibliography

PRIMARY SOURCES

MANUSCRIPT COLLECTIONS

Boston Public Library
      William Lloyd Garrison Papers
      Weston Family Papers
      Amos Phelps Papers
      Orange Scott Papers
      Abolition Papers

Boston University School of Theology
      New England Methodist Historical Society Papers
      Luther Lee Papers

Drew University
      Nathan Bangs Papers
      Joshua Soule Papers

Oberlin College Library
      Theodore Dwight Weld Papers

Schlesinger Library, Radcliffe College
      Blackwell Papers

Syracuse University
      Gerrit Smith Collection
      Silas Comfort Papers

Wesleyan University
    Wilbur Fisk Papers

Western Reserve Historical Society, Cleveland, Ohio
    Elizur Wright Sr. Papers

NEWSPAPERS AND PERIODICALS

American Wesleyan, The (New York City, Syracuse, N.Y.)
American Wesleyan Observer (Lowell, Mass.)
Anti-Slavery Examiner (New York City)
Anti-Slavery Lecturer (Utica, N.Y.)
Anti-Slavery Record (New York City)
Anti-Slavery Reporter (New York City)
Christian Advocate (New York City)
Christian Advocate and Journal (New York City)
Christian Examiner and General Review (Boston)
Christian Reflector (Boston)
Christian Register (Boston)
Christian Secretary (Hartford, Conn.)
Church Review, The (New Haven, Conn.)
Cincinnati Weekly Herald and Philanthropist, The
    (New Richmond, Ohio)
Colonizationist and Journal of Freedom (Boston)
Colored American (New York City)
Daily Standard (Syracuse, N.Y.)
Emancipator (New York City and Boston)
Evangelist and Religious Review or *New York Evangelist*
    (New York City)
Flint Daily News, The (Flint, Mich.)
Friend of Man (Utica, N.Y.)
Herald of Freedom (Concord, N.H.)
Liberator, The (Boston)
Maine Wesleyan Journal (Hallowell, Maine)
Michigan Christian Advocate (Mich.)
Milford Times (Milford, Mich.)
National Anti-Slavery Standard (New York City)
New England Christian Advocate (Lowell, Mass.)

New York Daily Tribune (New York City)
New York Herald (New York City)
New York Times (New York City)
New York Tribune (New York City)
Niles' National Register (Washington, D.C.)
Northern Christian Advocate (Auburn, N.Y.)
Northville Record (Northville, Mich.)
Pennsylvania Freeman,The (Pa.)
Philanthropist (Cincinnati, Ohio)
Phrenological Journal of Science and Health
　　　(New York City)
Recorder, The (Flint, Mich.)
Standard (Syracuse, N.Y.)
True Wesleyan, The (Boston, New York City)
Trumpet and Universalist (n.p.)
Western Anti-Slavery Herald (Concord, N.H.)
Western Christian Advocate (Cincinnati, Ohio)
Wolverine Citizen, The (Flint, Mich.)
Zion's Herald (Boston)
Zion's Watchman (New York)

PUBLISHED WORKS BY LUTHER LEE

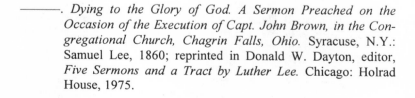

Lee, Luther. *Autobiography of the Rev. Luther Lee, D.D.* New York: Phillips & Hunt, 1882; Cincinnati, Ohio: Walden & Stowe, 1882.

———. *A Defense of the Organization of the Wesleyan Methodist Connection.* Syracuse, N.Y.: Samuel Lee, Publisher, 1862.

———. *Dying to the Glory of God. A Sermon Preached on the Occasion of the Execution of Capt. John Brown, in the Congregational Church, Chagrin Falls, Ohio.* Syracuse, N.Y.: Samuel Lee, 1860; reprinted in Donald W. Dayton, editor, *Five Sermons and a Tract by Luther Lee.* Chicago: Holrad House, 1975.

————. *Ecclesiastical Manual, or Scriptural Church Government Stated and Defended.* New York: Wesleyan Methodist Book Room, 1850.

————. *Elements of Theology or an Exposition of the Divine Origin, Doctrines, Morals and Institutions of Christianity.* Syracuse, N.Y.: S. Lee, 1856.

————. *The Evangelical Pulpit.* 3 Vols. Syracuse, N.Y.: Lee & Masters, 1854, 1856, 1864.

————. *The Revival Manual.* New York: Wesleyan Methodist Book Room, 1850.

————. *A Sermon for the Times: Prohibitory Laws.* New York: Wesleyan Book Room, 1852; reprinted in Donald W. Dayton, editor and Introduction, *Five Sermons and a Tract by Luther Lee.* Chicago: Holrad House, 1975.

————. *A Sermon Preached in the Methodist Episcopal Church, in the Village of Fulton, N.Y., Sabbath Evening, December 3d, 1837, on the Occasion of the Death of the Reverend E. P. Lovejoy Who Was Murdered by a Mob at Alton, Ill., November 7th, 1837.* Fulton, N.Y.: T. Johnson, 1838; reprint in Donald W. Dayton, editor and Introduction, *Five Sermons and a Tract by Luther Lee.* Chicago: Holrad House, 1975.

————. *Slavery Examined in the Light of the Bible.* Syracuse, N.Y.: Wesleyan Methodist Book Room, 1855; reprinted., Detroit: Negro History Press, n.d.

————. *The Supremacy of the Divine Law. A Sermon, preached on the occasion of the death of Reverend Charles Turner Torrey.* [Published by request]; in Dayton, *Five Sermons and a Tract by Luther Lee.* n.p., n.d.; reprint in Donald W. Dayton, editor, *Five Sermons and a Tract by Luther Lee.* Chicago: Holrad House, 1975.

————. *Woman's Right to Preach the Gospel, A Sermon Preached at the Ordination of the Reverend Miss Antoinette L. Brown, at*

South Butler County, N. Y., Sept. 15, 1853. Syracuse, N.Y.: By the Author, 1853; reprint in Donald W. Dayton, editor, *Five Sermons and a Tract by Luther Lee.* Chicago: Holrad House, 1975.

————. *Wesleyan Manual: A Defense of the Organization of the Wesleyan Methodist Connection, With an Introduction by Reverend Cyrus Prindle.* Syracuse, N.Y.: Samuel Lee Publisher, 1862.

————. *Universalism Examined and Refuted, and the Doctrine of the Endless Punishment of Such as Do Not Comply with the Conditions of the Gospel in this Life, Established.* Watertown, N.Y.: Knowlton and Rice for the author, 1836.

Lee, Luther, and Reverend E. Smith, eds. *The Debates of the General Conference of the M. E. Church, May, 1844.* New York: O. Scott for the Wesleyan Methodist Connection of America, 1845.

Lee, Luther. Letters to Antoinette Brown, August 22, 1853 and April 30, 1855 in the Blackwell Collection, Schlesinger Library, Radcliffe College.

PAMPHLETS AND PUBLISHED REPORTS

American Anti-Slavery Society, *Annual Report of the American Anti-Slavery Society* (title varies with the designation of which annual report). New York: William S. Dorr, 1838; reprint, New York: Krause Reprint Co., 1972.

Doctrines and Discipline of the Methodist Episcopal Church, Place of publication and publisher varies, 1789, 1791, 1798, 1804, 1808, 1812, 1820, 1824, 1828, 1836, 1840, 1844.

Journals of the General Conference of the Methodist Episcopal Church, 1796-1836. New York: Carlton & Phillips, 1855.

Journal of the General Conference of the Methodist Episcopal Church, 1840-1844. New York: Carlton & Phillips, 1855.

Minutes of the Annual Conferences of the Methodist Episcopal Church, 3 vols. New York: T. Mason and G. Lane, 1796-1845.

Minutes of the Annual Conferences of the Methodist Episcopal Church, Fall Conferences of 1890. New York: Hunt & Easton; Cincinnati: Cranston & Stowe, 1890.

"Minutes of the New England Conference of the Methodist Episcopal Church," 2 vols. Typescript copy at Duke University prepared by the New England Methodist Historical Society at Boston in 1912.

PUBLISHED LETTERS, DIARIES, MEMOIRS,
AUTOBIOGRAPHIES, AND CONTEMPORARY HISTORIES

Annual Report of the Board of Managers of the New England Anti-Slavery Society. 2 vols. 1833; reprinted Westport, Conn.: Negro Universities Press, 1970.

Bangs, Nathan. *A History of the Methodist Episcopal Church.* 4 vols. New York: Mason & Lane, 1838-42.

Barnes, Gilbert H., and Dwight L. Dumond, eds. *Letters of Theodore Weld, Angelina Grimké Weld, and Sarah Grimké, 1822-1844.* 2 vols. New York: D. Appleton-Century Company, 1934.

Birney, James G. *The American Churches: the Bulwarks of American Slavery.* Boston: n.p. 1843; reprinted New York: Arno Press, 1969.

————. *Debate on "Modern Methodism," in the General Conference on the Methodist Episcopal Church, May 1836.* Cincinnati: Ohio Anti-Slavery Society, 1836.

Blassingame, John W. *The Frederick Douglass Papers, Series One:*

Speeches, Debates, and Interviews. Vol. 3: 1855-63. New Haven, Conn.: Yale University Press, 1985.

Boyeson, Persis E. "Early History of Heuvelton Methodist Church" Unpublished essay. Heuvelton, N.Y.: Heuvelton United Methodist Church, 1993.

Bucke, Emory Stevens, ed. *The History of American Methodism.* 3 vols. New York: Abingdon Press, 1964.

Buckley, James M. *A History of Methodism in the United States.* 2 vols. New York: Christian Literature, Co., 1897.

―――. *Constitutional and Parliamentary History of the Methodist Episcopal Church.* New York: n.p. 1912.

―――. *A History of Methodists in the United States.* New York: Charles Scribner's Sons, 1899.

Campbell, George. *The Philosophy of Rhetoric.* London and Edinburgh, 1776; reprint, Lloyd F. Bitzer, ed., *The Philosophy of Rhetoric by George Campbell*, Carbondale: Southern Illinois University Press, 1963.

Cartwright, Peter. *Autobiography of Peter Cartwright, The Backwoods Preacher.* Cincinnati, Ohio: Cranston and Curtis, 1856.

Child, Lydia Maria. *An Appeal in Favor of the Class of Americans Called Africans.* Boston: n.p. 1833.

Clark, D. W. *Life and Times of Reverend Elijah Hedding, D.D.* New York: Carlton & Phillips, 1856.

Clark, Elmer C., J. Manning Potts, and Jacob S. Payton, eds. *The Journal and Letters of Francis Asbury.* 3 vols. Nashville, Tenn.: Abingdon, 1958.

Conable, F. W. *History of the Genesee Conference of the Methodist Episcopal Church.* New York: n.p. 1876.

Discipline of the Wesleyan Methodist Connection of America. Boston: Published by O. Scott, 1843.

Dorchester, David. "The Relations of the Churches and Mr. Garrison to the American Anti-Slavery Movement," *Methodist Quarterly Review* 63 (July 1881): 474-501.

Drinkhouse, Edward J. *History of Methodist Reform in the Methodist Protestant Church.* 2 vols. Baltimore, Md.: Board of Publication of the Methodist Protestant Church, 1899.

Dumond, Dwight L., ed. *Letters of James Gillispie Birney, 1831-1857.* 2 vols. New York: Appleton-Century, 1938.

Edmonds, John W. *Reports of Select Cases Decided in the Courts of New York, Not Heretofore Reported, or Reported Only Partially.* 2 vols. New York: S. S. Peloubet & Co., 1883.

Emory, Robert. *History of the Discipline of the Methodist Episcopal Church.* New York: n.p. 1844.

Fifth Annual Report of the Executive Committee of the American Anti-Slavery Society, with the Minutes of the Meetings of the Society for Business, and the Speeches Delivered at the Anniversary Meeting on the 8th May, 1838. New York: Printed by William S. Dorr, 1837; reprint, New York: Kraus Reprint Co., 1972.

Flood, Theodore, and John W. Hamilton. *Lives of Methodist Bishops.* New York: n.p. 1882.

Garrison, Wendell Phillips, and Francis Jackson. *William Lloyd Garrison, 1805-1879: The Story of His Life, Told by His Children.* 4 vols. New York: Houghton Mifflin Co., 1894.

Goodell, William. *Slavery and Anti-Slavery; A History of the Great Struggle in Both Hemispheres; With a View of the Slavery Question in the United States.* n.p.: William Harned, 1852; New York: Negro Universities Press, 1968.

Gorrie, P. Douglas. *Black River and Northern New York Conference Memorial. Second Series. Sketches of the Life and Character of the Deceased Members of the Above Conferences, Not Included in the Former Work.* Watertown, N.Y.: Charles E. Holbrook, 1881.

Historical, Collections, and Researches Made by the Michigan Pioneer and Historical Society, Michigan Historical Commission, vol. XVII. Lansing, Mich.: Robert Smith & Co., 1892.

Hughes, George. *Days of Power in the Forest Temple: A Review of the Wonderful Work of God at Fourteen National Camp-Meetings, From 1867 to 1872.* Boston: John Bent & Co., 1873; reprint, Salem, Ohio: Allegheny Publications, 1975.

Jennings, Arthur T. *History of American Wesleyan Methodism.* Syracuse, N.Y.: Wesleyan Methodist Publishing Association, 1902.

Kingsley, Calvin. *Round the World: A Series of Letters by Calvin Kingsley, D.D., Late Bishop of the Methodist Episcopal Church.* Cincinnati, Ohio: Hitchcock and Walden, 1870.

Lee, William. *John Leigh of Agawam (Ipswich) Massachusetts 1634-1671 and His Descendants of the Name of Lee with Genealogical Notes and Biographical Sketches of ALL His Descendants, So Far as Can Be Obtained: Including Notes on Collateral Branches.* Albany, N.Y.: Joel Munsell's Sons, 1888.

Martin, Joel L. *The Wesleyan Manual, or History of Wesleyan Methodism.* Syracuse, N.Y.: Wesleyan Methodist Publishing House, 1889.

Matlack, Lucius C. *The Anti-Slavery Struggle and Triumph in the Methodist Episcopal Church.* New York: Phillips & Hunt, 1881; reprint, New York: Negro Universities Press, 1969.

———. *Discussion of the Doctrine of the Trinity, between Luther Lee,*

Wesleyan Minister, and Samuel J. May, Unitarian Minister. Syracuse, N.Y.: Wesleyan Book Room, 1854.

————. *The History of American Slavery and Methodism from 1780 to 1849, and History of the Wesleyan Methodist Connection of America in Two Parts.* New York: C. Prindle and L. C. Matlack, 1849; reprint, Freeport, N.Y.: Books for Libraries Press, 1971.

————. *The Life of the Reverend Orange Scott: Compiled from His Personal Narrative, Correspondence, and Other Authentic Sources of Information, In Two Parts.* New York: C. Prindle and L. C. Matlack, 1847; reprint, Freeport, N.Y.: Books for Libraries Press, 1971.

May, Samuel J. *Some Recollections of Our Antislavery Conflict.* Boston: Fields, Osgood, & Co., 1869; reprint New York: Arno Press and New York Times, 1968.

Merrill, Walter M., ed. *The Letters of William Lloyd Garrison: I Will Be Heard, 1822-1835.* 6 vols. Cambridge: Harvard University Press, 1971-81.

Mudge, James. *History of the New England Conference of the Methodist Episcopal Church, 1796-1910.* Boston: Published by the New England Conference, 1910.

Pegler, George. *Autobiography of the Life and Times of the Reverend George Pegler.* Syracuse, N.Y.: Wesleyan Methodist Publishing House, 1875.

Proceedings of the New England Anti-Slavery Convention Held in Boston, May 24, 25, 26, 1836. Boston: Isaac Knapp, 1936.

Ruchames, Louis, ed. *The Letters of William Lloyd Garrison: A House Dividing against Itself, 1836-1840.* Vol. 2. Cambridge: Belknap Press of the Harvard University Press, 1971.

Scott, Orange. *Address to the General Conference of the Methodist Episcopal Church by the Reverend O. Scott, A Member of*

That Body. New York: n.p. 1836.

————. *The Grounds of Secession From the M. E. Church, or Book for the Times: Being an Examination of Her Connection with Slavery, and Also of Her Form of Government, Revised and Corrected to Which Is Added Wesley Upon Slavery*. New York: C. Prindle, 1848; reprint, New York: Arno Press and New York Times, 1969.

Sixth Annual Report of the Executive Committee of the American Anti-slavery Society, with the Speeches Delivered at the Anniversary Meeting Held in the City of New York, On the 7th of May, 1839, and the Minutes of the Meetings of the Society for Business, Held on the Evening and the Three Following Days. New York: William S. Dorr, 1839.

Stevens, Abel. *History of the Methodist Episcopal Church in the United States of America*. 4 vols. New York: Carlton & Porter, 1864.

Stone, William L. *Letters on Masonry and Anti-Masonry Addressed to the Hon. John Quincy Adams*. New York: O. Halstead, 1832.

Sunderland, La Roy. *The Testimony of God Against Slavery, Or A Collection of Passages from the Bible, Which Show the Sin of Holding Property in Man. With Notes*. Boston: Webster & Southard, 1835; reprint, St. Clair Shores, Mich.: Scholarly Press, 1970.

Suttler, Boyd B., to Edwin N. Cotter Jr., 20 November 1967. Held by Edwin N. Cotter Jr., Lake Placid, New York.

Whately, Richard. *Elements of Rhetoric: Comprising an Analysis of the Laws of Moral Evidence and of Persuasion, with Rules for Argumentative Composition and Elocution*. [1826]; reprint, Carbondale, Ill.: Southern University Press, 1962.

Whittier, John Greenleaf. "The Anti-Slavery Convention of 1833." *Atlantic Monthly* 33 (Feb. 1874): 166-72.

Woman's Rights Conventions: Seneca Falls & Rochester, N.Y., July &

August, 1848. New York: Robert J. Johnston, 1870; reprint, New York: Arno and New York Times, 1969.

Woods, Leonard. *History of Andover Theological Seminary.* Boston: Andover Theological Seminary, 1885.

Wright, Elizur. "Slavery and Its Ecclesiastical Defenders." *Quarterly Anti-Slavery Magazine* 1 (July 1836): 341-74.

LOCAL AND REGIONAL HISTORIES

Bangs, John. *History of Delaware County, N.Y., with Illustrations, Biographical Sketches and Portraits of Some Pioneers and Prominent Residents.* New York: W. W. Munsell & Co., 1880.

Blakeslee, C. T. *History of Chagrin Falls and Vicinity.* Chagrin Falls, Ohio: By the author, 1874.

Bowen, G. Byron, ed. *History of Lewis County New York, 1880-1965.* Board of Legislators of Lewis County, 1970.

French, J. H. *Gazetteer of the State of New York: Embracing a Comprehensive View of the Geography, Geology, and General History of the State, and a Complete History and Description of Every County, City, Town, Village, and Locality.* Syracuse, N.Y.: R. Pearsall Smith, 1860.

Historical and Statistical Gazetteer of New York State. Syracuse, N.Y.: R. P. Smith, 1860.

Hough, Franklin B. *A History of Lewis County in the State of New York from the Beginning of Its Settlement to the Present Time.* Merrick, N.Y.: Richwood Publishing Co., n.d.

————. *A History of St. Lawrence and Franklin Counties, New York from the Earliest Period to the Present Time.* Albany, N.Y.: Little & Co., 1853.

Landon, Harry R. *The North Country: A History Embracing Jefferson,*

St. Lawrence, Oswego, Lewis and Franklin Counties, New York. Indianapolis, Ind.: Historical Publishing Co., 1932.

Roscoe, William E. *History of Schoharie County, New York.* Syracuse, N.Y.: D. Mason & Co., 1882.

Simms, Jeptha R. *History of Schoharie County and Border Wars of New York.* Bowie, Md.: Heritage Books, Inc. Facsimile reprint, n.d.

Smithers, Cortland F. *History of Heuvelton and Vicinity.* Published by the author, 1971.

Spafford, Horatio Gates. *A Gazetteer of the State of New York: Embracing an Ample Survey and Description of Its Counties, Towns, Cities, Villages, Canals, Mountains, Lakes, Rivers, Creeks, and Natural Topography.* Interlaken, N.Y.: Heart of the Lakes Publishing, 1981.

Yates, A. P., ed. *The Utica Directory and City Advertiser: Arranged in Five Parts, for 1839-40.* Utica, N.Y.: R. Northway Jr., Printer, 1899.

SECONDARY LITERATURE

Abzug, Robert H. *Passionate Liberator: Theodore Dwight Weld and the Dilemma of Reform.* New York: Oxford University Press, 1980.

Ahlstrom, Sydney E. *A Religious History of the American People.* New Haven, Conn.: Yale University Press, 1972.

Altschuler, Glenn C., and Jan M. Saltzgaber. *Revivalism, Social Conscience, and Community in the Burned-Over District: The Trial of Rhoda Bement.* Ithaca, N.Y.: Cornell University Press, 1983.

Barkun, Michael. *Crucible of the Millennium: The Burned-Over District of New York in the 1840s.* Syracuse, N.Y.: Syracuse

University Press, 1986.

Barnard, John. *From Evangelism to Progressivism at Oberlin College, 1866-1917.* Columbus, Ohio: Ohio State University Press, 1969.

Barnes, Gilbert H. *The Antislavery Impulse, 1830-1844.* New York: Harcourt, Brace & World, 1933.

Benson, Lee. *The Concept of Jacksonian Democracy: New York as a Test Case.* Princeton, N.J.: Princeton University Press, 1961.

Biographical Directory of the United States Congress, 1774-1989, Bicentennial Edition. Washington, D.C.: Government Printing Office, 1989.

Bormann, Ernest G. *The Force of Fantasy: Restoring the American Dream.* Carbondale, Ill.: Southern University Press, 1985.

Cameron, Richard M. *Methodism and Society in Historical Perspective. Vol. I. Methodism and Society.* Nashville, Tenn.: Abingdon Press, 1961.

Carwadine, Richard. *Trans-atlantic Revivalism: Popular Evangelicalism in Britain and America, 1790-1965.* Westport, Conn.: Greenwood Press, 1978.

Cassara, Ernest, ed. *Universalism in America: A Documentary History.* Boston: Beacon Press, 1971.

Cazden, Elizabeth. *Antoinette Brown Blackwell: A Biography.* Old Westbury, N.Y.: The Feminist Press, 1983.

Cole, Charles C. *The Social Ideas of Northern Evangelists.* New York: Columbia University Press, 1954.

Craven, Avery O. *The Coming of the Civil War.* Chicago: University of

Chicago Press, 1957.

Cromwell, Otelia. *Lucretia Mott.* Cambridge: Harvard University Press, 1958.

Cross, Whitney R. *The Burned-over District: The Social and Intellectual History of Enthusiastic Religion in Western New York, 1800-1850.* New York: Harper and Row, 1965.

Cunningham, Charles E. *Timothy Dwight, 1752-1817: A Biography.* New York: Macmillan, 1942.

Curry, Richard O., ed. *The Abolitionists: Reformers or Fanatics?* New York: Holt, Rinehart & Winston, 1965.

Dayton, Donald W. *Discovering an Evangelical Heritage.* New York: Harper & Row, 1976.

————. *The American Holiness Movement: A Bibliographic Introduction.* Wilmore, Ky.: B. L. Fisher Library of Asbury Theological Seminary, 1971.

————, editor. *Five Sermons and a Tract by Luther Lee.* Chicago: Holrad House, 1975.

Dieter, Melvin Easterday. *The Holiness Revival of the Nineteenth Century.* Metuchen, N.J.: The Scarecrow Press, Inc., 1980.

Dillon, Merton L. *Benjamin Lundy and the Struggle for Negro Freedom.* Urbana: University of Illinois Press, 1966.

————. *Elijah P. Lovejoy, Abolitionist Editor.* Urbana: University of Illinois Press, 1961.

Donald, David. *Lincoln Reconsidered.* New York: Alfred A. Knopf, 1956.

Duberman, Martin, ed. *The Antislavery Vanguard: New Essays on the Abolitionists.* Princeton, N.J.: Princeton University Press, 1965.

————. *Charles Francis Adams. 1807-1886.* Boston: Houghton Mifflin, 1961.

DuBois, Ellen Carol, ed. *Elizabeth Cady Stanton, Susan B. Anthony: Correspondence, Writings, and Speeches.* New York: Schocken Books, 1981.

————. *Feminism and Suffrage: The Emergence of an Independent Women's Movement in America, 1848-1869.* Ithaca, N.Y.: Cornell University Press, 1978.

Du Bose, Horace M. *Life of Joshua Soule.* Nashville, Tenn.: Publishing House of the M. E. Church South, 1911.

Dumond, Dwight L. *Antislavery: The Crusade for Freedom in America.* Ann Arbor: The University of Michigan Press, 1961.

Elkins, Stanley M. *Slavery: A Problem in American Institutional and Intellectual Life.* Chicago: University of Chicago Press, 1959.

Epstein, Barbara L. *The Politics of Domesticity: Women, Evangelism, and Temperance in Nineteenth-Century America.* Middletown, Conn.: Wesleyan University Press, 1981.

Filler, Louis J. *The Crusade against Slavery, 1830-1860.* New York: Harper & Row, 1960.

Fladeland, Betty. *James Gillespie Birney: Slaveholder to Abolitionist.* Ithaca, N.Y.: Cornell University Press, 1955.

Fletcher, Robert Samuel. *A History of Oberlin College: From Its Foundation Through the Civil War.* Vol. 1. Oberlin, Ohio: Oberlin College, 1943.

Foner, Eric. *Free Soil, Free Labor, Free Men: The Ideology of the Republican Party before the Civil War.* New York: Oxford University Press, 1970.

Formisano, Ronald P. *The Transformation of Political Culture: Massachusetts Parties, 1790s-1840s.* New York: Oxford University Press, 1983.

Friedman, Lawrence J. *Gregarious Saints: Self and Community in American Abolitionism, 1830-1870.* Cambridge: Cambridge University Press, 1982.

Gates, Paul Wallace. *Fifty Million Acres: Conflicts over Kansas Land Policy, 1854-1890.* Ithaca, N.Y.: Cornell University Press, 1954.

Gattell, Frank O. *John Gorham Palfrey and the New England Conscience.* Cambridge: Harvard University Press, 1963.

Gausted, Edwin S. *Historical Atlas of Religion in America.* Rev. ed. New York: Harper & Row, 1976.

———, ed. *The Rise of Adventism: Religion and Society in Mid-nineteenth Century America.* New York: Harper & Row, 1974.

Gerlach, Luther P., and Virginia H. Hine. *People, Power, Change: Movements of Social Transformation.* Indianapolis, Ind.: Bobbs-Merrill, 1970.

Gerteis, Louis S. *Morality and Utility in American Antislavery Reform.* Chapel Hill: University of North Carolina Press, 1987.

Goodheart, Lawrence B. *Abolitionist, Actuary, Atheist: Elizur Wright and the Reform Impulse.* Kent, Ohio: Kent State University Press, 1990.

Greven, Philip, Jr. *The Protestant Temperament: Patterns of Child-Rearing, Religious Experience, and the Self in Early America.* New York: Knopf, 1977.

Griffin, Clifford S. *Their Brothers' Keeper: Moral Stewardship in the United States, 1800-1865.* New Brunswick, N.J.: Rutgers University Press, 1960.

Gross, Robert A. *The Minutemen and Their World.* New York: Hill & Wang, 1976.

Gurko, Miriam. *The Ladies of Seneca Falls: The Birth of the Woman's Rights Movement.* New York: Macmillan Publishing Co., Inc., 1974.

Hardman, Keith J. *Charles Grandison Finney, 1792-1875: Revivalist and Reformer.* Grand Rapids, Mich.: Baker Book House, 1990.

Harlow, Ralph V. *Gerrit Smith, Philanthropist and Reformer.* New York: Holt, 1939.

Harrold, Stanley. *Gamaliel Bailey and the Antislavery Union.* Kent, Ohio: The Kent State University Press, 1986.

Hatch, Nathan. *The Democratization of American Christianity.* New Haven, Conn.: Yale University Press, 1989.

Helfaer, Philip M. *The Psychology of Religious Doubt.* Boston: Beacon Press, 1972.

Henretta, James A. *The Evolution of American Society, 1700-1815.* Lexington, Mass.: D. C. Heath, 1973.

Hersh, Blanche Glassman. *The Slavery of Sex: Feminist-Abolitionists in America.* Urbana: University of Illinois Press, 1978.

Hewitt, Nancy A. *Women's Activism and Social Change: Rochester, New York, 1822-1872.* Ithaca, N.Y.: Cornell University Press, 1984.

Hofstadter, Richard. *Anti-intellectualism in American Life.* New York: Alfred A. Knopf, 1966.

Howe, Daniel Walker. *The Political Culture of the American Whigs.* Chicago: University of Chicago Press, 1979.

———. *The Unitarian Conscience: Harvard Moral Philosophy,*

1805-1861. Cambridge: Harvard University Press, 1970.

Hunter, Carol M. *To Set the Captives Free: Reverend Jermain Wesley Loguen and the Struggle for Freedom in Central New York, 1835-1872.* New York: Garland Publishing, Inc., 1993.

Hyman, Harold M., and Leonard W. Levy, eds. *Freedom and Reform: Essays in Honor of Henry Steele Commager.* New York: Harper & Row, 1967.

Isaac, Rhys. *The Transformation of Virginia, 1740-1790.* New York: W. W. Norton & Co., 1988.

James, William. *Varieties of Religious Experience.* New York: Longmans Green, 1904.

Johnson, Curtis D. *Islands of Holiness: Rural Religion in Upstate New York, 1790-1860.* Ithaca, N.Y.: Cornell University Press, 1989.

Johnson, Paul. *Shopkeeper's Millennium: Society and Revivals in Rochester, N.Y.,1815-1837.* New York: Hill & Wang, 1978.

Jones, Charles E. *A Guide to the Study of the Holiness Movement.* Metuchen, N.J.: Scarecrow Press, 1974.

————. *Perfectionist Persuasion: The Holiness Movement and American Methodism, 1867-1936.* Metuchen, N.J.: Scarecrow Press, 1974.

Keniston, Kenneth. *Young Radical: Notes of Committed Youth.* New York: Harcourt, Brace & World, 1968.

Kett, Joseph. *Rites of Passage: Adolescence in America 1790 to the Present.* New York: Basic Books, 1977.

Kilby, Clyde S. *Minority of One: The Biography of Jonathan Blanchard.* Grand Rapids, Mich.: William B. Eerdmans Publishing Co., 1959.

Kraditor, Aileen S. *Means and Ends in American Abolitionism: Garrison and His Critics on Strategy and Tactics, 1834-1850.* New York: Pantheon, 1967.

————, ed. *Up from the Pedestal.* Chicago: Quadrangle Books, 1968.

Kraut, Alan M., ed. *Crusaders and Compromisers: Essays on the Relationship of the Antislavery Struggle to the Antebellum Party System.* Westport, Conn.: Greenwood Press, 1983.

Krout, John Allen. *The Origins of Prohibition.* New York: Alfred A. Knopf, Inc., 1925; reprint, New York: Russell & Russell, 1967.

Lee, Robert, and Martin Marty, eds. *Religion and Social Conflict.* New York: Oxford University Press, 1964.

Lipson, Dorothy Ann. *Freemasonry in Federalist Connecticut.* Princeton, N.J.: Princeton University Press, 1977.

Litwack, Leon F. *North of Slavery: The Negro in the Free States, 1790-1860.* Chicago: University of Chicago Press, 1961.

Macmillen, Margaret Burnham. *The Methodist Church in Michigan: The Ninetenth Century.* Grand Rapids, Mich.: Michigan Area Methodist Historical Society and William B. Eerdman's Publishing Company, 1967.

Magdol, Edward. *The Antislavery Rank and File: A Social Profile of the Abolitionists' Constituency.* Westport, Conn.: Greenwood Press, 1986.

Mandel, Bernard. *Labor—Free and Slave: Workingmen and the Anti-Slavery Movement in the United States.* New York: Associated Authors, 1955.

Marsden, George. *The Evangelical Mind and New School Presbyterian Experience: A Case Study of Thought and Theology in Nineteenth-Century America.* New Haven, Conn.: Yale University Press, 1970.

————. *Religion and American Culture.* San Diego: Harcourt Brace Jovanovich, 1990.

Mathews, Donald G. *Slavery and Methodism: A Chapter in American Morality 1780-1845.* Princeton, N.J.: Princeton University Press, 1965.

Matthews, Glenna. *"Just a Housewife": The Rise and Fall of Domesticity in America.* New York: Oxford University Press, 1987.

Mayfield, John. *Rehearsal for Republicanism: Free Soil and the Politics of Antislavery.* Port Washington, New York: Kennikat Press, 1980.

McFeely, William S. *Frederick Douglass.* New York: W. W. Norton & Co., 1991.

McKivigan, John R. *The War against Proslavery Religion: Abolitionism and the Northern Churches, 1830-1865.* Ithaca, N.Y.: Cornell University Press, 1984.

McLeister, Ira Ford. *History of the Wesleyan Methodist Church of America.* Marion, Ind.: Wesleyan Press, 1959.

McLoughlin, William G. *Modern Revivalism: Charles Grandison Finney to Billy Graham.* New York: Ronald Press, 1959.

————. *Revivals, Awakenings and Reform: An Essay on Religion and Social Change in America, 1607-1977.* Chicago: University of Chicago Press, 1978.

————, ed. *The American Evangelicals, 1800-1900: An Anthology.* New York: Harper Torchbooks, 1968.

McPherson, James M. *The Struggle for Equality: Abolitionists and the Negro in the Civil War and Reconstruction.* Princeton, N.J.: Princeton University Press, 1964.

Meyer, Jacob C. *Church and State in Massachusetts from 1740-1830.*

New York: Russell and Russell, 1968.

Nissenbaum, Stephen. *Sex, Diet, and Debility in Jacksonian America: Sylvester Graham and Health Reform.* Chicago: Dorsey Press, 1980.

Norwood, Frederick A., ed. *Sourcebook of American Methodism.* Nashville, Tenn.: Abingdon, 1982.

Nye, Russell B. *Fettered Freedom, Civil Liberties and the Slave Controversy, 1830-1860.* Urbana: University of Illinois Press, 1972.

Oakley, Mary Ann B. *Elizabeth Cady Stanton.* Old Westbury, N.Y.: Feminist Press, 1972.

Odell-Scott, David W. *A Post-Patriarchal Christology.* Atlanta: Scholars Press, 1991.

Pease, Jane H., and William H. Pease. *Bound with Them in Chains: A Biographical History of the American Antislavery Movement.* Westport, Conn.: Greenwood Press, 1972.

Perry, Lewis. *Radical Abolitionism: Anarchy and the Government of God in Antislavery Thought.* Ithaca, N.Y.: Cornell University Press, 1980.

Perry, Lewis, and Michael Fellman, eds. *Antislavery Reconsidered: New Perspectives on the Abolitionists.* Baton Rouge: Louisiana State University Press, 1979.

Persons, Stow. *Free Religion: An American Faith.* New Haven, Conn.: Yale University Press, 1947.

Pessen, Edward. *Jacksonian America: Society, Personality, and Politics.* Urbana: University of Illinois Press, 1985.

Peters, John L. *Christian Perfection and American Methodism.* Nashville, Tenn.: Pierce & Washabaugh, 1956; reprint, Grand Rapids, Mich.: Zondervan Publishing House, 1985.

Rhodes, James Ford. *History of the United States from the Compromise of 1850.* New York: Macmillan & Co., 1906.

Riegel, Robert E. *American Feminists.* Lawrence, Kans.: University of Kansas Press, 1963.

Roberts, Allen E. *Frontier Cornerstone: The Story of Freemasonry in Ohio, 1790-1980.* n.p.: Published by the Grand Lodge of Free and Accepted Masons of Ohio, n.p., 1980.

Robinson, Dune L., compiler. *General Catalogue of Middlebury College.* Middlebury, Vt.: Publications Department, 1950.

Robinson, Elmo Arnold. *American Universalism: Its Origins, Organization and Heritage.* New York: Exposition Press, 1970.

Rorabaugh, William J. *The Alcoholic Republic: An American Tradition.* New York: Oxford University Press, 1979.

Rowe, David L. *Thunder and Trumpets: Millerites and Dissenting Religion in Upstate New York, 1800-1850.* Chico, Calif.: Scholars Press, 1985.

Ruchames, Louis. *The Abolitionists: A Collection of Their Writings.* New York: G. P. Putnam's Sons, 1963.

Ruether, Rosemary Radford, and Rosemary Skinner Keller, *Women and Religion in America, Vol. 1: The Nineteenth Century.* San Francisco: Harper & Row, 1981.

Runyan, William M. *Life Histories and Psychobiography: Exploration in Theory and Method.* New York: Oxford University Press, 1982.

Sargant, William. *Battle for the Mind: A Physiology of Conversion and Brain-Washing.* New York: Doubleday, 1957; reprint, Penguin Books, Inc., 1961.

Schwartz, Harold. *Samuel Gridley Howe: Social Reformer, 1801-*

1876. Cambridge: Harvard University Press, 1956.

Scott, Donald M. *From Office to Profession: The New England Ministry, 1750-1850.* Philadelphia: University of Pennsylvania Press, 1978.

Sernett, Milton C. *Abolition's Axe: Beriah Green, Oneida Institute, and the Black Struggle.* Syracuse, N.Y.: Syracuse University Press, 1986.

Sewell, Richard H. *Ballots for Freedom: Antislavery Politics in the United States, 1837-1860.* New York: Oxford University Press, 1976.

————. *John P. Hale and the Politics of Abolition.* Cambridge: Harvard University Press, 1965.

Smith, H. Shelton. *Changing Conceptions of Original Sin: A Study in American Theology since 1750.* New York: Scribner, 1955.

Smith, Timothy L. *Revivalism and Social Reform in Mid-Nineteenth-Century America.* New York: Abingdon Press, 1957.

Sorin, Gerald. *The New York Abolitionists: A Case Study of Political Radicalism.* Westport, Conn.: Greenwood Press, 1971.

Stameshkin, David M. *The Town's College: Middlebury College 1800-1915.* Middlebury, Vt.: Middlebury College Press, 1985.

Stange, Douglas C. *Patterns of Antislavery among American Unitarians, 1831-1860.* Cranbury, N.J.: Associated University Presses, Inc., 1977.

Stewart, James B. *Holy Warriors: The Abolitionists and American Slavery.* New York: Hill & Wang, 1976.

Stout, Harry S. *The Divine Dramatist: George Whitefield and the Rise of Modern Evangelicalism.* Grand Rapids, Mich.: William B. Eerdmans Publishing Co., 1991.

Stromberg, Peter G. *Symbols of Community: The Cultural System of a Swedish Church.* Tucson: University of Arizona Press, 1986.

Swaney, Charles. *Episcopal Methodism and Slavery.* Boston: Gorham Press, 1926.

―――. *Episcopal Methodism with Sidelights on Ecclesiastical Politics.* Boston: Gorham Press, 1926.

Sweet, William Warren. *Methodism in American History.* New York: Holt, Rinehart & Winston, 1932.

Swierenga, Robert P., ed. *Beyond the Civil War Synthesis: Political Essays of the Civil War Era.* Westport, Conn.: Greenwood Press, 1975.

Sydnor, Charles S. *The Development of Southern Sectionalism, 1819-1848.* Baton Rouge: Louisiana State University Press, 1948.

Taylor, Clare. *British American Abolitionists: An Episode in Transatlantic Understanding.* Edinburgh: Edinburgh University Press, 1974.

Taylor, Gordon R. *The Angel Makers: A Study in the Psychological Origins of Historical Change, 1750-1850.* London: Heinemann, 1958.

Thistlethwaite, Frank. *The Anglo-American Connection in the Early Nineteenth Century.* Philadelphia: University of Pennsylvania Press, 1959.

Thomas, John L. *The Liberator: William Lloyd Garrrison, A Biography.* Boston: Little and Brown, 1963.

Thonssen, Lester, and A. C. Baird. *Speech Criticism.* New York: Ronald Press, 1948.

Thrift, Menton. *Memoir of the Reverend Jessie Lee with Extracts from His Journals.* New Haven, Conn.: Yale University Press, 1989.

Tyler, Alice Felt. *Freedom's Ferment: Phases of American Social History from the Colonial Period to the Outbreak of the Civil War.* New York: Harper & Row, Publishers, 1944.

Walker, Peter F. *Moral Choices: Memory, Desire, and Imagination in Nineteenth Century American Abolitionism.* Baton Rouge: Louisiana State University Press, 1967.

Walters, Ronald. *American Reformers, 1815-1860.* New York: Hill & Wang, 1978.

———. *The Antislavery Appeal: American Abolitionism after 1830.* Baltimore, Md.: Johns Hopkins University Press, 1978.

Ward, John William. *Andrew Jackson, Symbol for an Age.* New York: Oxford University Press, 1953.

Ward, William Ralph, Jr. *Faith in Action: A History of Methodism in the Empire State, 1784-1984.* Rutland, Vt.: Academy Books, 1984.

Weinstein, Fred, and Gerald M. Platt. *Psychoanalytic Sociology: An Essay on the Interpretation of Historical Data and the Phenomena of Collective Behavior.* Baltimore, Md.: Johns Hopkins University Press, 1973.

Weisberger, Bernard A. *They Gathered at the River: The Story of the Great Revivalists and Their Impact on Religion in America.* Chicago: Quadrangle Press, 1966.

Whalen, William J. *Christianity and American Freemasonry.* Milwaukee, Wisc.: Bruce Publishing Company, 1958.

White, Charles Edward. *Beauty of Holiness: Phoebe Palmer as Theologian, Revivalist, Feminist.* Grand Rapids, Mich.: Asbury Press, 1986.

Williams, T. Harry. *Lincoln and the Radicals.* Madison, Wisc.: University of Wisconsin Press, 1941.

Wolf, Hazel Catherine. *On Freedom's Altar: The Martyr Complex in the Abolition Movement.* Madison, Wisc.: University of Wisconsin Press, 1952.

Wyatt-Brown, Bertram. *Lewis Tappan and the Evangelical War against Slavery.* New York: Atheneum, 1971.

Yacovone, Donald. *Samuel Joseph May and the Dilemmas of the Liberal Persuasion, 1797-1871.* Philadelphia: Temple University Press, 1991.

ARTICLES

Banner, Lois. "Religious Benevolence as Social Control: A Critique of an Interpretation." *Journal of American History* 60 (June 1973): 23-41.

Brackney, William H. "The Fruits of a Crusade: Wesleyan Opposition to Secret Societies." *Methodist History* 17 (July 1979): 239-52.

Brooks, Elaine. "Massachusetts Anti-Slavery Society." *Journal of Negro History* 30 (1945): 311-30.

Carwadine, Richard. "The Second Great Awakening in the Urban Centers: An Examination of Methodism and the 'New Measures.'" *Journal of American History* 52 (February 1972): 327-34.

Coppedge, Alan. "Entire Sanctification in Early American Methodism: 1812-1835." *Wesleyan Theological Journal* 13 (Spring 1978): 34-50.

Cotter, Edwin N., Jr. "John Brown in the Adirondacks." *Adirondack Life* 9 (Summer 1972): 9-12.

Curry, Richard O., and Lawrence B. Goodheart. "Knives in Their Heads': Passionate Self-Analysis and the Search for Identity in Recent Abolitionist Historiography.'" *Canadian Review of*

American Studies 19 (1983): 401-14.

Davis, David B. "The Emergence of Immediatism in British and American Antislavery Thought." *Mississippi Valley Historical Review* 49 (September 1962): 209-30.

Dayton, Lucile Sider, and Donald W. Dayton. "'Your Daughters Shall Prophesy': Feminism in the Holiness Movement." *Methodist History* 14 (October 1975): 67-93.

Dillon, Merton L. "The Abolitionists: A Decade of Historiography, 1959-1969." *Journal of Southern History* 35 (February-November 1969): 500-22.

————. "The Failure of the American Abolitionists." *Journal of Southern History* 25 (May 1959): 159-77.

Duberman, Martin. "The Abolitionists and Psychology." *Journal of Negro History* 47 (July 1962): 183-91.

Fladeland, Betty. "Who Were the Abolitionists?" *Journal of Negro History* 59 (1964): 99-115.

Friedman, Lawrence J. "'Historical Topics Sometimes Run Dry': The State of Abolitionist Studies." *The Historian* 43 (February 1981): 177-94.

————. "The Gerrit Smith Circle: Abolitionism in the Burned-Over District." *Civil War History* 26 (March 1980): 18-38.

Harwood, Thomas F. "British Evangelical Abolitionism and American Churches in the 1830's." *Journal of Southern History* 28 (August 1962): 287-306.

Hatch, Nathan O. "Demand for a Theology of the People." *Journal of American History* 67 (December 1980): 545-67.

Hewitt, Nancy A. "Feminist Friends: Agrarian Quakers and the Emergence of Woman's Rights in America." *Feminist Studies* 12 (Spring 1986): 27-49.

Isaac, Rhys. "Evangelical Revolt: The Nature of the Baptists' Challenge to the Traditional Order in Virginia, 1765-1775." *William & Mary Quarterly* 31 (July 1974): 345-68.

Jacob, J. R. "LaRoy Sunderland: The Alienation of an Abolitionist." *Journal of American Studies* 6 (April 1972): 1-17.

Jernegan, Marcus W. "Slavery and Conversion in the American Colonies." *American Historical Review* 21 (April 1916): 504-27.

Jervis, Edward D. "LaRoy Sunderland: *Zion's Watchman.*" *Methodist History* 6 (April 1968): 16-32.

————. "LaRoy Sunderland: 'Prince of the Sons of Mesmer.'" *Journal of Popular Culture* 9 (April 1976): 1010-26.

Johnson, Reinhard O. "The Liberty Party in Massachusetts, 1840-1848: Antislavery Third Party Politics in the Bay State." *Civil War History* 28 (March 1982): 237-65.

Kostlevy, William C. "Luther Lee and Methodist Abolitionism." *Methodist History* 20 (January 1982): 90-103.

Lerner, Gerda. "The Lady and the Mill Girl: Changes in the Status of Women in the Age of Jackson." In Jean E. Friedman, William G. Shade, and Mary Jane Capozzoli, eds. *Our American Sisters; Women in American Life and Thought, 125-38.* Lexington, Mass.: D. C. Heath, 1987.

Main, Jackson Turner. "Government by the People: The American Revolution and the Democratization of the Legislatures." *William & Mary Quarterly* 23 (July 1966): 391-407.

Mathews, Donald G. "The Abolitionists on Slavery: The Critique Behind the Social Movement" *The Journal of Southern History* 33 (May 1967): 163-82.

————. "The Second Great Awakening as an Organizing Process, 1780-1830." *American Quarterly* 21 (Spring 1969): 23-43.

Morrow, Ralph E. "The Proslavery Argument Revisited." *Mississippi Valley Historical Review* 48 (June 1961): 79-94.

Myers, John L. "The Beginning of Anti-Slavery Agencies in New York State, 1833-1836." *New York History* 43 (April 1962): 149-81.

Nye, Russell B. "The Slave Power Conspiracy, 1830-1860." *Science and Society* 10 (Summer 1946): 262-74.

Odell-Scott, David W. "Women Speaking in Corinth." *Biblical Literacy Today* (Spring 1989): 14-15.

Perkal, M. Leon. "American Abolition Society: A Viable Alternative to the Republican Party?" *Journal of Negro History* 65 (Winter 1980): 57-71.

Porter, James. "General Conference of 1844." *Methodist Quarterly Review* 53 (April 1871): 234-50.

Pritchard, Linda K. "The Burned-Over District Reconsidered: A Portent of Evolving Religious Pluralism in the United States." *Social Science History* 8 (Summer 1984): 243-65.

Purifoy, Lewis M. "The Methodist Anti-Slavery Tradition, 1784-1844." *Methodist History* 4 (July 1966): 3-15.

Ryan, Mary P. "The Power of Women's Networks: A Case Study of Female Moral Reform in Antebellum America." *Feminist Studies* 5 (Spring 1979): 66-85.

Skotheim, Robert A. "A Note on Historical Method: David Donald's 'Toward a Reconsideration of Abolitionists.'" *Journal of Southern History* 25 (August 1959): 356-65.

Staiger, C. Bruce. "Abolitionism and the Presbyterian Schism of 1837-1838." *Mississippi Valley Historical Review* 36 (December 1949): 391-414.

Stewart, James B. "The Aims and Impact of Garrisonian Abolitionism,

1840-1860." *Civil War History* 15 (September 1969): 197-209.

————. "Politics and Belief in Abolitionism: Stanley Elkins' Concept of Anti-institutionalism and Recent Interpretations of American Antislavery." *South Atlantic Quarterly* 75 (Winter 1975): 94-97.

Strong, Douglas M. "Partners in Political Abolitionism: The Liberty Party and the Wesleyan Methodist Connection." *Methodist History* 23 (January 1985): 103-04.

Tracy, F. P. "Historical View of Universalism in the United States." *Methodist Magazine and Quarterly Review* 19 (October 1937): 390-404.

Welter, Barbara. "The Cult of True Womanhood, 1820-1860." *American Quarterly* 18 (Summer 1966): 151-64.

Wetherwax, John R. "The Secularization of the Methodist Church: An Examination of the 1860 Free Methodist-Methodist Episcopal Schism." *Methodist History* 20 (April 1982): 156-63.

Williamson, Douglas J. "The Rise of the New England Methodist Temperance Movement, 1823-1836." *Methodist History* 21 (October 1982): 3-28.

————. "Wilbur Fisk and African Colonization: A 'Painful Portion' of American Methodist History." *Methodist History* 23 (January 1985): 79-98.

Zorn, Roman J. "The New England Anti-Slavery Society: Pioneer Abolition Organization." *Journal of Negro History* 47 (July 1957): 157-76.

DISSERTATIONS, THESES, AND
OTHER UNPUBLISHED MATERIALS

Brackney, William. "Religious Antimasonry: The Genesis of a Political Party." Ph.D. dissertation, Temple University, 1976.

Cotter, Edwin N., Jr. "John Brown at North Elba," unpublished essay, Superintendent of the John Brown Farm and Grave, North Elba, N.Y., n.d.

Heisey, D. Ray, and Paul L. Kaufman. "Luther Lee: 19th Century Evangelical Debater and Reformer," an unpublished essay to be presented to the Religious Speech Communication Association Convention, New Orleans, November, 1994.

Henderson, Alice Hatcher. "The History of the New York State Anti-Slavery Society." Ph.D. dissertation, University of Michigan, 1963.

Hendricks, John R. "The Liberty Party in New York State, 1838-1848." Ph.D. dissertation, Fordham University, 1959.

Howard, Victor B. "The Anti-Slavery Movement in the Presbyterian Church, 1835-1861." Ph.D. dissertation, Ohio State University, 1961.

Kraut, Alan Morton. "The Liberty Men of New York: Political Abolitionism in New York State, 1840-1848." Ph.D. dissertation, Cornell University, 1975.

Myers, John Lytle. "The Agency System of the Anti-Slavery Movement, 1832-1837 and Its Antecedents in Other Benevolent and Reform Societies." Ph.D. dissertation, University of Michigan, 1960.

Senior, Robert C. "New England Congregationalists and the Anti-Slavery Movement 1830-1860." Ph.D. dissertation, Yale University, 1954.

Wellman, Judith. "The Burned-over District Revisited: Benevolent

Reform and Abolitionism in Mexico, Paris, and Ithaca, New York, 1825-1842." Ph.D. dissertation, University of Virginia, 1974.

Williams, Thomas Leonard. "The Methodist Mission to the Slaves." Ph.D. dissertation, Yale University, 1943.

Index

About the Author

Paul Leslie Kaufman (B.A., Allegheny Wesleyan College; M.A., Baltimore Hebrew University; M.Th., Antietam Biblical Seminary; S.T.M., Lutheran Theological Seminary at Gettysburg; Th.D., Antietam Biblical Seminary; Ph.D., Kent State University) is professor of church history and academic dean at Allegheny Wesleyan College. He was a teaching fellow at Kent State University, has served as adjunct professor of history at Malone College for many years and currently is adjunct professor of church history at Ashland Theological Seminary. He has presented numerous papers on abolitionism and the Methodist Episcopal Church at Western Reserve University, Syracuse University, and Cleveland State University. He is an ordained minister in the Wesleyan Methodist Church, and a member of Phi Alpha Theta and the Wesleyan Theological Society. He resides at Quincy Hall near Salem, Ohio, with his wife, Pearl.